D0700029

THE RESTORATION RAKE-HERO

THE RESTORATION RAKE-HERO

Transformations in
Sexual Understanding in
Seventeenth-Century England

HAROLD WEBER

The University of Wisconsin Press

Published 1986

The University of Wisconsin Press
114 North Murray Street
Madison, Wisconsin 53715

The University of Wisconsin Press, Ltd.
1 Gower Street
London WC1E 6HA, England

First printing

Printed in the United States of America

For LC CIP information see the colophon

ISBN 0-299-10690-X

For my parents, Gerald and Bernice,
and my sister and brother, Fran and Philip

CONTENTS

ACKNOWLEDGMENTS

I compose these acknowledgments with a tremendous sense both of relief, for they conclude a project that has occupied me for too many years, and of pleasure, because they allow me to recognize those individuals whose help has been an integral part of writing this book. The willingness of colleagues to spend their time and energy in my behalf marks my most rewarding experience of the intellectual community that I regard as the academy's rarest and perhaps highest achievement. I hope that the sincerity of my thanks emerges from the formality of these acknowledgments.

I owe my largest debt of gratitude to Morris Eaves, A. H. Scouten, J. L. Simmons, and Maaja Stewart. Without their intellectual stimulation and prodding this book would be a far inferior work; without their emotional support and encouragement it might not have been written at all. For reading large parts of the manuscript and making helpful criticisms and suggestions I thank Barbara Ewell, Michelle Massé, Ellen Rosenman, and Jerry Speir. I am obliged to Gordon Hutner for introducing me to the University of Wisconsin Press, and I wish to thank all those individuals at the press who helped transform manuscript into book: Allen Fitchen, Peter Givler, Jack Kirshbaum, Carolyn Moser, and Carol Olsen. I am particularly indebted to my demanding and still anonymous readers.

I would like to acknowledge my debt to the William Andrews Clark Memorial Library in Los Angeles. Their financial assistance, in the form of an Ahmanson Fellowship for the summer of 1982, merits my appreciation; yet even more significant was the proficiency, consideration, and friendliness of the library's staff. Much of the research for this book was performed at the Clark during the summers of 1980 through 1983. I returned regularly not simply because of the excellence of the collection, nor even the proximity of the

Pacific surf, but because of the pleasure of being a part of the library's community. I thank everyone associated with the Clark for realizing my ideal of the research library.

Portions of chapters 1, 2, 3, and 4 appeared earlier in different form as "Rakes, Rogues, and the Empire of Misrule," *Huntington Library Quarterly* 47 (1984); "Horner and His 'Women of Honour': The Dinner Party in *The Country-Wife*," *Modern Language Quarterly* 43 (1982); "The Rake-Hero in Wycherley and Congreve," *Philological Quarterly* 61 (1982); and "The Female Libertine in Southerne's *Sir Anthony Love* and *The Wives Excuse*," *Essays in Theatre* 2 (1984).

University, Alabama
December 1985

THE RESTORATION RAKE-HERO

INTRODUCTION

My argument is shaped by the assumption that the Restoration rake-hero's most distinctive, and therefore most important, characteristic is his sexuality. The singularity of his sexual nature reveals how fundamentally he differs even from most of the figures usually related to him, for the rake is the first character type in the history of English literature to derive his definition primarily from his eroticism:

> Cupid and Bacchus my saints are:
> May drink and love still reign.
> With wine I wash away my cares,
> And then to cunt again.[1]

Like Rochester, the rake is too complex and enigmatic a figure to be reduced to a sexual machine: his love of disguise, need for freedom, and fondness for play all establish the complexity of the rakish personality. Yet, like Rochester, the rake most compellingly expresses these complexities through his overwhelming desire for sexual pleasure, transforming the world's great stage into a playground for his amours. Most rakes possess little identity outside of the love game, their lives responding largely to the rhythms of courtship and seduction, pursuit and conquest, foreplay and release. Characters like Wycherley's Horner and Etherege's Dorimant maintain no past that cannot be encompassed by a list of previous mistresses; their appetites are so immense and indiscriminate that all differences are annihilated by the simple mechanism of desire:

> I love the frolick, the precise,
> The reverend Lady, that is wise;
> The Wife, the Maid, the Widow too,
> All that is Woman, and will Do.[2]

Horner, the exuberant and coarse lover, and Dorimant, the
frigid Machiavellian seducer, are very different figures, but
these differences express themselves primarily in variant attitudes toward the sexual pleasure that both obsessively pursue.

I do not claim, of course, that English literature prior to the
Restoration encompasses no characters preoccupied with sexual satisfaction, no traditions concerned with the erotic: the
sexual energy of Chaucer's Wife of Bath and Shakespeare's
Cleopatra defines an essential feature of their individuality,
while picaresque prose fiction and Elizabethan sonnet se-
quences contain important erotic elements. Yet the rake of
Restoration comedy marks a significant departure from earlier
characters and traditions, not simply because of his compulsive nature, the way in which the erotic determines, almost to
the exclusion of all else, his behavior, but also because of his
overt concern with the sexual act itself:

> The powerful cunt! whose very name
> Kindles in me an amorous flame!
> Begins to make my pintle rise,
> And long again to fight Love's prize!
> .   .   .   .
> This shows Love's chiefest magic lies
> In women's cunts, not in their eyes.[3]

The irony with which Etherege mocks conventional love lyrics
emphasizes the distinction between the subtle eroticism of
Elizabethan love poetry and the frank appetites of the Restoration rake. Rogues such as Jacke Wilton (in Thomas Nashe's
The Unfortunate Traveller [1594]) and Meriton Latroon (in
Richard Head's *The English Rogue* [1665]) indulge in countless
sexual intrigues, but their erratic movement from city to city
and occupation to occupation depends primarily on their financial manipulations and not on their sexual knavery. The rake,
like Rochester's Charles II, responds primarily to his prick,
"the sauciest prick that e'er did swive," for "love he loves, for
he loves fucking much."[4]

While in the last twenty-five years modern criticism has
certainly not ignored the rake's sexuality, it has tended to explore different facets of his character and other issues his be-

havior raises. Studies of the rake have helped us to understand, for instance, Restoration conceptions of wit, and the desires for personal power and autonomy that underlie libertine beliefs; analyses of his personality have demonstrated his desire to participate in a world of play, a holiday realm freed from responsibility and constraint.[5] In centering my work on the rake's sexuality I propose a shift of emphasis based on the conviction that this central quality generates the manifold complexities of his personality. Recent studies subordinate the rake's eroticism to his other traits, defining his sexual nature in the context of his more general desires for freedom or play or power. In assuming the primacy of the rake's sexuality, I would thus argue that the rake's very real needs for freedom, play, and power are themselves given form and meaning through his sexual desires. While the rake's energies certainly seek an outlet in a holiday existence freed from the briars of "this working-day world," this liberty for him takes a primarily erotic form. Even the rake's manipulation of language and understanding of the distinction between substance and mask, though it helps us to distinguish a true wit from a witwoud, proves most compelling when it reveals the sexual tensions that animate his multitudinous relations to women.

This rakish lust for sexual variety is the most direct and powerful expression of the individual will, just as Western society's attempts to restrict each man to one woman and each woman to one man represent the fundamental social necessity of subordinating the individual to the group: according to Freud, "this replacement of the power of the individual by the power of a community constitutes the decisive step of civilization."[6] The rake's sexual antics and bedroom romps thus reflect the inherent tensions that divide an individual from society. Rakes do not represent Freud's "civilized man" willing to exchange "a portion of his possibilities of happiness for a portion of security,"[7] but those individuals who in rejecting the basic social unit—the family—cut themselves off from the moral center of society:

> Our civilization is, generally speaking, founded on the suppression of instincts. . . . Over and above the struggle for existence, it is chiefly family feeling, with its erotic roots, which has induced the

individuals to make this renunciation. . . . The man who in conse-
quence of his unyielding nature cannot comply with the required
suppression of his instincts, becomes a criminal, an outlaw, unless
his social position or striking abilities enable him to hold his own as
a great man, a "hero."[8]

The rake represents just such a "hero." As Freud's ambivalent use of the term demonstrates, such figures generate contradictory responses, for they reveal the tensions between our
own conflicting desires for the security of order and the pleasures of misrule. The rake necessarily raises ambivalent responses, for the sexual energy that he represents threatens the
stability of the social order even while it promises to provide
the vitality that must animate the structures of that order.
These conflicting desires govern not only our responses to the
rake, but the form of Restoration comedy itself, which normally asserts the efficacy of traditional notions of order—
through the institution of marriage—while at the same time
recognizing the power and attractiveness, even the necessity,
of those forces threatening to disrupt it. The rake's rebellion is
usually frustrated, his energies redirected in the service of conventional order when his fifth-act conversion transforms him
from a wanton lover into a satisfied husband. The metamor-
phosis of the rake is thus a necessary part of his dramatic character and function; his movement from sexual adventure to
domesticity qualifies his initial sexuality but does not deny it.
Though recent scholarship has demonstrated that the rake
and "gay couple" did not "dominate" the theatre as critics
long assumed, the rake was one of the most popular of stock
theatrical types, surely the most notorious both during the
Restoration and after. At the same time, the libertine-rake's
sexual licentiousness made him a primary target for moralists
lamenting the corruptions of the age. The rake's behavior on
the stage, according to the anonymous author of *Reflexions on
Marriage, and The Poetick Discipline* (1673), taught people not
"to burn like *Heroes*, . . . [but] love like Beasts; and all the industry of the Stage, has helpt them to nothing more refin'd in
that passion, than what is common to the Goat, and the
Bull."[9] Sir Richard Blackmore represents another voice in a

conservative chorus that used the rake as a symbol for social disorder and evil:

> Our Poets seem engag'd in a general *Confederacy* to ruin the End of their own Art, to expose *Religion* and *Virtue*, and bring *Vice* and *Corruption of Manners* into Esteem and Reputation. The Poets that write for the Stage (at least a great part of 'em) seem deeply concern'd in this *Conspiracy*. . . . If any Man thinks this an unjust Change, I desire him to read any of our modern Comedies, and I believe he will soon be convinc'd of the Truth of what I have said.
>
> The *Man of Sense* and the *Fine* Gentleman in the *Comedy*, who as the chiefest Person propos'd to the Esteem and Imitation of the Audience . . . will appear a *Finish'd Libertine*.
>
> And as these Characters are set up on purpose to ruin all Opinion and Esteem of Virtue . . . whence the Youth of the Nation have apparently receiv'd very bad Impressions. The *universal* Corruption of Manners and irreligious Disposition of Mind that infects the Kingdom, seems to have been in a great Measure deriv'd from the Stage, or has at least been highly promoted by it. . . . Sure some Effectual Care should be taken that these Men might not be suffer'd by Debauching our Youth, to help on the *Destruction* of a brave Nation.[10]

Blackmore's tirade against the stage, contained in his Preface to *Prince Arthur* (1695), participates in the earnest attempt to reform the theatre that we now call the Jeremy Collier stage controversy. What interests me here, however, is not primarily the social context of Blackmore's remarks, but their reflection of Blackmore's own relationship to that which he attacks. Blackmore has, apparently, no difficulty in separating himself from the *"Finish'd Libertine"* who blights the nation. Though the *"Fine* Gentleman in the *Comedy"* "infects" the rest of the kingdom with a *"universal* Corruption," Blackmore proceeds with the assurance that he himself has escaped contagion. Indeed, the anger that these pages display—their extravagant movement from the hypothetical ("Our Poets seem engag'd in a general *Confederacy"*) to the certain ("these Characters are set up on purpose")—appears to stem from Blackmore's knowledge that figures so black remain nonetheless so appealing. Though Blackmore himself seems not to feel the libertine's attraction, evidently others do, for the passage twice returns to the "Debauching [of] our Youth." Blackmore's anger waxes eloquent because he can distance himself from an evil that he attributes only to others.

Though written thirty-five years earlier and directed against a very different type of evil, two passages from Dryden's "Astraea Redux" provide an instructive contrast to Blackmore's prose. While these passages reveal a similar detestation of ungovernable passions, they also admire a vitality that denies conventional constraints:

> The Rabble now such Freedom did enjoy,
> As Winds at Sea that use it to destroy:
> Blind as the *Cyclops*, and as wild as he,
> They own'd a lawless salvage Libertie,
> Like that our painted Ancestours so priz'd
> Ere Empires Arts their Breasts had Civiliz'd.[11]

This passage begins with the same distinction between a despised Other and the Self. Dryden portrays the civil war rebels as a "rabble" who pervert the precious freedom that they enjoy; they employ their liberty only for destruction, their energies at once "blind," "wild," "lawless," and "salvage." The allusion to the Cyclops fixes their nature as primitive, antisocial, and inhuman: such creatures, this image suggests, exist outside the realm of common humanity. The last couplet, however, with its abrupt shift from "they" to "our," implies that the poet and his audience cannot hold themselves entirely aloof from that which they despise. Our ancestors once resembled such individuals, and though civilization has transformed us, the frightening energies characteristic of the rabble remain nonetheless a part of our past. Dryden makes such a connection as tenuous as possible, balancing the couplet on the analogic "Like," and using "painted" to comically reduce our ancestors. Yet the final couplet, however hesitantly, does establish a relationship between the author and the hated evil. Indeed, the celebratory nature of the poem depends on our intimacy with such an inhuman Other: only the blessed return of Charles stands between an England of law and a state of nature in which human life is "solitary, poore, nasty, brutish, and short."

Dryden's ambivalences are confirmed not a hundred lines later when he returns to the years of civil war. Again he explicitly condemns the rabble freedom of the war years, rejecting the chaos of Charles's "Too, too active age." Yet the hesitations of the first passage become here a surprising reevaluation of disorder, as Dryden expresses a curious contempt for those epochs that have not experienced a like perturbation:

> Some lazy Ages lost in sleep and ease
> No action leave to busie Chronicles;
> Such whose supine felicity but makes
> In story *Chasmes*, in *Epoche's* mistakes;
> O're whom *Time* gently shakes his wings of Down
> Till with his silent sickle they are mown.[12]

In both passages Dryden happily places the chaos of the pre-Restoration years at a distance; yet the vague ambivalences of the first passage give way in the second to a celebration of the transforming power and value of such unrest. The civil war, despite its violence, formed a vital identity denied other ages and cultures, whose ease and felicity lead only to a silent, anonymous, and inevitable decay. The energy unleashed by the civil war, however much it frightened and repelled Dryden, emerges here as a necessary condition for England's greatness.

Disorder assumes vastly different forms for Blackmore and Dryden: Blackmore opposes a subtle infection that insidiously corrupts, whereas Dryden portrays an apocalyptic violence that would level all. Yet both confront threats to the nation's order and security, to conventional definitions of virtue and law. Both Blackmore and Dryden are motivated by a fear of the chaos that society keeps at bay only through its ability to enforce its civilizing will over the individual. And both writers, in very different ways, reveal the fragility of the social balance toward which civilization strives. Blackmore the moralist has no trouble remaining aloof from the behavior he condemns, though the extravagance of his rhetoric indicates how isolated he feels, how few follow his example. Dryden, on the other hand, finds himself implicated in that which he fears. Both writers, in short, reveal the attraction of the disorder they loathe.

This book will deal with this fundamental ambivalence as it reveals itself in the character and treatment of the Restoration rake-hero. In focusing on the rake's extravagant sexuality and on the way in which his career on the Restoration stage becomes a metaphor for that larger tension between order and misrule apparent in both Blackmore and Dryden, I will demonstrate that the rake illuminates a profound transformation in seventeenth-century English perceptions of human sexuality. In Chapter 1 an examination of the erotic vocabulary of Elizabethan and Jacobean England will disclose a rhetoric of demonic sexuality that conditioned Renaissance understandings of how eroticism contributed to the establishment of the Self. This language reveals a significant distrust of extravagant sexuality and shapes comic form in ways alien to the rake's obsessive pursuit of sexual pleasure. The rake stands at the beginning of what Michel Foucault regards as a new consciousness of the way in which sexuality helps to generate the individual personality and to govern the relations of the individual and society:

> Rather than the uniform concern to hide sex, rather than a general prudishness of language, what distinguishes these last three centuries is the variety, the wide dispersion of devices that were invented for speaking about it, for having it be spoken about, for inducing it to speak of itself, for listening, recording, transcribing, and redistributing what is said about it: . . . Rather than a massive censorship, beginning with the verbal proprieties imposed by the Age of Reason, what was involved was a regulated and polymorphous incitement to discourse.[13]

Changing attitudes towards, and conceptions of, the erotic constitute a history of sexuality. This book stems from the conviction that the rake's career on the Restoration stage initiates the modern "discourse" on sexuality, for the rake represents the initial attempts of English culture to transfer control of sexuality from the divine to the secular world.

In succeeding chapters my insistence on the primacy of the rake's sexuality clarifies the large differences that exist between different types of rakes. The modern recognition that a variety of rakes populated the Restoration stage has greatly increased our understanding of the Restoration theatrical world. The rake was not a static creation, for conceptions of his character changed to accommodate changes in the tastes, expectations, and composition of Restoration audiences. Concentrating on the essential sexuality of the rake does not deny the important distinctions between polite rake and debauchee, philosophical libertine and Hobbesian libertine, but redraws them. Sexual desires express themselves in diverse words and actions, while sexual pleasure fulfills itself in many different fashions: Chapters 2 and 3 will examine the ways in which different rakes define and enjoy pleasure.

This rakish obsession with pleasure involved a new understanding of both male and female sexuality, even though the masculine pronoun I have used throughout this introduction to refer to the rake would seem to imply the latter's neglect. The term "rake," however, like the term "prostitute," is sex-specific; to refer to the opposite sex one must speak of a female rake or, analogously, a male prostitute. The sexual specificity of such terms, of course, is not accidental, but points to the social and economic contexts that determine our apprehension of gender. During the Restoration the types of sexual freedom imaginatively as well as socially available to men and women differed greatly. Yet the new perception of sexuality that concerns this book encompasses women as well as men, for the Elizabethan and Jacobean language of demonic sexuality particularly conditioned understandings of female eroticism. Women were intimately involved in the transformation of sexual identity that separated the second half of the seventeenth century from the first. The female rake must differ from her male counterpart, for the male takes his definition precisely from those social conventions that assume male aggression and enforce female passivity. Yet Restoration comedy presents a select number of women determined to enjoy the sexual freedoms available to men. The career of the female rake—the subject of Chapter 4—particularly because of its divergence from male patterns, reveals just how men understood women as sexual beings, for the female rake exists as a projection of the ambivalent feelings aroused in men by female eroticism.

Locating the rake within a complex shift in sexual understanding will illuminate the particular terms of the rake's rebellion as well as the transformation in sexual attitudes that

shaped it. The rake's hatred of marriage reflects his more pervasive contempt for all of society's efforts to restrain the
natural passions of men and women; in the face of the order demanded by society, the rake pursues an erotic dream of un-
limited power and freedom. In my final chapter I will examine
how the rake's dreams of sexual freedom were adapted and
transformed by eighteenth-century literary forms outside of
the comedy of manners in which the rake first appears. By
examining the rake's sexual discourse in the eighteenth century, I intend to show how the rake changed to accommodate
new perceptions of the relationship between the individual and
society, new understandings of the tension between erotic license and social order.

CHAPTER 1

The Rake and the Devil:
The Rhetoric of Demonic
Sexuality in Jacobean Drama

I

Attempts to trace a native English genealogy for the Restoration rake-hero, and for the gay couple in which he often appears, provide a substantial list of forebears. Behind the polished raillery of Dorimant and Harriet stands a gallery of witty lovers in Shakespeare and Shirley, Fletcher and Killigrew; behind the libertine-rake we can detect the traditions of the medieval Vice and the Jacobean trickster-hero, the figures of Fletcher's Mirabel (*The Wild-Goose Chase*) and Don John (*The Chances*).[1] Literary history, we today insist, represents a complex interaction between past and present, tradition and innovation, conservative parents and radical offspring. Literary creation does not occur *ex nihilo*, and the rake hardly springs full-grown and furiously erect from the head of John Dryden or James Howard or Sir George Etherege.

Yet no such list can entirely explain the rake's prominence on the Restoration stage or his importance in Restoration society. According to Peter Holland, "however much one might wish to establish its roots in Shirley, Brome or Davenant, the 'gay couple' was the most distinctive new contribution to comedy of the 1660s, the first new change in the comic form in the Restoration."[2] The distinctiveness of the rake's personality brings home this truth, for the very extravagance of his sexual desires distinguishes him from previous literary types and intimates some of the dangers that lurk within his excess.

Comparing the rake to Mosca, one of the figures from Eliza-

bethan and Jacobean drama who most resembles him, illuminates the extent of the rake's singularity. In his understanding of, and ability to manipulate, the differences between surface and substance, the trickster-hero of Jacobean comedy has
often reminded critics of the Restoration rake-hero. The two
characters share a love of disguise, a joy in playing with the
masks that all people assume in society, that grants them the
perspective of outsiders. Both figures recognize, as Volpone's
great parasite explains, the freedom that exists in the ability to

> rise
> And stoop, almost together, like an arrow;
> Shoot through the air as nimbly as a star;
> Turn short as doth a swallow; and be here,
> And there, and here, and yonder, all at once;
> Present to any humor, all occasion;
> And change a visor swifter than a thought.[3]

Mosca's celebration of his powers contains a sensuality that
reinforces the trickster-hero's relationship to the rake, whose
love of disguise reveals the sophisticated sense of play that
manifests itself in his sexual enthusiasms. This mastery of
disguise suggests the potentially leviathan capacities of the
rake's identity, his desire to change shape and transform the
self. Horner, as the eunuch in *The Country-Wife*, and Bellmour,
as the pious parson Spintext in Congreve's *The Old Batchelour*, relish the opportunity to mask; but they adopt their
disguises primarily to advance their sexual intrigues. Rochester, enjoying the favors of the City ladies as the Italian mounte-
bank Alexander Bendo, exemplifies the rake's characteristic
linking of disguise and sexual intrigue.

In Mosca's speech, however, the sensuality is only latent,
subtly expressed in the force of the verbs ''rise and stoop,'' or
in the polymorphous desire to ''be here, / And there, and here,
and yonder, all at once.'' Mosca responds here to disguise
itself, his excitement generated by a general appreciation of the
ability to shift shape and confound others, not, as with the
rake, by the potential sexual conquests such behavior may
secure. The trickster simply overlooks the sexual implications
of disguise that most concern the rake. Indeed the only explicit

connection between disguise and sexuality in this play is in
Volpone's attempt to seduce Celia, when he imagines for her
the varieties of sexual play available to Protean lovers:

Whilst we, in changèd shapes, act Ovid's tales,
Thou like Europa now, and I like Jove,
Then I like Mars, and thou like Erycine;
So of the rest, till we have quite run through,
And wearied all the fables of the gods.
Then will I have thee in more modern forms,
Attirèd like some sprightly dame of France,
Brave Tuscan lady, or proud Spanish beauty;
Sometimes unto the Persian Sophy's wife,
Or the Grand Signior's mistress; and, for change,
To one of our most artful courtesans,
Or some quick Negro, or cold Russian;
And I will meet thee in as many shapes;
Where we may, so, transfuse our wand'ring souls [Kissing her.]
Out at our lips and score up sums of pleasures.

                                                    (III.vii.221–35)

Though Volpone is not a rake, the outsized nature of his passions here place him in a similar realm of sexual obsession and
extravagance; like the rake, he responds primarily to the sexual implications of disguise.

The moment that the sexual nature of disguise becomes apparent, however, those sexual desires are judged not only as
perverse but sinful. Throughout Volpone's scene of seduction
Celia prays to "God, and his good angels," beseeching the
"holy saints, or heaven" to "let me 'scape." Volpone possesses no real interest in their "wand'ring souls," in the
spiritual ecstasy of love, but only in the physical "sums of
pleasures" they can acquire. The economic metaphor suggests
what Bonario makes clear as he drives off the "Foul ravisher!
libidinous swine": that Volpone has cut himself off from true
spirituality by worshipping "before this altar, and this dross,
thy idol" money (lines 267–75). Volpone's "gorgeous language"[4] is framed by a moral and divine hierarchy that exposes
the sinfulness of his sexual obsessions. His inverted values,
symbolized by his first-act worship of gold, transform his sexual extravagance into an expression of a corrupt and sinful pas-

sion. Volpone damns himself not only by worshipping a false god, but by pursuing his bestial sexual obsessions.

It is not accidental that in this scene Volpone's lust finds expression only when juxtaposed to the spirituality of Celia and Bonario. The contrapuntal movement from Volpone's visions of sexual extravagance to Celia's prayers shapes our responses to his evil, indicating the absolute distance between sexual vice and spiritual goodness; the extent to which Volpone's lust separates him from God is understood only when seen in the light of Celia's true piety. Relying on the Renaissance psychology that normally binds uncontrollable human sexuality to expressions of a sinful and infernal passion, Elizabethan and Jacobean dramatists inevitably expressed the relations between men and women in terms of a divine hierarchy most completely realized, according to Jean Hagstrum, in Milton's *Paradise Lost:* "For Milton, a divinely ordained hierarchy governs the relations of God, man, and woman; and a gulf yawns between love and lust, between Edenic sexuality and sin."[5]

In Jacobean literature this divine hierarchy, as well as the tension it reflects between the sexual and the spiritual, is probably most familiar to modern audiences in the poetry of Donne. Even with his proud and defiant celebrations of intercourse in "The Sun Rising" and "Elegy XIX," Donne seems unable to accommodate both his desire and his repulsion, his physical needs and his spiritual aspirations. The elaborate attempts of "The Ecstasy" to rationalize the sexual act with its spiritual aspects indicate this tension between his love of God and his love of woman, and his lingering disdain for a passion in which "my man / Can be as happy as I can." The power of some of his *Holy Sonnets* stems from their use of a sexual vocabulary borrowed from the secular *Songs and Sonnets:*

> Betray kind husband thy spouse to our sights,
> And let myne amorous soule court thy mild Dove,
> Who is most trew, and pleasing to thee, then
> When she'is embrac'd and open to most men.[6]

Donne's attempt to create a divine sexuality, to locate physical passion not at the demonic but at the divine end of the hierarchy, reached its fullest expression a half-century later when Milton's passionate espousal of "the Rites / Mysterious of connubial Love" in Book IV of *Paradise Lost* strains against the "Hypocrites" who fail to grant the possibility of a sanctified sexuality.

While literature of the sixteenth and early seventeenth centuries reveals a powerful urge to idealize the human body and its passions, Elizabethan and Jacobean England rarely iden tified sexual passion with the divine. Antony, in Shakespeare's *Antony and Cleopatra*, may commemorate the sensual powers of his love for Cleopatra in a "new heaven, new earth," but in the sixteenth and early seventeenth centuries passionate love seldom escaped moral and religious censure. Renaissance psychology and medical theory treated erotic love as a disease, "lovesickness" as a form of insanity. During the Renaissance erotic sinners suffered under a compulsive passion imaged as a type of madness. Raleigh's "A Farewell to false Love" characterizes Love as "A bastard vile, a beast with rage possest: / A way of error, a temple ful of treason, / In all effects, contrarie vnto reason."[7] In Shakespeare's *Love's Labour's Lost*, the desire for women stands as the chief obstacle thwarting the king and his gentlemen's attempt to "war" against their "own affections / And the huge army of the world's desires" (I.i.9–10). When Berowne first realizes that he has betrayed their ideal kingdom by falling in love, he sees himself as "toiling in a pitch,—pitch that defiles: defile! a foul word. . . . By the Lord, this love is as mad as Ajax: it kills sheep, it kills me, I a sheep: well proved again o' my side! I will not love; if I do, hang me; i'faith, I will not. O! but her eye" (IV.iii.2–9).[8] In Elizabethan and Jacobean England the triumph of love normally marked the defeat of reason. Submitting to the power of love represented an inability to control the bestial in the individual personality. In elevating the flesh over the spirit, individuals delivered themselves to "a beast with rage possest," became, in Berowne's comic image, "sheep."

Today, of course, we remain familiar with love portrayed as a sickness or madness; the metaphors are common property, available even to schoolchildren who grow faint and tremble in their infatuations. In Elizabethan and Jacobean England, however, at the furthest range of metaphor, eroticism was also un-

derstood as a symptom of demonic possession. Such metaphors reveal most explicitly Elizabethan and Jacobean fears of
sexual obsession, for they represent the sexual impulse, not as
the bestial part of the individual that has slipped all controls,
but as an imposition from outside the human personality. The
erotic sinner is possessed by the devil, and the individual identity, the Self, has been overcome by an external power, the
Other, over which the individual has no control.

When placed within a divine hierarchy, sexuality enjoyed
outside of marriage becomes an emblem of our fallen state, the
sexual act itself a manifestation of satanic passion. In the
comic drama, this sexual-demonic vocabulary prevents the gay
couple and the rake from achieving dramatic prominence. In a
society that normally linked uncontrollable sexual appetites to
the demonic, the elevation of the sexually compulsive rake to
the status of a comic hero is unimaginable, no matter how
morally ambiguous his presentation or how convincing his
final conversion. But in Restoration comedy, sexuality is
displaced from this divine hierarchy, only inconsistently
associated with the demonic, thus allowing the rake to indulge
his sexual appetites. These appetites are not morally condoned, but they are no longer judged as expressions of absolute
evil.

Restoration dramatists do not, of course, abandon the
demonic vocabulary that characterizes sexuality during the Renaissance, but they use it inconsistently, as a language of hysterical outburst rather than as a primary mode of linguistic
understanding; the language remains, though its meaning and
power have changed. As J. M. Armistead suggests in his revaluation of the occult in Restoration drama, "The question is
not whether occultism rose or fell but rather what forms it
took and how these forms can help us to understand an important element of the period's sensibility."[9] In England, legal activity against witchcraft declined substantially after 1650, and
though the language of demonic sexuality remains a part of
Restoration comic drama, it is no longer animated by the same
forms of demonic belief that inspired it during the sixteenth
and early seventeenth centuries. The rake can disport himself
freely only when attitudes towards sexuality have become sec-

ularized; after the Restoration, sex remains a dangerous and unpredictable passion, harboring a potential for destruction, but a power no longer seen invariably in terms of the divine or the demonic.

The rake thus represents something quite new not only in literature but in society's apprehension of human sexuality as well. After the Restoration, of course, people did not cease to believe in the corruption of their physical being or to mistrust their sexual natures; the Restoration does not mark the beginning of a long "liberation" of sex that has culminated in our own halycon days. What changes is not the painful ambivalences of Elizabethan and Jacobean attitudes towards sexuality —ambivalences that mark us just as surely today—but the way in which those doubts are understood and expressed. There is, of course, a great deal of difference between attributing the violence and unpredictability of sex to demonic possession, or, as we might today, to a powerful and unconscious id. The implications of this transformation are immense, for they reveal, as Michel Foucault insists, very different ways of thinking about our relations to self, other, and society:

> We have arrived at the point where we expect our intelligibility to come from what was for many centuries thought of as madness; the plenitude of our body from what was long considered its stigma and likened to a wound; our identity from what was perceived as an obscure and nameless urge. Hence the importance we ascribe to it, the reverential fear with which we surround it, the care we take to know it. Hence the fact that over the centuries it has become more important than our soul, more important almost than our life; and so it is that all the world's enigmas appear frivolous to us compared to this secret, minuscule in each of us, but of a density that makes it more serious than any other.[10]

And yet in spite of these changes, both the Jacobean habit of defining sexuality as an expression of demonic imposition and the modern impulse to portray it as the manifestation of an unconscious id are attempts to deal with our sexual fears and needs and with the tension between our intellectual structures and physical desires. The id has no more objective reality than the demons who possessed our Jacobean forebears; the language of psychoanalysis is as metaphorical as the language of demonology. Both are systems for dealing with fundamental insecurities about ourselves.

Restoration drama certainly did not anticipate this modern sexual vocabulary, but by weakening the link between the sexual and the demonic it allowed new perceptions of the nature of human sexual potential. The importance of the rake on the Restoration stage, and his essentially sexual being, point to a new concern with the sexual act that Foucault sees as central to the modern sensibility: "What is peculiar to modern societies, in fact, is not that they consigned sex to a shadow existence, but that they dedicated themselves to speaking of it *ad infinitum*, while exploiting it as *the* secret."[11] The appearance of the rake reflects this modern obsession with the sexual, revealing a historical shift in society's understanding of the relationship between character and sexuality, the individual personality and the sexual self. Modern conceptions of character locate our sexual natures at the core of the individual being; we no longer relegate our sexuality to the periphery, but attend to it as the center of our individuality. In spite of this change, sexuality remains opaque, a "secret" that our incessant speech will never succeed in fully revealing. Yet sex now represents not an alien power, an intrusion of a demonic Other, but the central mystery of the Self.

II

Though medieval Catholic Europe possessed a religious tradition deeply uncomfortable with the human body and the sexual act, as well as a belief in and fear of witchcraft, in England the specific connection between sexuality and witchcraft did not arise until after the Reformation. Prior to the establishment of the Church of England, the fear of witches was held in check by the protective ecclesiastical magic of Roman Catholicism: "In medieval England a man need not be hurt by witches, so long as he observed the prescriptions of the Church." Legal activity against witchcraft began in England "only with the great breach effected by the Reformation. It was then that the protective armour of ecclesiastical magic was broken down."[12]

The extent to which sixteenth- and early seventeenth-century England possessed a genuine belief in the devil is not given to precise measurement. Clearly, not everyone believed in such spiritual phenomena, and I am not arguing that all people in Elizabethan and Jacobean society believed in demonic possession or apprehended sexuality as a satanic passion. Yet Keith Thomas, whose *Religion and the Decline of Magic* is one of the most authoritative modern studies of magical beliefs, insists that "for most men the literal reality of demons seemed a fundamental article of faith": "The battle with Satan and his hierarchy of demons was . . . a literal reality for most devout Englishmen."[13] In the last fifteen years social historians have increasingly turned to court records in order to chart the frequency of witchcraft prosecutions and the dimensions of belief in witches; their findings have demonstrated that particularly during the years 1580–1650, witchcraft prosecutions constituted a significant percentage of all criminal proceedings.[14] A.D.J. Macfarlane, for instance, in studying the Essex assizes, discovered that "between 1580 and 1599 an average of five or six people a year were tried at Essex assizes on charges of witchcraft. . . . In the years 1580–89, 118 of the 890 indictments for all offences concerned witchcraft, approximately 13 per cent of all the prosecutions. The trial of witches was second only to the trial of thieves. It was not a peripheral and marginal crime, but of central importance." Yet such statistics, Macfarlane reminds us, "seriously underestimate the amount of formal and informal accusation concerning this crime," and Keith Thomas agrees: "Legal proceedings for witchcraft . . . represent the tip of an iceberg of unascertainable dimensions."[15] Even if the more extravagant manifestations of the satanic world were derided by individuals, the universal fear of damnation was not.[16]

During the years 1500–1700 the great witch-hunts of Europe claimed thousands of lives. During these centuries the fear of damnation that helped generate these witch-hunts contained an important and highly visible sexual component. Around the belief in demons and witches grew an elaborate sexual mythology that indicates just how potent was the connection between the sexual and demonic worlds. Gatherings of witches and demons, the infamous "witches' sabbat," allegedly involved sexual orgies as well as promiscuous intercourse between mortals and spirits, scenes in which "eroticism . . . [went] hand in hand with apostasy."[17] Diabolic incubi and succubi supposedly visited men and women at night in order to enjoy sexual pleasure and bind souls more securely to the devil: James I, in his *Daemonologie* (1597), twice repeats the tale "of a Monasterie of Nunnes which were burnt for their being that way abused."[18] Of more importance, because it represented a witch belief peculiar to Christian Europe, was the demonic pact, in which the witch renounced her baptism and dedicated her soul to Satan; the pact was normally consummated with the witch's acceptance of the devil's mark and acts of intercourse.[19]

Demonology in England, however, must be considered apart from both Scotland and the Continent, for English legal activity directed against witchcraft was predicated on a very different understanding of witchcraft and witch-beliefs. In the first place, the English prosecution of witchcraft began later and ended earlier than elsewhere. Parliament passed the first statute against witchcraft in 1542, and though it remained a crime until 1736, by 1650 most of the prosecutions had ended. In Essex, for example, there were only thirty-nine presentments against witches between 1647 and 1680, and twenty of these were rejected as *ignoramus*.[20] Legal prosecutions of witchcraft in England were restricted primarily to the years 1580–1650, and by 1624 the majority of English executions for witchcraft had already occurred. The 1650s and 1660s saw the publication of a number of works deriding belief in witches; by 1677, John Webster, in his *The Displaying of Supposed Witchcraft*, sounds confident that he and his fellow skeptics have helped undermine serious belief in witchcraft and demonology: "The gross, absurd, impious and Popish opinions of the too much magnified powers of Demons and Witches, in this Nation, were pretty well quashed and silenced by the writings of *Wierus, Tandler*, Mr. *Scot*, Mr. *Ady*, Mr. *Wagstaff* and others; and by the grave proceedings of many learned Judges, and other judicious Magistrates."[21]

In the second place, legal authorities in England prosecuted witchcraft primarily as a crime against society, not as a heresy. By directing the law against those who were thought to have harmed others, rather than against worship of the devil or those thought to have gained occult powers through a compact with Satan, England avoided the more hysterical religious excesses of the Continental witch-hunts. Finally, England also rejected the more sensational sexual-demonic beliefs found in other countries. English law, at least at first, did not consider the devil's pact, and its culminating act of intercourse, one of the primary activities of witchcraft, nor did the English dwell quite so insistently on the alleged sexual extravagances of witches' communal gatherings.[22]

Yet even in England, particularly during the reign of James I, the sexual aspects of demonic belief were persistent and important. Continental witch-beliefs were certainly known in England, where they influenced both popular belief and legal activity. Keith Thomas notes that many English intellectuals and theologians were converted "more or less totally" to the Continental conception of witchcraft, while an even wider public read the occasional translations of Continental demonologists.[23] The full title of Webster's book, for instance, testifies to the carnal details that most excited the popular imagination: *The Displaying of Supposed Witchcraft. Wherein is affirmed that there are many sorts of Deceivers and Impostors, and Divers persons under a passive Delusion of Melancholy and Fancy. But that there is a Corporeal League made betwixt the Devil and the Witch, Or that he sucks on the Witches Body, has Carnal Copulation, or that Witches are turned into Cats, Dogs, raise Tempests, or the like, is utterly denied and disproved.* Thomas Ady's *A Perfect Discovery of Witches* (1661) also exploits the sexual component of witchcraft even as it tries to discredit demonic beliefs; four of the first eleven questions he asks concerning the scriptural evidence for witch belief deal with sexual matters: "2 Where is it written, that Witches have Imps sucking on their bodies? . . . 11 Where do we read of a he devill, or a she devill, called *incubus* or *succubus*, that useth generation or copulation with Witches, or Witches with them?"[24] Continental beliefs even influenced English legal proceedings. The first two statutes against witchcraft, passed in 1542 and 1563, made no mention of the demonic pact. The third and final statute of 1604, however, clearly refers to the Continental doctrine of the diabolical compact, though Keith Thomas demonstrates that even during the seventeenth century it was not an "indispensable feature" of witch trials.[25]

Yet even apart from Continental influences, England possessed its own traditions of demonic sexuality. Thomas Ady may question the biblical warrant for the existence of succubi and incubi, but evidence exists that copulation with the devil was a belief in tenth-century England.[26] According to Thomas, "there were plenty of medieval stories about men who made sacrifices to the Devil and of women who succumbed to the embraces of a demon lover."[27] The notorious possession of William Sommers of Nottingham in 1597–98 featured an act of bestiality with a dog in front of many onlookers, while a law student from the north of England named Briggs testified in 1574 that he was tempted by a seductive painted woman who sang and danced for him;[28] such a seductive female demon appears prominently, as we shall see, in Thomas Middleton's *A Mad World, My Masters*. Though such cases are mild by Continental standards, they point to a durable connection in England between sexual guilt and demonic belief.

Such guilt is visible not only in the sexual details of witchcraft, which represent only the most sensational aspects of the connection between sexuality and the demonic, but in a persistent strain of metaphor identifying the devil with intercourse. The following passage from Richard Sibbes' *The Soules Conflict with it selfe, and Victory over it selfe by Faith* (1635) ascribes to the act of intercourse an explicitly demonic dimension: "Satan oftentimes casts a mist before our *imagination*, that so we might have a mishapen conceit of things; . . . Imagination is the *wombe*, and Satan the *father* of all monstrous *conceptions* and disordered *lusts*, which are well called *deceitfull lusts*, and *lusts of ignorance*, foolish and noysome lusts, because they both spring from errour and folly, and lead unto it."[29] Describing Satan as the "father of evil," of course, is hardly unusual, though in this passage the quite literal understanding of the image, with Satan impregnating the "wombe" of imagination and giving birth to "monstrous" deformities, indicates the implicit sexual properties of the common metaphor. From this image Satan emerges as a frightening phallic presence, a grotesque parody of human eroticism.

Milton, in the allegory of Sin and Death that concludes Book II of *Paradise Lost*, provides the most memorable extension of such a vision. In Milton's allegory Satan's daughter Sin appears much like Spenser's Duessa, "Woman to the waist, and fair, / But ended foul in many a scaly fold / Voluminous and vast"(II.650–52). Satan's impregnation of his narcissistic creation leads to the birth of Death, whose rape of his mother engenders those "monstrous" forms who so horrify Sibbes:

> in embraces forcible and foul
> Ingend'ring with me, of that rape begot
> These yelling Monsters that with ceasless cry
> Surround me, as thou saw'st, hourly conceiv'd
> And hourly born, with sorrow infinite
> To me, for when they list, into the womb
> That bred them they return, and howl and gnaw
> My Bowels, thir repast.
>
> (II.793–800)

In this terrible nightmare of ceaseless demonic birth, Death stalks the created world as a result of a satanic act of incest.

A related metaphor, even more indicative of Jacobean sexual fears, explicitly associates the penis with the devil. This link between the male organ and the demonic exposes a phallic evil that threatens to pollute the source of generation itself:

> as sure as God is, there be *Devils*, and some *Devils* must have some Power, and their Power is in this World, . . . and if the *Devil* hath any Power, it is over the Flesh, rather over the filthiest and most sinful part thereof, whereunto orginal Sin is soldred; as God, before and under the Law, to shew *officialem* of purging Man's original Sin, ordained the *Praeputium* of the Foreskin: and to exempt this of our Profession from the Power of Witchcraft, is a Paradox never yet maintained by any learned or wise man.
>
> . . . if the Power of Witchcraft may reach to our Life, much more to a Member, not so governed by the Fancy, wherein the Devil hath his principal Operation.[30]

James I articulated this famous description of the genital demonic during the Somerset affair of 1613, when James was eager to secure a divorce for Frances Howard, wife of the earl of Essex, so that she could marry James's favorite, Robert Carr, earl of Somerset. James's sentiments proved prophetic, for two years later, in 1615, the poisoning of Sir Thomas Overbury demonstrated all too clearly the demonic aspects of the original affair.[31] Witchcraft and sorcery, spells and potions and poisoning, were brought together in one vast sexual stew that vividly documents Jacobean fears of unleashed sexual desires. Apparently the Overbury scandal was not an isolated event either. In 1625, when the duke of Buckingham's sister-in-law, Lady Purbeck, gave birth to a male heir, there were rumors of both adultery (the child's father was held to be Sir Robert Howard) and sorcery (witchcraft and a picture of Buckingham in wax were spoken of).[32] And it was another notorious sexual scandal, involving the earl of Castlehaven in 1630–31, that provided the occasion for Milton's *Comus*, where a Lady committed to the "serious doctrine of virginity" must confront "a Sorcerer," "Deep skill'd in all his mother's witcheries" (line 523), who would, with his "monstrous rout," "roll with pleasure in a sensual sty" (line 77).[33]

While the penis might be linked to the devil, the vagina could become hell itself. Shakespeare's great sonnet 129, "Th'expense of spirit in a waste of shame," concludes with just such a metaphor:

> All this the world well knows, yet none knows well
> To shun the heav'n that leads men to this hell.[34]

Spenser's *The Faerie Queene* also reveals the female body deformed by an association with the demonic. In Book I Duessa appears in her true shape as "A filthy foule old woman":

> Her neather partes misshapen, monstrous,
> Were hidd in water, that I could not see,
> But they did seeme more foule and hideous,
> Then womans shape man would beleeve to bee.
> (I.ii.41)

This Elizabethan and Jacobean link between the sexual and the demonic is most profoundly realized in the drama of the period. Lear's terrible lament, that "to the girdle do the Gods inherit, / Beneath is all the fiend's: there's hell, there's dark-

ness, / There is the sulphurous pit" (IV.vi.128–30), represents only the most famous statement of a demonic sexuality
that pervades tragedies such as Middleton and Rowley's *The
Changeling*, Ford's *'Tis Pity She's a Whore*, and Webster's *The
White Devil* and *The Duchess of Malfi*.

In examining how this vocabulary of demonic sexuality
shaped the forms of Elizabethan and Jacobean tragedy and comedy, I do not, of course, mean to suggest that demonic eroticism represented a quotidian understanding of sexuality; eroticism was not consistently or even usually comprehended as a
satanic passion. What it indicates instead are beliefs on the
margins of discourse, fears that a compulsive sexuality un-
checked by conventional social mechanisms could overcome
the individual personality and annihilate the ability to preserve a coherent identity. Demonic sexuality was not a consistent habit of mind but a projection of the age's most extreme
anxieties; people's deepest fears about themselves, about their
place in the world and relationship to self, gained expression
through sexual demonism. Today we regard sexuality as central to our identities, a necessary if enigmatic part of the individual personality, a fundamental source of personal vitality.
For Elizabethan and Jacobean England, however, the sexual
self was not so easily integrated into the rest of the personality.
Its power mistrusted, its sources feared, eroticism represented
not an essential part of the human identity, but a threat to it.
To yield to the power of sexuality, to encourage its unlawful
demands and pleasures, was to court a satanic power that
threatened to overwhelm one's essential integrity.

III

Few Jacobean dramatists express these fears as profoundly
as John Webster. His two dark tragedies present worlds so
frightening and horrific that they almost seem to deny the possibility of light and salvation. Both rival *King Lear* in their depiction of a society out of balance, a universe inhospitable and
without pity for the human creatures who inhabit it. An examination of *The White Devil* (1612) testifies not only to the
range and pervasiveness of the Jacobean experience of sexual

demonism but, through a comparison to Thomas Otway's *Venice Preserv'd* (1682), also reveals the uniqueness of the Elizabethan and Jacobean apprehension of sexual-demonic possession. Both plays portray through demonic imagery a corrupt and decaying social order; both also locate a diseased sexuality at the center of the violence, corruption, and ruin that overtake the world. Webster's tragedy, however, posits a necessary relation between the two that Otway's play pursues only inconsistently. *The White Devil* creates an identity between the sexual and the demonic, whereas *Venice Preserv'd* suggests the connection as only one among many attempts to articulate the central anxiety of characters living in a world over which they have lost control. This fundamental difference reveals the transformation in belief that divided Jacobean and Restoration understandings of sexuality.

The White Devil, as M. C. Bradbrook has noted, suggests the theme of diabolic possession in Bracciano's first words to Flamineo: "Quite lost Flamineo."[35] From this initial hint of damnation the play develops a totally corrupt society whose decay is realized and explored through a pervasive pattern of demonic imagery. Hardly a major character in the play escapes being stigmatized as a devil: Vittoria, of course, is repeatedly labeled a devil, but at other points Lodovico, Bracciano, Flamineo, Monticelso, Zanche, even Isabella, and Marcello, are all associated with the demon.[36]

Yet such specific connections to the devil do not suggest the full extent of the satanic subversion of the moral and social order. Flamineo, while feigning a madness that allows him to speak the truth, uses excremental imagery to link society's political leaders to the devil: "In this a politician imitates the devil, as the devil imitates a cannon. Wheresoever he comes to do mischief, he comes with his backside towards you" (III.iii.16–19). But as Monticelso emphasizes in the very next scene, the servants of the great imitate this same corruption—he knows because their names inhabit his demonic "black book": "Well may the title hold: for though it teach not / The art of conjuring, yet in it lurk / The names of many devils" (IV.i.34–36). The world exists, finally, as a vast elaboration of the demonic, as Flamineo suggests when he briefly sketches his great chain of evil: "As in this world there are degrees of evils: / So in this world there are degrees of devils" (IV.ii.58–59). Flamineo, of course, is the worst of devils, his mind a horrid confusion of sex, religion, and witchcraft. Yet the satanic measure of the natural world overwhelms the play, its presence so characteristic of Webster's tragedy that it cannot be dismissed as merely the depraved perception of one or two characters. The play contains a darkness, a "mist," that obscures a vision of any world not steeped in infernal blackness.

Otway's masterpiece portrays an analogous vision of earthly torment, perversity, and damnation. Again we inhabit an Italian scene—and its associations with the popish Antichrist—that seems always under the cloak of night: the conspirators gather at midnight, the Senate meets at "this late hour." Again we discover a host of characters who are designated devils—Pierre, Jaffeir, Antonio, Renault—and occupy a realm where the demonic haunts almost every important character and action. Jaffeir, driven to the conspiracy by "worldly Want! that hungry meager Fiend," predictably awaits his midnight rendezvous with his imagination fixed on hell:

> I am here, and thus, the Shades of Night around me,
> I look as if all Hell were in my Heart,
> And I in Hell. Nay, surely 'tis so with me; —
> For every step I tread, methinks some Fiend
> Knocks at my Breast, and bids it not be quiet:
> I've heard, how desperate Wretches, like my self,
> Have wander'd out at this dead time of Night
> To meet the Foe of Mankind in his walk:
> Sure I am so Curst, that, tho' of Heav'n forsaken,
> No Minister of Darkness cares to Tempt me.
> Hell! Hell! why sleepest thou?[37]

The entrance of Pierre immediately answers Jaffeir's question: "I but half wisht / To see the Devil, and he's here already" (II.99–100).

While Otway consistently characterizes the conspirators as devilish, so too does he represent the Senate. Aquilina scorns Antonio as that "pampered Devil" and laments that the judi-

cial murder of the conspirators is "that hellish Sentence." The
entire city, in Jaffeir's ultimate vision of destruction, comes to
represent hell:

> Final destruction seize on all the world:
> Bend down, ye Heavens, and shutting round this earth,
> Crush the Vile Globe into its first confusion;
> .   .   .   .
> .   .   .   .   .   but let *Venice* burn
> Hotter than all the rest: Here kindle Hell
> Ne'r to extinguish and let souls hereafter
> Groan here, in all those pains which mine feels now.
>
> (V.219–27)

In Jaffeir's frenzied imagination the world returns to unformed
matter, its Miltonic chaos juxtaposed, in this revised cos-
mology, not to Pandemonium but to Venice.[38]

Both plays emphasize the demonic nature of the worlds
they depict; at the same time they both project a morbid sexuality at the center of the social frame. The very title of Webster's play points to the sexually depraved woman whose
attraction and appetite rend the social fabric. The uncontrollable lust of Vittoria and Bracciano dominates the play as the
essential spring of the action. *Venice Preserv'd*, though ostensibly more political in its motivations, breathes an even more
perverse and obscene atmosphere. The degraded sadomaso-
chism of Aquilina and Antonio, particularly in their bedroom
scene in Act III, scene i, where "Nacky" beats the howling
Antonio out of doors, provides a grotesque tone hardly equalled
in the earlier play even by the voyeurism and pandering of Flamineo. Flamineo's sexual behavior remains always at the service of his ambition, his enjoyment of evil secondary to its
utility. Antonio's perversions, however, serve no larger purpose. Situated at the center of the play, his long scene with
Aquilina at the beginning of Act III moves the plot forward not
at all; in the tableau of Antonio on his knees being kicked and
beaten we see no ambition or recognition of a larger world,
merely his desire to satisfy degraded passions. And even the political motivations of *Venice Preserv'd* are suspect, so dependent are they on the sexual: Pierre creates the conspiracy only
because a senator steals Aquilina from him; Jaffeir leaves the

conspiracy only because Renault sexually threatens Belvidera; Antonio's speech on the conspiracy reveals the same intellectual and moral vacuity apparent in his sexual antics.[39]

Both plays, then, insist on the primacy of the sexual and the demonic. Both portray sexuality as the chief engine of human motivation, while both envisage a frightening world lost in the corrupt, perverse, and demonic. But Webster's play understands the sexual almost entirely in terms of the demonic. At the climax of the play Flamineo curses the weakness of men and the complicity of women when he characterizes the sexuality that has driven the play to its end as an implicit pact with the devil. "Trust a woman?—never, never; Bracciano be my precedent: we lay our souls to pawn to the devil for a little pleasure, and a woman makes the bill of sale. That ever man should marry!" (V.vi.160–63). Even the sacrament of marriage, suggests Flamineo's final scornful lament, cannot cleanse the impurity of women, whose inherently more evil natures indicate their inherently more sexual natures: for this play the two are one. Their essential intimacy with the demonic grants women a superior power that renders men their playthings; this inversion of the "natural" hierarchy, in which men should dominate women, makes this demonic power even more terrible. It is Vittoria, after all, who relates in Act I, scene ii, the dream that leads Bracciano to conceive of the dual murders. As Flamineo remarks, overhearing their conversation, "Excellent devil. / She hath taught him in a dream / To make away his duchess and her husband" (I.ii. 256–58). The dream itself is a tissue of demonic details, its references to midnight, graveyards, cross-sticks, and black thorns all possessing significance in the rites of witchcraft.[40]

Significantly, Vittoria relates her dream immediately after the sexual play, observed by her mother and brother, on the carpet and "two fair cushions" readied by Zanche. As Cornelia notes in horror as she watches the "happy union" of her daughter and Bracciano, "Earthquakes leave behind, / Where they have tyrannized, iron, or lead, or stone, / But—woe to ruin—violent lust leaves none" (I.ii.218–20). In this play sexuality exists almost exclusively as a power of darkness and destruction. The conjurer who in Act II, scene ii, arranges and reveals in dumb show the deaths of Isabella and Camillo enters with Bracciano at "dead midnight," the hour when witches' sabbats traditionally begin, the moment when the Prince of Darkness most freely displays his power, the moment, according to Flamineo, when women reveal their uncontrollable lusts most clearly: "Come, sister, darkness hides your blush, —women are like curst dogs, civility keeps them tied all day-time, but they are let loose at midnight, then they do most good or most mischief" (I.ii.198–201).[41] Midnight reveals not only the Prince of Darkness but the darkness of sexuality: Lodivico curses the great, who pretend "modest form"

> when their thoughts are loose,
> Even acting of those hot and lustful sports
> Are to ensue about midnight.
>   (IV.iii.147–49)

To a large extent the terrible power of *The White Devil* stems from its insistence on yoking one of our essential passions with the necessarily evil. In Webster's play we are unable to assert ourselves against a sexuality that moves inevitably to our ruin and damnation. As in the Overbury scandal, the genital demonic again serves to fix the identity between the sexual and the demonic worlds that dooms us to our inevitable fall; in the final act Flamineo's pun on tumescence relates the penis to the devil: "'Tis not so great a cunning as men think / To raise the devil: for here's one up already,— / The greatest cunning were to lay him down" (V.i.88–90). And when Bracciano lies dying near the play's conclusion the devil seems to him an overwhelming phallic specter, appearing

> In a blue bonnet, and a pair of breeches
> With a great codpiece. Ha, ha, ha,
> Looke you his codpiece is stuck full of pins
> With pearls o'th'head of them.
>   (V.iii.98–101)

People in this world act as if *possessed*—the language of the play treats this quite literally—driven by the demons of a sexuality outside their control.

Otway severs this identity between the sexual and the demonic, though his play does contain a number of links between the two. Renault, particularly, represents a degraded sexuality imaged as a demonic passion. Belvidera, after being attacked, compares him to Tarquin, "gastely with infernal Lust" (III.ii.7); later, when complaining to Jaffeir, she calls her attacker "that old Son of Mischief" who "mutter'd vows to Hell" (III.ii.180, 193). Renault is sexually portrayed as "that Infernal Devil, that old Fiend / That's Damn'd himself and wou'd undo Mankind" (IV.30-31).

But even in the person of Renault this identity between the sexual and the demonic is but inconsistently pursued. More often Otway's play captures the essence of sexuality through animal imagery that conveys the bestial nature of degraded sexuality. Jaffeir curses Renault as "the old Fox" who "stunk . . . / When the rank fit was on him" (III.ii.245-46), while Antonio and Aquilina express their perverse lusts almost exclusively in animal images. Aquilina would "rather meet a Toad in my dish than that old hideous Animal in my Chamber to Night" (III.i.11-13), and when Antonio does enter her chamber, he pursues his pleasures in sundry animal guises: "Come let's to bed—you Fubbs, you Pugg you—you little Puss—Purree Tuzzey"; "Then look you now, suppose me a Bull, a *Basan*-Bull, the Bull of Bulls, or any Bull. Thus up I get and with my brows thus bent—I broo, I say I broo, I broo, I broo"; "Ah toad, toad, toad, toad! spit in my Face a little, *Nacky* —spit in my Face prithee, spit in my Face, never so little"; "I'l give thee this to'ther purse to let me be a Dog—and to use me like a Dog a little" (III.i.19-98). Even the others describe Antonio's sexuality in bestial terms: Pierre scorns him as a "filthy Cuckoo," "the rank old bearded *Hirco*" who "uses Beauty like a Lambskin" (I.186-93).

Animal imagery, to be sure, can represent the demonic world: Satan's various disguises in *Paradise Lost* demonstrate the power of such images as they link his movement down the chain of being with his impotence and increasing sexual frustration. Yet in *Venice Preserv'd* Otway does not link the bestial to the demonic; while his animal imagery primarily indicates the perversity of sex, it also expresses other facets of passion. Jaffier can even overturn the crucial association between midnight and demonic sexuality when he pictures himself as a dove returning to Belvidera. Here the conventional ro-

matic image emphasizes the real love that Jaffeir and Belvidera
share:

> Anon at Twelve!
> I'l steal my self to thy expecting Arms,
> Come like a Travell'd Dove and bring thee Peace.
>   (III.ii.207–9)

Because sexuality is not necessarily demonic, people succumb
to a lesser self only when they lose themselves:

> Heav'n! where am I? beset with cursed Fiends,
> That wait to Damn me: What a Devil's man,
> When he forgets his nature—
>   (III.ii.302–4)

Jaffeir never sees himself as *possessed*; he is instead *beset*, his
love for Belvidera overwhelmed by the perverse society they
inhabit.

The contrast between Webster's *The White Devil* and Otway's *Venice Preserv'd* indicates that we must take seriously
the figurative language of the earlier play and its portrayal of a
world in which sexuality exists as a manifestation of the demonic. While Otway's play describes as emphatically the
power of sex to corrupt, its irresistible force and potential for
evil, *Venice Preserv'd* does not insist that the devil lives in the
mundane world through the expression of people's sexuality.
For Otway the vocabulary of demonic sexuality represents
only one of a number of attempts to discover an articulation for
human anxiety. His characters search for a language capable of
expressing and containing their fears, though Belvidera's climactic descent into madness demonstrates the futility of their
efforts: "Murmuring streams, soft shades, and springing
flowers, / Lutes, Laurells, Seas of Milk, and ships of Amber"
(V.368–69). The strangely beautiful, but chaotic and meaningless, vocabulary of madness is all the play leaves her. In *The
White Devil*, however, the power of the metaphorical language
of Jacobean sexual possession depends on the fusion of the sexual and the demonic. Otway at times employs this vocabulary,
but its inconsistency and its subordination to other sexual
vocabularies reveal that for him it is a dead language, aestheti-

cally but not metaphysically satisfying. In *Venice Preserv'd*
the language of demonic sexuality remains merely ornamen-
tal; in *The White Devil* it is primary, an essential part of the
way in which characters perceive and understand their world.

IV

The Jacobean vocabulary of demonic sexuality compels
belief even when removed from the tragic stage; though apparently antithetical to the comic vision, which historically celebrates sex, the association between the demonic and the sexual
has its place in Jacobean comic drama. Thomas Middleton's *A
Mad World, My Masters* (1605) and John Marston's *The Dutch
Courtesan* (1605) demonstrate not simply the presence of a
comic sexual demonism, but also its importance in determining the structure of comic action. Both plays are notable because they depend on characters who bear a close relationship
to the rake and gay couple. In both cases, however, the insistence on the sexually demonic inhibits the development and
importance of such characters; neither rake nor gay couple can
achieve their fullest potential when inhabiting a society in
which sex bears the burden of the demonic.

In Middleton's city comedy, Follywit emerges as an almost
perfect example of what Robert Jordan has called the "extravagant rake." His name alone indicates two of these characters'
most distinctive traits: their propensity for finding themselves
in ridiculous predicaments, and their impudent wit and exaggerated language. Follywit also shares their impulsive and
unruly behavior, their love of disguise and play, their self-satis-
faction, lack of pretension, and cynical if good-humored
knowledge of self and other. The exuberant center of the comic
action, Follywit dominates the play and provides the ultimate
excuse for joining its two major plots. In addition, he participates in the final rejection of a youthful humor that ill suits the
adult world of marriage and responsibility; Jordan says: "The
extravagant rake in his own person is actually filling a carnival
role. . . . In him customary restraints are thrown off with a
wild exuberance and an unashamed joy, and if he does finally
dwindle into a husband this could be said to mark the passing
of carnival and the acceptance of responsibility."[42]

Yet for all of this, Follywit lacks the taste for sexual extravagance that is a necessary part of the rake's personality. Even Jordan—who by no means emphasizes the sexual as I have—recognizes an extravagant rake's "promiscuity" and "obsession with love"; and this obsession does not touch Middleton's hero. Follywit's chief passions involve the love of play, money, and drink; though we may assume his sexual licentiousness, we see or hear very little of it. We share, of course, much bawdy talk when he impersonates his uncle's courtesan, Frank Gullman, but during his elaborate masquerade we discover little about his own sexual interests. And when he finally falls in love with the real Gullman, we still do not get a very precise sense of his sexual appetites. A man who assures us that "If e'er I love, or anything move me, / 'Twill be a woman's simple modesty"[43] does not indulge his madcap personality as a lover. Though Follywit is clearly a sensual being, Middleton takes great care that Follywit's evident passion never assumes an explicitly sexual form. For all of his exuberance and sensuality, Follywit distinguishes himself as remarkably ignorant in sexual matters. Middleton clearly wishes to isolate Follywit from the sexual: how else to account for this master trickster being gulled by the whore he has impersonated, mistaking a well-used piece for a modest virgin? That Follywit's otherwise penetrating insight into others abandons him when he confronts Gullman points to Middleton's determination that Follywit not be tainted by any clear relationship to the sexual.

The character who does exhibit the obsession with sex that we expect to see in the play is Master Penitent Brothel, whose opening-scene observations on Follywit at once establish his distance from, but relationship to, the "mad-brain" youth:

> Here's a mad-brain o'th' first, whose pranks scorn to have precedents, to be second to any, or walk beneath any mad-cap's inventions; . . . hating imitation, a fellow whose only glory is to be prime of the company . . .
>> But why in others do I check wild passions,
>> And retain deadly follies in myself?
>> I tax his youth of common receiv'd riot,
>> Time's comic flashes, and the fruits of blood;

And in myself soothe up adulterous motions,
And such an appetite that I know damns me.
(I.i.83-95)

The play develops from this point as if Follywit's sexual energies had been displaced onto Penitent, who in his own dull fashion pursues a course of sexual duplicity and obsession. The play proceeds in this way because sexual obsession clearly remains outside of "time's comic flashes"; Penitent's "adulterous motions" represent instead "deadly follies" that would compromise Follywit's comic nature were he too clearly to expose his sexual inclinations. Follywit's pranks can all be innocent as long as he does not explicitly reveal the one "appetite" that "damns." Sexual extravagance must be sundered from the comic hero in order for him to escape our moral censure. Follywit thus emerges from the drama as an innocent figure of play; distanced from the sexual he can indulge in the sheer creative play that celebrates basic human energies.

In Middleton's play sexual passion represents one of these basic energies only when enjoyed in lawful marriage. Sexuality apart from marriage is invariably perverse in this play, expressing itself in the ludicrous behavior of Sir Bounteous—an object of derision for his insistence on enjoying passions he can no longer fulfill—or in the hellish adultery of Penitent Brothel and Mistress Harebrain, who expose a "lechery that's damn'd to th' pit-hole" (I.ii.133). Follywit's innocence takes shape against the sexual obsessions of both his uncle and the adulterous couple. Thus, sexuality as play cannot really express itself in this society, so narrowly confined are its moral limits.

Middleton's determination to exert such a strict control over the sexual extravagances of his "mad world" accounts for the disturbing appearance of the succubus in Act IV, scene i. This intrusion of the demonic realm certainly leads to a marvellously comic scene. Breaking in upon Penitent while he castigates himself for his sexual weakness, the succubus amusingly highlights this earnest speech of remorse in which Penitent exposes his self-loathing—"To dote on weakness, slime, corruption, woman!"—and fear that "to please the flesh, [I have] blotted out . . . [my] name." The succubus' obscene wit —"What, at a stand? The fitter for my company"—and sexual

enticements perfectly set off Penitent's trembling fear and
resolution. She dances round him repeating lascivious verse in
rhymed hexameters ("wanton and effeminate rhymes" he
later calls them), only to disappear when he finally conjures
the devil himself to "leave this chamber freed from thy
damn'd art." The scene is all the more comic because Penitent
thinks the spirit is a real woman; a witty director would have
him tremble as much with desire as fear.

In spite of its wit and humor, however, the scene also reflects the serious moral dimension of the play's sexual concerns. Even if we assume that Middleton did not believe literally in demons—and that the scene may in fact satirize such
beliefs—the scenes that follow the succubus' appearance emphasize the genuineness of Penitent's peril. In Act IV, scene iii,
Follywit, now dressed as his uncle's whore, wonders why
Gullman never before thought to steal the jewels he is now
about to remove: "If I do not wonder how the quean 'scap'd
tempting, I'm an hermaphrodite! Sure she could lack nothing
but the devil to point to't, and I wonder that he should be missing. Well, 'tis better as it is; this is the fruit of old grunting
venery" (IV.iii.39–43). This insistence on the intimate connection between sex, the devil, and women is further established in the next scene when Penitent finally discovers the
true identity of the spirit that visited him. His moralizing on
the incident condemns not only adultery—his particular sin—
but all sex enjoyed outside of marriage: "What knows the
lecher when he clips his whore / Whether it be the devil his
parts adore?" (IV.iv.55–56). The association of the phallus
with the devil again emphasizes the inherent dangers of sexuality, the discomfort and fear that the organs of generation
themselves inspire. This phallic demonism leads naturally to
Penitent's final advice to Mistress Harebrain, in which he suggests, like Paul in his dictum "It is better to marry than to
burn" (1 Cor. 7:9), the human longing for an untormented virginity: "Live honest, and live happy, keep thy vows; / She's
part a virgin whom but one man knows."

The insistent moralizing that the succubus' intervention
generates has disturbed most critics of the play. Richard Levin
asserts that her appearance "drops [the play] out of the comic
framework," whereas Anthony Covatta feels that with her ap-

pearance the ''subplot sits uncomfortably beside the main action. It is a long jump from hell to the world of Dick Follywit, but Middleton asks us to make it.''[44] The strain in the comic structure that these critics recognize is forced upon Middleton by the assumptions that underlie the rhetoric of demonic sexuality. The play must take its audience on that long jump from hell because Penitent's sexual obsessions clearly stand outside of the comic world of the play; they represent a ''madness'' not endorsed or even condoned by the exhilaration of the play's title, *A Mad World, My Masters*. The appreciation of misrule, the joy in anarchic energy, that the title and action of the play celebrate thrives only when separated from the explicitly sexual: the tonal, formal, and moral gulfs between the Follywit and Penitent plots point to this necessity. The play's comic resolution, therefore, must reveal the sexual demonic displaced by the divine: Mistress Harebrain must ''keep her vows,'' remain ''part a virgin,'' while even Frank Gullman must promise to ''have a soul true to both thee and heaven.''[45] Comedy, of course, normally moves from misrule to order; what distinguishes Jacobean from Restoration comedy is the divine hierarchy that in the former defines that transition. Sexuality as a form of play, as a natural and creative part of the human personality, is not ordinarily endorsed by the earlier drama, where the explicitly sexual must be kept at a distance, rendered strange, unhealthy, even alien. This does not mean that the later drama necessarily celebrates sexual obsession, or conceives of it as other than a dangerous and potentially destructive form of play. Defined, however, as a more fully human passion, sexuality and the attempt to control it pass from the divine to the human world. Restoration comedies dealing with the rake insist on the social terms of the limitations they place on sexuality; marriage qualifies sexuality not because it is a sacrament representing the divine, but because as a social institution it may be molded to suit individual passions and needs.

Another instructive example of the strain that this divine framework places on the structure of Jacobean comedy can be found in Marston's *The Dutch Courtesan*, where sexual obsession again fractures a play's tone and action. Here the plot involving Cocledemoy and Mulligrub remains sundered from

the Freevill-Franceschina-Malheureux plot in much the same
way as Follywit's escapades were separated from Penitent's.
This remains true even though Cocledemoy is clearly a more
sexual being than Follywit: his initial trick on Mulligrub—only reported to us by Freevill—involved "his movable
chattel, his instrument of fornication, the bawd Mistress Mary
Faugh."[46] Cocledemoy shares an intimacy with the
prostitute's world that leads to his amusing celebration of their
"trade": "Only my smooth-gumm'd bawd lives by others'
pleasure, and only grows rich by others' rising. O merciful
gain! O righteous income!" (I.ii.46–48). Yet in spite of his
evident sexual sophistication, we see none of his energy directed to sexual goals in the play; all of his vitality spends itself
in his endless gulling of Mulligrub. Though Cocledemoy's
vigor may always threaten to erupt into sexual form, it never
quite does. He remains an "innocent" trickster, his playful
spirits never quite tarnished by the corruption of sexuality.

The power of sexuality to corrupt presents itself in the
other half of the play, where the sexual obsessions of Franceschina and Malheureux reveal two souls in pawn to the devil.
The Dutch courtesan of the title is damned from the beginning
of the play. Such a broad caricature that she hardly exists as a
genuine character, Franceschina early warns us that "the
world sall know the worst of evils: / Woman corrupted is the
worst of devils" (II.ii.196–97); her behavior consistently confirms this initial judgment. Even a casual reference by Cocledemoy establishes that a woman can be marked by "the nim-
ble devil in her buttock" (II.i.152), and Franceschina's behavior reveals a woman totally lost to these twin powers of sex and
evil: "O Divila, life o' mine art! Ick sall be reveng'd! Do ten
tousand hell damn me" (II.ii.40–41). If, as Freevill ironically
remarks during an early defense of prostitution, "Every man
must follow his trade, and every woman her occupation"
(I.i.94–95), Franceschina has willfully chosen one occupation
that must inevitably damn her. The patron saint of prostitution is the devil himself.

Malheureux has not betrayed himself to such an extent, but
his own torment proves the truth of his rueful lament, "When
woman's in the heart, in the soul hell" (IV.ii.30). Hurried
away from himself by a passion he cannot control, Malheureux

exemplifies the betrayal of human divinity that overtakes one
who would place lust above all else. Malheureux admits that
"I do malign my creation that I am subject to passion"
(III.i.241), defining extravagant passion as a revelation of non-
being, an annihilation of proper human identity; there is, Malheureux insists, "no God in blood" (IV.ii.13). Again we
inhabit a society in which the genital demonic reveals the
ultimate fear of inevitable sexual damnation: "*Diaboli virtus
in lumbis est!*" (II.i.89, translated by John Florio, in his edition of Montaigne, as "The divels master-point lies in our
loines"). Freevill's allusion to Montaigne's quotation from
Saint Jerome in "On some verses of Virgil" establishes once
again the essential identity of sexual obsession and demonic
possession.

The moral climax of the play comes in the fifth act, when
Freevill describes the divine hierarchy that enforces a strict
dichotomy between the chaste love of heaven and the demonic
sexuality of hell. Having just watched Malheureux taken off to
prison while cursing that "wicked, wicked devil" Franceschina, Freevill soliloquizes on the gulf between the "hellish"
passions she exemplifies and the "holy union" of a "lawful
bed." Franceschina is fit only for hell, "unreprievable, beyond
all / Measure of grace damn'd immediately!" (V.i.60–61). She
epitomizes a "vile" world of "blood and hell" that stands in
sharp contrast to the "joys of chaste sheets" whose "modest
pleasures" heaven blesses. Imaged by the "cataracts of Nile"
that "take away sense," sexual obsession stands revealed as a
frenzy that destroys the "very music of life." The speech gains
power because Freevill himself stands between the unlawful
pleasures that he now despises but once enjoyed, and the
chaste passion that he will soon share with Beatrice. Franceschina represents a world he has rejected, and his speech ends
with the appearance of Franceschina and Freevill's final curse
upon her: "How monstrous is thy devil! / The end of hell as
thee!" In this soliloquy Freevill treats Franceschina as the
demonic Other; he directs his curses not at himself or Malheureux but at the woman who "bewitched" them into exposing
their weaknesses.

Freevill's soliloquy marks Marston's most forceful delinea-
tion of what the opening "Fabulae Argumentum" describes as

"the difference betwixt the love of a courtesan and a wife."
Marston, as Paul Zall argues, wishes to dramatize "that passions in themselves were vital to the organic process." Yet the
extravagance of Freevill's language, and the exaggerated distinction he draws between the two types of love and the two
women who externalize them, attest to Marston's difficulty in
creating a clear relationship between lust and love: "It is
through the medium of the body that ideal love, whose seat is
in the soul, can best be effected and expressed. And yet love, as
lust, was 'the strongest argument that speaks against the
soul's eternity.'"[47] Freevill, after all, begins the play as one
who would enjoy the natural passions, "love[,] the life's
music." By the time of his soliloquy, however, he can find
those passions natural only when sanctified by marriage;
otherwise they appear as the grotesque and frightening com-
pulsions of a Franceschina or a Malheureux, who between
them disclose an uncontrollable sexual world of bawds, prostitutes, and murderers. Marston has difficulty defining any middle ground between Franceschina, the devil, and Beatrice, the
angel, between the hellish sexual world of taverns and
brothels, and the heavenly love found in Beatrice's home.[48]
The play's inability to do so reveals Marston's failure to resolve the essential sexual paradox of the Montaigne essay, "On
some verses of Virgil," to which the play often alludes: "On
the one side nature urgeth us unto it, having thereunto combined, yea, fastned the most noble, the most profitable, and
the most sensually-pleasing of all her functions; and on the
other suffereth us to accuse, to condemne and to shunne it, as
insolent, as dishonest, and as lewder to blushe at it, and allow,
yea, and to commend abstinence."[49] Marston does not commend abstinence, but the care with which he describes the
"chaste sheets" and "holy union" of marriage greatly limits
the expression of natural passion.

The rigorous morality of this sexual plot bears little resemblance to the relaxed and generous license that allows us to
enjoy the tricks and plots of Cocledemoy in the play's other
major plot. In spite of his willful disregard for law and close relationship to the Vice, Cocledemoy emerges as a gamboling
child who avoids moral censure because he inhabits a juvenile

realm of play. In both *A Mad World, My Masters* and this play, that realm can exist only because it has been carefully isolated from the sexual ambivalences that characterize the rest of the two plays. In *The Dutch Courtesan* Marston so successfully divides the two worlds that through most of the eighteenth and nineteenth centuries his play was most often revived as a farce involving only the trickster Cocledemoy and his eternal victim, Mulligrub. The "main" plot, in fact, is completely detachable, so fractured is the play's action, so schizophrenic its moral tone.

The play's major attempt to bridge this gap, to create a natural relationship between lust and love, comes in the wooing of Beatrice's sister Crispinella by her "blunt gallant" Tysefew. This couple indulges in the witty play typical of the gay couple, employing a language that at once preserves their innocence yet discloses the sexual excitement they share. In contrast, the relationship between Beatrice and Freevill cannot admit the desires available to the gay couple; restricted by the moral limits of Marston's action, they cannot enjoy a passion that might link them to the demonic world of Malheureux and Franceschina. Thus, as Beatrice and Freevill move closer to marriage, Beatrice must assure both her fiancé and the audience that "your virtue won me; faith, my love's not lust" (III.i.201). The conventional distinction between lust and love reinforces their purity and their relationship's absolute distance from the sexual demonism that disfigures Franceschina and Malheureux.

On the margins of the play, however, basically irrelevant to the workings out of the moral significance of the comic action, Crispinella and Tysefew can comport themselves in a much livelier fashion. Crispinella first enters at the beginning of Act III, immediately overturning the circumscribed moral world of her sister by announcing "Let's ne'er be ashamed to speak what we be not asham'd to think. I dare as boldly speak venery as think venery" (III.i.25–27). Crispinella then launches into a series of long speeches that scandalize her fastidious sister by questioning the strict demarcation between the proper and the improper upon which Beatrice insists. Crispinella ends with a glance at marriage that presents a much more casual, more cynical view of marriage than Beatrice can allow: "Virtuous marriage! There is no more affinity betwixt virtue and marriage than betwixt a man and his horse. Indeed, virtue gets up upon marriage sometimes and manageth it in the right way, but marriage is of another piece; for as a horse may be without a man, and a man without a horse, so marriage, you know, is often without virtue, and virtue, I am sure, more oft without marriage" (III.i.82–88). After this speech Tysefew enters, and he and Crispinella begin the repartee that leads eventually to their marriage. Their conversations contain much personal abuse, more than an occasional double entendre, and a wit and irreverence most closely associated in the play with the extravagance of Cocledemoy. They are, in short, a fully formed gay couple.

Precisely for that reason their role is strictly limited: for all the undeniable excitement that they bring to the stage, they have only one major scene together, Act IV, scene i, and even that lasts only sixty lines. Otherwise their wooing—in, for example, Act III, scene i, or Act V, scene ii—is only a small part of a larger action, as in the latter scene, where news of Freevill and Malheureux overshadows their witty exchanges. The play even avoids bringing much attention to their marriage: Tysefew's announcement that "marriage and hanging are spun both in one hour" (V.iii.150–51) is hurried into just a few lines at the play's conclusion. After the Restoration Crispinella and Tysefew would probably form the focus of the comic action; here, not only are they tangential to that action, but also the implicit comparison between their love and Beatrice and Freevill's serves primarily to reinforce our perception of the principal couple's superiority.[50] If Crispinella's speech about marriage offends her sister, it also clashes with the conception of marriage on which the play itself finally insists. Opposed to the unholy sexual alliance of Franceschina and Malheureux, Beatrice and Freevill must participate in a sacramental rite that cannot afford qualification by the witticisms of the two extravagants. The high-spirited freedom, cynicism, and irreverence of Crispinella and Tysefew are values that the play can fully countenance only when enjoyed in the juvenile world of Cocledemoy and Mulligrub; the sexual focus of the gay couple's remarks remains at odds with the main comic

action.[51] Their presence cannot be ignored, but the values the
gay couple advances carry little weight in the society of the
play.

V

In his remarkable book *The World We Have Lost*, Peter Laslett argues that "nothing in the documents confirms that there
was a change in sexual habits to correspond with that license
and licentiousness which has always been associated with the
Restoration as a whole period of time." For late-sixteenth-cen-
tury as well as late-seventeenth-century England,

> it would seem impossible to cite statements which contemplated
> permissiveness of any sort in such matters except for those which
> made full use of poetic licence, and except for some of the speeches
> heard in the London Playhouses during the Restoration period. Ordi-
> nary people can rarely be heard on this subject. But when they spoke
> their minds as witnesses in ecclesiastical courts they left no doubt
> that sexual intercourse outside marriage was universally con-
> demned.[52]

Loss of belief in demonic sexuality does not imply that between the courts of James I and Charles II sexual behavior
became radically more promiscuous, that adultery became acceptable, premarital sex common, Pauline morality banished.
My concern with demonism has not necessarily involved different degrees of sexual license, but different perceptions of
human sexuality. That Restoration society may have distanced
itself from a pervasive sense of the sinfulness of sexuality—
whose particular nature I have located in the sexually demonic
—does not mean that sex suddenly became a mundane activity
unconnected to guilt, casually enjoyed by all. What the transformation from Jacobean to Restoration society does reveal are
the complexities of human sexuality taking new form. When
the rake replaces the witch as a primary image of social disorder and erotic compulsion, new perceptions of human sexual
potential reveal themselves. Subsequent chapters will describe
some of these understandings and their implications for both
the individual and society.

It is foolish to assume that this shift would necessarily lead to a liberation from all sexual fears; promiscuity is not the only conceivable response to a loss of belief in sexual demonism. And even when outlandish promiscuity does result, as in Rochester's "The Fall," sexuality remains an ambiguous part of life and experience:

> How blest was the created state
> Of man and woman, ere they fell,
> Compared to our unhappy fate:
> We need not fear another hell.
>
> Naked beneath cool shades they lay;
>   Enjoyment waited on desire;
> Each member did their wills obey,
>   Nor could a wish set pleasure higher.
>
> But we, poor slaves to hope and fear,
>   Are never of our joys secure;
> They lessen still as they draw near,
>   And none but dull delights endure.[53]

In spite of the allusion to hell, Rochester's poem is not concerned with the demonic aspects of sexuality; he laments not an evil passion, but a fallen passion that, because of the male failure to control erection and ejaculation, by its very nature pits will against pleasure, enjoyment against desire, and leads inevitably to dissatisfaction and frustration. While Rochester may not fear sexuality because its evil threatens to undermine his fragile identity, his sexual world remains a prey to guilt and pain, not at all the erotic paradise imagined by popular belief. As Carole Fabricant has demonstrated, Rochester normally presents a frightening sexual world filled with images of violence, disease, and mechanization.[54] Rochester's secularized myth of a sexual fall bears little resemblance to Jacobean thought—where theologians occasionally envisioned an Edenic state *sans* sexual intercourse—but the transformation has not liberated him from a mistrust or fear of the erotic.

Yet such a radical change in understanding is sure to have left its mark, though its results need not be manifested in more permissive forms of sexual activity. Far more likely are changes in the social institutions involved with human sexuality. David Foxon, for instance, argues that the rapid development of pornography in the three or four decades after 1650 depends on a changing relationship between authority and sexuality. Foxon links the religious and political ferment of seventeenth-century England to increased sexual license, arguing that all three constitute a general revolt against traditional modes of authority.[55]

Foxon even suggests that this revolt may be related to parallel changes in the raising of children, thus anticipating the current historical debate over transformations in family structure and relationships. Social historians have yet to generate a convincing model for such changes, and research continues into how, if at all, the family changed during the seventeenth and eighteenth centuries. Lawrence Stone, in *The Family, Sex, and Marriage in England, 1500–1800,* has set the parameters for this debate by insisting that at least three important transformations in family structure began during the Restoration: changes in child-rearing practices among the middle class, upper bourgeoisie, and squirarchy; the undermining of rigorous patriarchal authority by the institution of "strict settlements" (the allocation of portions to unborn children at the time of marriage); and the movement of mating arrangements from parents to children. For Stone all of these changes involve a movement from arranged marriages that stressed economic, political, and kinship concerns towards marriages in which mutual affection and love were primary: "This shift of emphasis towards the nuclear family was given powerful support by Reformation theology and practice. The medieval Catholic ideal of chastity . . . was replaced by the ideal of conjugal affection."[56] If Stone is correct, the changes he defines may mark another social phenomenon that can be linked to new appreciations of the erotic. An increased emphasis on love and friendship between partners as a necessary condition of marriage might indicate a new role for marital sexuality. The changes suggested by Stone clearly relate to the concomitant shift in sexual attitudes developed in this chapter.

Part of the problem in dealing with Restoration comedy has been the belief that the rake's rhetoric of sexual liberation would necessarily manifest itself in society with the same promiscuity celebrated on stage. But the connection between

the theatre and life is not so simple and direct. The rake
initiates a complex and deeply ambivalent sexual discourse,
and only by recognizing this can we make sense of the cultural
significance of the rake and his place in Restoration comedy
and society.

CHAPTER 2

The Hobbesian Libertine Rake and Restoration Definitions of Pleasure

I

How pleasanter it is to jolt about in poor hackney Coaches to find out the harmless lust of the Town than to spend the time in a Roome of State in whispers to discover the ambitious designs of Princes. A letter from you so fires me with the thought of the life I have lead that I can hardly forbear railing at that I am condemn'd to.
—Sir George Etherege to William Jephson
8 March 1688

Etherege's complaints about his life as a diplomat in Ratisbon perfectly display the rake's indifference to the great affairs of the world. Overturning conventional expectations of how people should most properly live, Etherege prefers "poor hackney Coaches" to "a Roome of State," the "harmless lusts of the Town" to the "ambitious designs of Princes." Etherege takes little pleasure in frequenting the corridors of power, suggesting that the rake's obsessive pursuit of sexual satisfaction stems at least in part from the conviction that people normally invest their energies in unworthy, if serious, concerns. A 1676 letter from Rochester to his friend Savile replaces Etherege's indifference to conventional ambition with contempt, Etherege's neat antitheses with a bitter imagery that reduces the exercise of power to mere child's play: "They who would be great in our little government seem as ridiculous to me as schoolboys who with much endeavour and some danger climb a crab-tree, venturing their necks for fruit which solid pigs would disdain if they were not starving."[1] The characteristic

49

turn of Rochester's mind, which caustically deflates human
pretensions by comparing people to beasts, leads inevitably to
the Restoration metaphors of sex as appetite that consistently
define the rake's understanding of human needs. Our sexual
desires, like our hunger for food, are fundamental to the
organism; those who ignore or try to transcend their sexuality
are like "schoolboys," unaware of the true values of life.
Another of the court wits, Charles Sackville, earl of Dorset,
playfully uses this understanding of human nature to subvert a
conventional metaphor for the individual personality:

> Some do compare a man t'a bark—
> A pretty metaphor, pray mark—
> And with a long and tedious story,
> Will all the tackling lay before ye:
> The sails are hope, the masts desire,
> Till they the gentlest reader tire.
> But howsoe'er they keep a pudder,
> I'm sure the pintle is the rudder:
> The pow'rful rudder, which of force
> To town will shortly steer my course.[2]

In Restoration drama, the most famous statement of this
distinction between conventional and rakish judgments of
value is Jaspar Fidget's innocent remark to his wife and Horner
that they "go to your business, I say, pleasure, whilst I go to
my pleasure, business."[3] Jaspar Fidget's naive use of the terms
"business" and "pleasure" characterize an individual alive
only, as Sackville puts it, to the bark's "tackling"; Sir Jaspar
fails to recognize the powerful sexual urges that steer the
entire craft. The opening scene of Congreve's first comedy,
The Old Batchelour, takes up Wycherley's distinction between
pleasure and business, dramatically depicting the rakish disdain for the mere business of life:

> *Vainlove. Bellmour*, good Morrow—Why truth on't is,
>   these early Sallies are not usual to me; but Business as
>   you see Sir—(*Shewing Letters.*) And Business must be
>   follow'd, or be lost.
> *Bellmour*. Pox o' Business—And so must Time, my Friend,
>   be close pursued, or lost. Business is the rub of Life,

perverts our Aim, casts off the Bias, and leaves us wide
and short of the intended Mark.
Vainlove. Pleasure, I guess you mean.
Bellmour. Ay, what else has meaning?[4]

As Vainlove and Bellmour continue their conversation,
cataloging the women with whom they are, have been, or will
be involved, it quickly becomes apparent that the pleasure of
which they speak is primarily sexual; for Bellmour the only
significant question is whether his body can satisfy the
demands of his desire: "Flesh and Blood cannot bear it always"
(I.i.160-61).

Bellmour's casual dismissal of all other pursuits, his playful assumption that nothing else "has meaning," places us
firmly in a rakish world "consecrate"—as Rochester explains
in "A Ramble in St. James's Park"—"to prick and cunt."[5] In
this and the following chapter, I shall explore just what
"meaning" sexual pleasure possesses for such a world. In
Elizabethan and Jacobean comedy, sexual pleasure has a
restricted significance. As the plays examined in Chapter 1
demonstrate, sexual pleasure before the Restoration usually
emerges as a relatively limited quality, bounded and understood primarily through the "chaste sheets" of marriage or the
"monstrous" expressions of demonic sexuality. After the
Restoration pleasure becomes a more complex phenomenon,
assuming diverse shapes and meanings. The Elizabethan and
Jacobean forms remain, but even they take a different shape as
the divine hierarchy governing sexuality becomes less compelling. Thus, marriage, as I previously noted, becomes less a
holy or sanctified union than (through the mechanism of the
proviso scene) a social institution liable to redefinition by the
individual. As Susan Staves notes, the Civil Marriage Act of
1653 and the Interregnum transfer of jurisdiction over marriage
from the ecclesiastical courts to the state "unsettled assumptions about the sacramental character of marriage."[6] And
though sexuality after the Restoration still breaks out in
"monstrous" forms, these normally escape condemnation as
instances of demonic imposition. Rochester, for instance, well
understands the corrupt and frightening sexual practices that
deform his pastoral world "consecrate to prick and cunt":

Each imitative branch does twine
In some loved fold of Aretine,
And nightly now beneath their shade
Are buggeries, rapes, and incests made.

(lines 21–24)

Here Rochester brutally undercuts the pleasant sensuality of
the first couplet with the gross perversions of the second; but
the rhetoric of these lines has less to do with the language of
sexual demonism than with the clinical language of a modern
sex survey: "buggeries, rapes, and incests" reveal, for
Rochester's contemporaries, the deformed desires of the
sexually perverted individual, not the frightening manifestations of a demonic presence. These secularized attitudes
towards sexuality make it possible to provide a taxonomy for
rakish behavior in terms of the diverse permutations of sexual
desire.

In this chapter I will begin to sketch this taxonomy by
examining four plays produced before 1685 that present the
rake as a Hobbesian libertine. In the past, the tendency of
critics to view the plays of Wycherley, Etherege, and Congreve
in a single light depended on the mistaken notion that libertinism designated an organized philosophy that remained consistent throughout the period 1660–1700. Virginia Ogden Birdsall, for instance, makes precisely this mistake when she
describes rakes, "both as libertines and as persistent chal-
lengers who thrive on controversy," as "exemplary of the Hobbesian thinking which prevailed in court circles after the Restoration."[7] Both Robert Hume and Maximillian Novak,
however, demonstrate that "the libertinism of the nineties is
philosophically very different indeed from that of the seven-
ties,"[8] and they maintain that a substantial difference exists
between the Hobbesian libertine of Wycherley and Etherege
and the philosophical libertine of Congreve. The Hobbesian
libertine represents the first type of rake to pursue his lusts on
the Restoration stage. In examining his career in four plays, by
four different playwrights, we can begin to understand the
complex and often contradictory impulses that motivate the
rake's search for sexual satisfaction. In analyzing these plays I
will be concerned not primarily with whether the rake emerges

as a "hero" or a "villain"—he must, as I have indicated, be both[9]—but with the tensions between sensual and aggressive pleasure that characterize his assiduous pursuit of women.

II

Essential to an understanding of the Hobbesian libertine is a recognition of what Dale Underwood has identified as "a crux in libertine belief arising from the influence of contradic tory traditions." While the scepticism of the English libertine depended on the naturalism of Machiavelli and Hobbes—a tradition concerned with human self-interest, aggression, and conquest—it also recognized the primitivist's Golden Laws of Nature and a belief in the individual's natural affinity for freedom, indulgence, and pleasure. In the true Hobbesian libertine, as Underwood emphasizes, these two strands "were combined into a nature whose inconsistencies were sufficiently submerged to avoid practical embarrassment."[10] Such a nature, perhaps because of the tension between these two inconsistent beliefs, manifests a tremendous vitality best displayed in Restoration comedy by Wycherley's Horner. The exuberance and animation of *The Country-Wife* (1675), which are probably responsible for its position as the most frequently revived of Restoration comedies, stem primarily from Horner, in whom we find the finest expression of the libertine's diverse naturalistic impulses. The aggression that he directs against others, revealed in his outrageous attempt to dupe all society, including his friends, is matched only by his concern for sexual satisfaction. Horner takes an exquisite pleasure in both his sexual and social manipulations. The extravagant lie that he lives, as his conversations with the quack reveal, clearly stands as a source of pleasure in its own right, though he never loses sight of its ultimate sexual aim. Elaborate as his deception may be, he remains always aware that "ceremony in love and eating, is as ridiculous as in fighting, falling on briskly is all should be done in those occasions" (V.iv.87–88). The success of the china scene proceeds not simply from its crude sexual power, but also from the joy that Horner takes in revealing the hypocrisy of Lady Fidget and the stupidity of her husband.[11]

Horner achieves an equilibrium between his hedonistic and aggressive impulses because for the most part he directs his contradictory desires to different objects; while he recognizes the similarities between "fighting" and "love," he does not confuse them. His aggression expresses itself in his behavior towards his male victims, the Fidgets and Pinchwifes whom he cuckolds. The horns that they wear, and that his name signifies, represent his success on the battlefield. Yet the cruelty that he directs towards the men rarely appears in his dealings with women, where he proclaims his triumphs only through the exhaustion of his supply of china. While I do not wish to imply that Horner declares himself a radical feminist, Horner insists throughout the play on a just appreciation of women. Though his primary interest in women is sexual, he is nonetheless convinced that "wit is more necessary than beauty, and I think no young Woman ugly that has it, and no handsome woman agreable without it" (I.i.387–89). Horner's disguise, and the pleasure he takes in manipulating the manners of society, are directed primarily at the men in the play, for to achieve his sexual ends Horner must necessarily disclose his true identity to the women.

If one assumes that a healthy sexuality can express itself only through marriage and an enduring relationship with one partner, then Horner of course appears a perverse figure; and many critics have seen him as the pathetic playboy doomed to an eternal round of unsatisfactory affairs. Gerald Weales, for instance, in his introduction to his edition of Wycherley's plays, remarks that Horner's "seductions become merely mechanical. He is more like a chain smoker than a great lover." David Vieth feels that Horner's disguise "limits the nature of his masculine activities so drastically that in a sense he becomes the eunuch he pretends to be," and William Freedman echoes Vieth's point when he discusses how Horner exemplifies the impotence found in the play's other male characters.[12]

Yet I seriously doubt that *The Country-Wife* asks us to see Horner in such a light. As W. R. Chadwick suggests, "the principle that sex is fun, that it is pleasurable to sleep with as many attractive women as possible," would not be alien to either Restoration or modern audiences.[13] While Harcourt and

Alithea emerge by the play's end as an ideal couple, their love vindicated by Harcourt's faith in Alithea's innocence, their triumph in no way reduces Horner's. He remains at the center of the comic world, his sexual generosity and vitality undiminished at the play's close. His final advice—that "he who aimes by women to be priz'd, / First by the men you see must be despis'd" (V.iv.417–18)—reveals once again that genuine sexual gratification depends on the ability to separate the concerns of the bedroom from those of the battlefield. This is a lesson that the Fidgets and Pinchwifes refuse to accept, for they continue to treat their wives as spoils of war to be guarded and humiliated. The desire of Pinchwife and Fidget to maintain their illusions about Horner and their wives represents society's failure to penetrate its affectations and recognize the sexual element of human nature. Society's inability to embrace Horner's sexuality describes society's loss more than Horner's. In this instance I find myself in agreement with Birdsall's vision of the play's conclusion, in which an imaginative staging of the "dance of cuckolds" would place Horner "at the vital center of the circling dancers—the phallic symbol incarnate— . . . draw[ing] each of the ladies in turn into the center with him to dance a turn, for he represents, in all his impudence, the life force triumphant."[14]

Horner's joyous sexuality depends on his capacity to maintain an equilibrium between his appetite for lust and his appetite for power, and one way to appreciate the tension between these two sources of pleasure is to concentrate on characters and a scene normally given scant attention. Lady Fidget and her attendant "Women of Honour," Mrs. Dainty Fidget and Mrs. Squeamish, are generally dismissed as affected and hypocritical pretenders for whom both Horner and the audience share a justified contempt. Convinced that the three women remain unchanged in the course of the play, most critics describe these pretenders to honor as libidinal monsters and use them only to define the higher virtues of Alithea and the artless innocence of Margery Pinchwife.[15] But Lady Fidget and company are not static figures who remain locked within their initial conceptions of self and society. By examining their banquet with Horner in Act V, I wish to suggest that they achieve a harmony between social masks and natural desires denied to

most of the other characters, and that this banquet, in presenting an image of a genuine community that the play's larger
society moves to frustrate, displays the conception of human
nature that the play assumes and the values that it celebrates.
Thus the banquet illuminates the structure of the comic action
and Horner's role within that structure.

The few critics who have considered the place of the banquet in *The Country-Wife* usually react to it with a mixture of
disgust and contempt. W. R. Chadwick, for instance, describes
it as an "orgy of confession," insisting on its dark and menacing overtones: "In production this . . . scene should surely be
given a rather dark colouring, for what it in fact shows is three
bibulous women in the process of a physical debauch disclos-
ing, without even the comedy of affectation to lighten their
performance, the depth of their moral depravity." Rose Zimbardo, too, sees the scene in this fashion, for she proposes that
Wycherley modeled his banquet on the section in Juvenal's
sixth satire in which a gang of women display their bestiality
and shameless indifference to virtue while performing the rites
of *Bona Dea.* And in his recent book, *Restoration Theatre Production*, Jocelyn Powell imagines the scene as a "striking
climax" to the play's "growing sense of moral and physical
squalor."[16]

Behind such condemnations lie assumptions about the
nature and value of physical passion which, for my purposes,
are best revealed by the two related Renaissance topoi that
Frank Kermode has labeled the Banquet of Intellect, or Heavenly Love, and the Banquet of Sense.[17] The former, with its
roots in Plato's *Symposium* and Paul's passage on the Eucha-
rist in 1 Corinthians 10, represents an uplifting love of the soul
that proceeds from the highest senses to the intellect. This
banquet rejects mere pleasure and fulfills itself in a vision of
divine beauty and a true *convivium* of love. The Banquet of
Sense, on the other hand, evolved from commentaries on the
cup of Circe, the temptation of Hercules, and Paul's allusion to
"the table of devils" (1 Cor. 10:21) to define a natural love that
satisfied the senses. The Banquet of Sense completes itself in
the sensual *Voluptas*, which it views as the highest good.

I am not suggesting that Wycherley necessarily wrote his

banquet scene with such traditions in mind or that he intended his reader to judge the scene within the context provided by the Renaissance convention. Yet the Renaissance Banquet of Sense does provide a model for understanding Wycherley's banquet and for appreciating how the scene defines the nature of the sensual passions and sexual liberties that its participants celebrate. Such passions and liberties undoubtedly challenge the ideals of conventional morality that insist on the exalted nature of love; the derivation of the Banquet of Sense from the "table of devils" emphasizes the demonic sexuality that for the Renaissance condemns this celebration of physical passion. As Kermode points out, though "Renaissance Platonism made provision for the service of the terrestrial Venus . . . in general the Banquet of Sense is not regarded as a good thing. . . . The blandishments it represents are trials to be overcome."[18] It is from such a perspective that Chadwick, Zimbardo, and Powell criticize the banquet and its participants.

Within the context of the play, however, the honesty of the banquet's participants is a virtue, not a vice, and their frank acknowledgment of the sexual aspects of human nature marks a valuable departure from the negations of those characters who would deny the importance of their own desires. Audiences undoubtedly find what Chadwick calls the "comedy of affectation" a source of great amusement, but the play never suggests that such affectation represents a healthy alternative to a forthright acceptance of one's own sexual needs. Wycherley does not write from a Platonic tradition, but instead with the anti-*précieuse* attitudes so prevalent at the court of Charles II during the 1660s and 1670s.[19] Wycherley's banquet, like the Banquet of Sense, insists that the body must be served, and although as a symposium it does not conclude with a pure vision of spiritual love, it does allow its participants to admit and share their unaffected desires.

The banquet's achievement of this communion is emphasized by its opening allusion to a conversation in Act I between Horner, Harcourt, and Dorilant. There, Horner, attempting to persuade his friends of the truth of his impotence, had argued vociferously that "women serve but to keep a Man from better Company; . . . good fellowship and friendship, are lasting, rational and manly pleasures" (I.i.190–94). Dorilant and Harcourt object, but Horner maintains that "'tis as hard to be a good Fellow, a good Friend, and a Lover of Women, as 'tis to be a good Fellow, a good Friend, and a Lover of Money: You cannot follow both, then choose your side; Wine gives you liberty, Love takes it away" (203–6). Horner eventually converts Dorilant, though Harcourt remains unconvinced. But Horner's conclusion—"for my part I will have only those glorious, manly pleasures of being very drunk, and very slovenly" (218–19)—firmly establishes for his friends his disguise as a eunuch.

The audience knows, of course, that Horner wants merely to throw his friends off the scent, and the banquet begins by cleverly denying the truth of Horner's ironic remarks. If that earlier conversation defined women and wine, love and good fellowship, as mutually exclusive, the banquet immediately announces that in this small group the two can be combined:

> *La. Fid.* Now Ladies, supposing we had drank each of us
> our two Bottles, let us speak the truth of our hearts.
> *Dayn. and Squem.* Agreed.
> *La. Fid.* By this brimmer, for truth is no where else to be
> found, [Not in thy heart   [*Aside to Hor.*
> false man.
>
>   (V.iv.19–24)

Horner's role as the "false man" would, as always, seem to stand in the way of an honest relationship; indeed, we should not forget that this scene begins with Horner concealing Margery Pinchwife in the next room, the irony of the situation indicating his inability to share fully in the confidences of the banquet. Yet as the scene progresses, the honesty of these three women gradually strips away the barriers that men and women normally erect between one another in the course of the play. The ladies begin by admitting in their song the frustrations of the "dull bed" that their husbands ("our damn'd Tyrants") force them to endure. The song ends with a renewal of their pledge of honesty, for "in token of our openness and plain dealing, let us throw our Masques over our heads" (43–44). As the scene develops, images of masking and unmasking continue to suggest the ability of those present to acknowledge the social illusions that so hamper the freedom of the other characters:

> *La. Fid.* Our Reputation, Lord! Why should you not think,
> that we women make use of our Reputation, as you men
> of yours, only to deceive the world with less suspicion;
> our virtue is like the State-man's Religion, the Quaker's
> Word, the Gamesters Oath, and the Great Man's Honour,
> but to cheat those that trust us.
> *Squeam.* And that Demureness, Coyness, and Modesty,
> that you see in our Faces in the Boxes at Plays, is as
> much a sign of a kind woman, as a Vizard-mask in the
> Pit.
> *Dayn.* For I assure you, women are least mask'd, when
> they have the Velvet Vizard on.
>
> (98–108)

Here the reference to the "Velvet Vizard" and what it reveals about women explicitly denies the masks that these women habitually wear to disguise their desires. The admission is an important one in the play, for the ability of the women to admit their sexual natures, not just to Horner but to each other, demonstrates an acceptance of their instinctive passions and an understanding of how these desires animate their personalities.

If the banquet looks back to Horner's initial conversation with Dorilant and Harcourt, it also reminds us of the initial conversation between Lady Fidget, Mrs. Squeamish, and Dainty Fidget, and the contrast emphasizes the knowledge that they have acquired in the course of the play. The early conversation in Act II, where the three women discussed the social quality of the lovers they might take, seemed to promise an admission of their true desires. But Lady Fidget's failure to admit her lust for pleasure blocked that movement and forced the scene to conclude instead with her shallow recitation of socially approved morality:

> *Lad.* How! no sure the Man of quality is likest one's
> Husband, and therefore the fault shou'd be the less.
> *Dain.* But then the pleasure shou'd be the less.

Lad. Fye, fye, fye, for shame Sister, whither shall we
ramble? be continent in your discourse, or I shall
hate you.

Dain. Besides an intrigue is so much the more
notorious for the man's quality.

Squeam. 'Tis true, no body takes notice of a private Man,
and therefore with him, 'tis more secret, and the crime's
the less, when 'tis not known.

Lad. You say true; y faith I think you are in the right
on't: 'tis not an injury to a Husband, till it be an injury
to our honours; so that a Woman of honour looses no
honour with a private Person; and to say truth—

Dain. So the little Fellow is grown a private Person—
with her—   [*Apart to* Squeamish.

Lad. But still my dear, dear Honour.

                                                          (II.i.374-90)

Even in private Lady Fidget cannot come to terms with the
nature of her desires. Her affected disdain for pleasure and her
incongruous attempts to reconcile her lust with her "dear,
dear Honour" reveal an individual ashamed of, and afraid to
admit, her natural passions. Even when talking to her friends,
Lady Fidget fears to admit the inadequacy of the conventional
social mask, the approved image of the chaste and honorable
female. In this scene the asides must bear the weight of the
truth, while the public masks that obscure the real personality
dominate the stage.

Only at the banquet do the three women finally talk hon-
estly to one another, and attention to the contrasting language
and syntax of the two scenes reveals the implications of this
movement from mask to substance. In the earlier scene Lady
Fidget's rationalizations lead to broken sentences in which
each phrase is keyed to the repetition of words such as "right,"
"truth," "faith," "honour": "You say true; y faith I think you
are in the right on't: 'tis not an injury to a Husband, till it be an
injury to our honours; so that a Woman of honour looses no
honour with a private Person; and to say truth—." The rambling and repetitive quality of her speech, with its staccato
rhythms and long pauses, reveals Lady Fidget in the act of constructing the vision of herself demanded by society. Her tor-
tuous and hypocritical evasions, all in the service of her

boasted honor, mark an individual adapting herself to "a forced disguise, / Leading a tedious life in misery / Under laborious, mean hypocrisy."[20] As Jocelyn Powell explains, the ladies must indulge in "fictional double-think" because they use "moral stricture in order to complain of sexual neglect."[21] Though Lady Fidget's thoughts are fixed on the infidelities she would enjoy, her language must create the picture of an honorable wife concerned not to commit "an injury to a Husband."

Contrast this speech with her consideration of reputation during the banquet: "Our Reputation, Lord! Why should you not think, that we women make use of our Reputation, as you men of yours, only to deceive the world with less suspicion; our virtue is like the State-man's Religion, the Quaker's Word, the Gamesters Oath, and the Great Man's Honour, but to cheat those that trust us." Here the strongly balanced phrases and vigorous wit indicate a sure awareness of the relationship of self to society, a refusal to indulge in polite fictions and degrading "double-think." Lady Fidget now employs a forceful "masculine language" normally used only by the play's men of sense, and in doing so she demonstrates her ability to disregard the unfulfilling identity society would force upon her. In the earlier scene she simply does not possess the vocabulary with which to discuss what society accepts only as a masculine activity—sexual promiscuity. By coming to terms with her passions, by publicly admitting her "dull bed" and "Tyrant" husband, her sexual dissatisfactions, Lady Fidget implicitly condemns the restricted stock of proper female roles that her society allows. Pinchwife's obsessive attempts to keep his wife within doors and to forbid Alithea the "innocent liberty" of the town are only the most brutal manifestations of a society unable to deal with the complexities of women's natures. As Pope explains to his friend Miss Blount, "Too much *your Sex* is by their Forms confin'd, / Severe to all, but most to Womankind."[22] Yet the amazement of the quack, when he is first confronted by the oddity of Horner's disguise, reveals a society blind to any but the most traditional understandings of male sexuality. For both men and women, the social world of the play can proffer only the most limited images of sexuality.

The banquet, then, functions as a scene of revelation, creating an atmosphere in which the women no longer feel the necessity to lie to each other. Significantly, it is Lady Fidget who begins the round of confidences culminating in the unmasking of Horner: "Come here's to our Gallants in waiting, whom we must name, and I'll begin, This is my false Rogue" (148–49). In the course of the banquet the "false Rogue" has acquainted himself with the secrets of the ladies while refusing to relinquish his own secret (the presence of Margery in the next room). Self-aware from the beginning of the play, Horner has not attained any new insight into his own personality. His understanding of sexuality has not changed at all, and his analogies between eating and love remind us that he continues to view sexuality as simply another appetite: "Why faith ceremony and expectation are unsufferable to those that are sharp bent, people always eat with the best stomach at an ordinary, where every man is snatching for the best bit" (80–82). Yet Horner has come to realize why his women so vociferously pretend to an honor for which they have contempt. The banquet provides him with an opportunity both to understand the frustrations that have made these women pretenders to honor and to recognize the kinship he shares with women he once despised. Horner, the self-confident male aggressor, has never before fully comprehended the social constraints that limit women in their pursuit of pleasure; during the banquet he comes to understand how much greater are the privileges males enjoy, how much larger are their spheres of action. Though he momentarily hesitates when his secret comes out —"So all will out now" (151)—this knowledge helps him to accept and even welcome the effect of his unmasking: "Well then, you are all three my false Rogues too, and there's an end on't" (160–61). All pretenses shed, the *ménage à quatre* no longer need assume virtues they have long ago rejected. All are "false Rogues," "false Villains"; and Lady Fidget's sense of her rivals as "Sister Sharers," and of Horner as "Harry Common," indicates the amused and tolerant response of all to their situation. Though cynicism certainly characterizes the ladies' easy acceptance of their situation, the revelations that all have shared signal a healthy occasion, for they have freed

these characters from social conventions and "ceremony" that
have little to do with their true natures:

> *La. Fid.* Well Harry Common, I hope you can be true
> to three, swear, but 'tis no purpose, to require your
> Oath; for you are as often forsworn, as you swear
> to new women.
> *Hor.* Come, faith Madam, let us e'en pardon one
> another, for all the difference I find betwixt we men,
> and you women, we forswear our selves at the
> beginning of an Amour, you, as long as it lasts.
>
> (170–75)

If for much of the play Horner and his women can satisfy
their desires only through the manipulation of manners, the
banquet represents a much more fulfilling ideal of personal
freedom; at least for the moment they need not isolate
themselves or deceive those around them in order to express
and satisfy their natures. The banquet marks the only occasion, except for the scenes between Horner and the quack and
between Alithea and Lucy, when all the characters gathered on
stage succeed in communicating without the barriers imposed
by the deceptions of other or self that so consistently define the
play's action. The play represents these barriers in its use of
double language, conversations whose true meaning is known
only to some of its participants. We discover such conversations everywhere in the play, particularly when Harcourt
makes love to Alithea in Sparkish's presence, but also, as in
the china scene, when Horner exploits his guise as a eunuch.
Such scenes, with their significant emphasis on the disjunction between appearance and reality, clearly represent the
degraded nature of the society depicted in the play, for they
reveal a world in which people are unable or unwilling to communicate with each other, isolated in the midst of social
rituals that serve not to unite but to divide them. The confidences of the banquet for once render such deceptions un-
necessary.

Though the banquet provides a glimpse of a momentary
honesty and fellow feeling in a society dedicated to the cruelty
of Pinchwife and the selfishness of Sparkish and Jaspar Fidget,

society triumphs in the next, and concluding scene of the play; the community forged by the four remains locked within the confines of the corrupt society of which it is but a part. The banquet is broken up by the intrusion of Jaspar Fidget, Old Lady Squeamish, and Pinchwife, precisely those individuals too affected to recognize the substance behind their social masks. These characters, the conclusion suggests, are all too ready to dupe themselves. Pinchwife confirms this truth when he declares, "For my own sake fain I wou'd all believe. / Cuckolds like Lovers shou'd themselves deceive" (V.iv. 410–11). Jaspar Fidget demonstrates it when he jumps at the chance to believe the quack instead of his reason: "Nay I do believe you truly—pardon me my virtuous Lady, and dear of honour" (347–48). The desire of such characters not to look beyond the manners and forms that define their society proves not only their inability to share in the confidences of the banquet, but the corruption of the society that they help to perpetuate. The play's conclusion dramatizes a society in which manners serve only to disguise human nature, and most individuals achieve happiness only when ignorant of the true characters of their peers.

Yet it will not do to talk of Horner solely as an innocent victim whose dream of an ideal community is frustrated by a society of fools and villains. The rake-hero, John Traugott notes, is an attractive but disturbing figure,[23] and if the banquet reveals what is most attractive about Horner—his frankness, vitality, and sexual enthusiasm—the scene that follows emphasizes his most disturbing qualities. In the concluding scene, Horner plays a significant role in preserving the deceptions that make impossible the enlargement of the community he has just enjoyed:

> *Har.* Madam, then have no trouble, you shall now see
> 'tis possible for me to love too, without being jealous,
> I will not only believe your innocence my self, but make
> all the world believe it—*Horner* I must now be
> concern'd for this Ladies Honour.   [*Apart to* Horner.
> *Hor.* And I must be concern'd for a Ladies Honour too.
> *Har.* This Lady has her Honour, and I will protect it.
> *Hor.* My Lady has not her Honour, but has given it me to
> keep, and I will preserve it.

Har. I understand you not.
Hor. I wou'd not have you.

(V.iv.250–61)

It is this exchange, rather than the banquet, that I find most menacing, for here Horner is not attacking the Pinchwifes and Fidgets—who, both Restoration and modern audiences would agree, deserve punishment—but an honorable couple trying to establish a relationship based on mutual love and respect.[24] The final scene hovers on the edge of social chaos, for even the two men of sense can no longer communicate intelligibly with each other. The double language that runs through the play culminates in this exchange, where the competing definitions of honor as reputation and as virtue collide and find no resolution. Horner's deliberate obfuscation of the truth reveals his love for the social confusion that allows his scheme to function: in preserving Margery's "honour," he also maintains his secret world of pleasure.

The betrayal of Harcourt in Act V is all the more disturbing because Horner, though he has never confided his secret to Harcourt, has hitherto at least aided the latter in his pursuit of Alithea. It is Horner who explains to Harcourt how best to secure Alithea from under the nose of her foolish fiancé. In his role as Harcourt's ally, Horner plays the part of the tricky slave, that figure, as Northrop Frye explains, "entrusted with hatching the schemes which bring about the hero's victory."[25] Harcourt does, of course, triumph when he demonstrates the trust that proves his love, but his success comes about in spite of Horner. In the final analysis, Horner becomes one of the play's blocking characters, a figure, like Pinchwife or Fidget, whose self-interest dictates that he help maintain the corrupt society with which the play begins.

Horner remains a difficult figure to come to terms with because his energies move to satisfy themselves in contradictory ways. On the one hand, he projects the warm and generous sexuality we have seen in the banquet. Though a number of critics have attempted to portray him as a brutal seducer, a type of Don Juan expressing "sexual hostility and aggression toward women,"[26] Horner emerges as the only male other than Harcourt who appreciates the needs of women. From the very start Horner insists that one gains pleasure from women only by giving pleasure in return: "Well, but let me tell you, Women, as you say, are like Souldiers made constant and loyal by good pay, rather than by Oaths and Covenants" (I.i.426–28). Horner is not, as the military metaphor might seem to imply, another battle-scarred knight engaged in the war between the sexes, for he specifically places men and women on the same side (though his metaphor of exchange reveals the hierarchical aspects of the relationship he assumes between men and women). He attracts women not because they desire a brutal tyrant—that is precisely what they wish to escape—but because they respond to his ebullient sensuality. In this play only a Pinchwife draws a real sword on a woman, only Sparkish threatens women with hatred, and the play savages such men, who regard marriage as a mere property settlement and women as nothing more than chattel.[27]

On the other hand, Horner's energies express themselves in his love of the isolation and detachment that his disguises and deception foster. Though he does find a confidant in the quack, Horner is without a true friend; the quack is only his tool, and even Harcourt, his ostensible friend, becomes the victim of his plot. As B. Eugene McCarthy notes, "Horner alters the friendship between Dorilant, Harcourt and himself into part of his pretense, or anti-friendship; it becomes as unnatural as the pimp's or quack's removal from natural sexuality or doctoring."[28] While the aim of Horner's elaborate scheme is sexual pleasure, its success depends on his ability to secure a freedom of action that the social forms of his society seek to deny.

In *The Country-Wife* Wycherley demonstrates just how difficult it is to achieve such a freedom. Throughout the play, the author distinguishes between hypocrisy and vanity, the deception of others and the deception of self. Horner's ability to dominate his society stems not from any moral virtues he may possess, but from his certain knowledge of his own desires and motivations: in deceiving others, he does not allow his social masks to blind him to his own personality. Horner's liberty lies in his skill in manipulating those masks to his own purposes, and his desire to dupe everyone suggests that he can achieve liberty only through a self-imposed isolation. He moves through much of the play as an immensely powerful but essentially solitary force. Bearing an identity known only to the quack, Horner plots in secret to satisfy his desires. He conducts his various sexual pursuits separately, and not until the play's penultimate scene does his left hand discover what his right is doing. Horner is, as he tells us, "a *Machiavel* in love" (IV.iii.63–64), and Lady Fidget is indeed correct when she notes that he cannot be true to all three. The banquet opens, as noted earlier, with Horner locking Margery Pinchwife away just as the "Women of Honour" enter: Horner's apartment comes to symbolize his personality, for it defines an area of separate and apparently unconnected rooms where affairs consummated in one go unnoticed in another, inconvenient lovers remove to make way for the satisfaction of a newer mistress, incredulous observers enjoy unnoticed the variety of scenes that present themselves. We might think of Horner as an industrious mole, working with unparalleled energy to create a palace of a burrow sunk beneath the notice of the larger world.

Horner's decision to keep his empire intact stems from his desire to remain an outsider, and it is this desire, even more than the self-deception of the other characters, that dictates the play's conclusion. Horner represents the energy that society must embrace if it is to maintain a fruitful and viable community, to extend the social intimacy revealed during the banquet beyond a small and isolated circle of knowing conspirators. While I do not question either the morality or attractiveness of the nominal hero and heroine, the success of Harcourt and Alithea remains peripheral to the play's major concerns because it lacks the power to change the humorous society that dominates the play. Their marriage represents a private rather than social triumph, for it does not succeed in dispelling the illusions caused by the disguise, obsession, and hypocrisy of the other characters.

Our ambivalent responses to Horner arise from our recognition that, although he possesses the vitality and self-knowledge to transform his society, he refuses to do so. He finds it more satisfying and convenient to secure his individual freedom by reinforcing, rather than removing, the illusions of his peers, for their illusions contribute to his power. The failure of the characters in *The Country-Wife* to reform them-

selves and their society makes the play characteristic of what
Frye calls the most ironic comic structure, the first phase of
comic action in which the humorous society triumphs or remains undefeated.[29] Despite the marriage of Harcourt and
Alithea, *The Country-Wife* lacks the festive resolution we normally ascribe to comedy, for its concluding dance—the parodic
"Dance of Cuckolds"—represents, not the birth of a new and
better society, but the triumph of the old. The "Dance of
Cuckolds" can be seen as the structural foil to the Banquet of
Sense that Horner and his women celebrate, for that banquet,
by suggesting the best that could possibly come of the comic
action, functions almost as a displaced comic resolution.
Horner thus emerges as a kind of Prospero figure around whom
a new society might possibly form, while Mary Knepp, as Lady
Fidget, gains a power that makes even more effective her
caustic Epilogue, in which she accuses her male audience of
impotence, hypocrisy, and affectation:

> *The World, which to no man his due will give,*
> *You by experience know you can deceive,*
> *And men may still believe you Vigorous,*
> *But then we Women,—there's no cous'ning us.*
> (30–33)

In the last decade, as we have studied more carefully the
range and variety of Restoration comedies, we have come to
understand the uniqueness of Wycherley's Horner. Critics
now mistrust what Robert Hume has called the myth of the
unrepentant rake[30] and recognize that the vast majority of
libertine rake-heroes, for all of their rhetoric and past sowing of
oats, quite tamely repent their sins when the fifth act is about
to end. The repentant rake is the accepted convention in
Restoration comedy, for the rake's transformation allows an
audience to enjoy his exhilarating freedom vicariously while
assuring them that freedom will be sacrificed in the end to the
demands of society. The greatness of *The Country-Wife* rests
on a number of factors, but surely one of the most important is
its ability to consider seriously the complexity of the rake's
personality. In not sacrificing Horner's rakish integrity,
Wycherley provides a fascinating portrait of libertine natural-

ism, revealing not only the various facets of the Hobbesian libertine's personality—its sexual exuberance and warmth, its destructive and antisocial power—but our own ambivalences toward the dream of freedom that such a figure represents.

III

The complexities of Wycherley's satire in *The Country-Wife*—which stem from the author's refusal to resolve an audience's ambivalent responses to a contradictory "hero"—make it likely that a number of questions raised about the play will never be answered with critical unanimity. Even such a basic problem as the objects of Wycherley's censure seems, particularly when related to Horner, resistant to conventional critical approaches. For every critic who insists that Horner is a "satiric spokesman" who both "draws our attention to the vice and hypocrisy before us" and "illustrates it in his own nature as well," there exists another who claims that "we are never invited to view Horner from the moral angle": "our moral awareness is always directed *by* Horner and not *at* him."[31]

Nathaniel Lee's *The Princess of Cleve* (1682) presents no such problems. In transforming Nemours, the polished and upright hero—"nature's masterpiece"—of Madame de Lafayette's original novel into "a Ruffian reeking from Whetstone's-Park," Lee makes clear from the beginning the moral bankruptcy of the rake's aggressive pursuit of pleasure.[32] In the figure of Nemours, Lee attacks not only the libertine philosophy that helped form the Hobbesian rake, but even (as Robert Hume has argued) the earl of Rochester, who exemplified for his contemporaries the type of life such a philosophy generated.[33] The brutality of the satire in *The Princess of Cleve* is invaluable in helping us to understand the complexities of the Hobbesian rake's desires because it throws into bold relief the full implications of the rake's obsessive need to satisfy his sexual and aggressive impulses. Though the play may not be of the first rank, it provides the intimate familiarity with evil that marks only the best satire. Rather than simplifying Nemours in order to attack him, Lee allows the duke to expose all the nuances and consequences of his rage for pleasure. A more

fastidious playwright than Lee might have produced a more
correct play, but such a play could not so completely have cap-
tured the excesses of Nemours' character.

Many Restoration plays, for example, emphasize the rake's
need for variety; Nemours' assertion that "I dye directly
without variety" (I.ii.33) and Tournon's claim that "his Soul
is bent / Upon variety" (I.i.60–61) are echoed in numerous
conventional comedies. What raises Lee's play above the level
of cliché is his ability to depict dramatically the overwhelming
power of the desire that makes such variety necessary. Few
Restoration comedies convince us of the rake's powerful sexual needs, for few playwrights demonstrate the willingness or
ability to dramatize the sexual extravagance that such a need
creates.

From the first scene, however, Lee suggests the sexual com-
pulsions that define Nemours' personality. Even as Nemours
sets in motion his seduction of the Princess of Cleve, we see
him unable to resist the charms of his male confidant Bellamore: "Now by this damask Cheek I love thee; keep but this
gracious Form of thine in health, and I'll put thee in the way of
living like a man"; "My bosom Dear—So young, and yet I
trust thee too"; "But be gone, and no more of this provoking
discourse, lest Ravishing shou'd follow thee at the heels"
(I.i.17–19, 32–33, 39–40). Act II makes explicit Nemours' sexual relationship to Bellamore when the duke praises his friend
as "Thou Dear Soft Rogue, my Spouse, my Hephestion, my
Ganymed, nay, if I dye to night my Dukedom's thine" (II.iii.1–
2). The significance of Nemours' bisexuality lies not simply in
the moral revulsion it would have raised in the audience,[34]
but in the genuineness of the passion, in our inability to differ-
entiate his sexual appreciation of men from his lust for
women. Nemours' bisexuality throughout the play possesses
none of the misogynous overtones that some of Rochester's
lyrics betray when the earl reveals his bisexuality; when
Rochester celebrates "a sweet, soft page of mine / Does the
trick worth forty wenches," we feel the revenge that he wishes
to take on women by proving that he doesn't need them to
satisfy his sexual urges:

> Let the porter and the groom,
> Things designed for dirty slaves,

> Drudge in fair Aurelia's womb
> To get supplies for age and graves.[35]

In Nemours, however, we discover a polymorphous desire that attracts him promiscuously to *all* flesh. For Nemours the human body possesses an ineffable attraction that makes him unable to think of intimacy without the fulfillment of physical desire. Even his ideal of masculine friendship contains an explicitly sexual component:

> If I must choose a Friend, grant me ye Powers
> The Man I love may seize my Heart at once;
> Guide him the perfect temper of your selves,
> With ev'ry manly Grace and shining Vertue;
> Add yet the bloom of Beauty to his Youth,
> That I may make a Mistress of him too.
> (IV.i.277–82)

The scene in which Nemours seduces the willing Celia reveals the extent to which his passion for the flesh dominates both his behavior and habitual mode of self-expression: "By Heav'n I'll eat thy hand—Thou dear sweet Seducer, how it fires my Fancy to steal into a Garden, to rustle through the Trees, to stumble up a narrow pair of back stairs, to whisper through the hole of the door, to kiss it open, and fall into thy Arms with a flood of Joy" (IV.i.19-23). This speech perfectly reflects the play's coarseness of tone, the almost hysterical air that suggests a certain lack of self-restraint on the playwright's part. Yet the speech strikes me as remarkable precisely because its very extravagance provokes a new life in what might otherwise seem mere cliché. Nemours' admission that the plot's elements of danger and subterfuge pique his "Fancy" is utterly conventional. Yet his exaggerated rhetoric, with its overheated eroticism, dramatically expresses the urgency and all-consuming nature of his passion: his overwrought "Fancy" sexualizes every part of reality, from the "narrow pair of back stairs," to the "hole of the door" that he will "kiss . . . open," to the "flood of Joy" that anticipates his sexual triumph. Similarly, Nemours' desire to "eat thy hand" demonstrates not only his inability to control himself, but the cannabalistic desires that can stand behind the conventional metaphors of sex as appetite. Nemours genuinely desires to "possess" the objects of his desire, not in the literally demonic fashion explored in Chapter 1, but in terms of ingesting them in order to satiate his uncontrollable appetite. Nemours is quite literally a man who cannot keep his hands to himself. He possesses an itch for human flesh, throughout the play constantly touching, caressing, fondling others; in the scene with Celia he doesn't merely kiss her hand, but devours it. Even in so slight a scene as Poltrot's demonstration of his vocal prowess, we find Nemours unable to resist the physical impulse to tease, tickle, finally ravish:

> *Nem.* For Heavens sake oblige us dear pleasant Creature—
> *Pol.* I'll swear I'm so ticklish you'll put me out my Lord,
>   for I am as wanton as any little Bartholomew Bore-Pig—
> *Vid.* Dear soft delicate Rogue sing.
> *Pol.* Nay, I protest my Lord, I vow and swear, but you'll
>   make me run to a Whore—Lord Sir, what do you mean?
> *Nem.* Come then begin—
>   (I.ii.158–64)

Though the published text provides no stage directions, the scene seems to make sense only if we see Nemours tickling, even assaulting Poltrot.

Nemours understands his life and relationship to the world entirely in sexual terms. Again the distinction between business and pleasure marks the rake's appreciation of human value—"Never let bus'ness Flatter thee Frank into Nonsense: Women are the sole Pleasure of the World; nay, I had rather part with my whole Estate, Health and Sense, than lose an Inch of my Love" (II.iii.49–52)—and again, Nemours' vulgar statement of the cliché remains distinctly his own. Nemours even expresses his disdain for marriage in terms that identify it with "the Cares of this World and its Inconveniences" (III.i.79). His desires express themselves so extravagantly that, like Mosca's, they reveal a longing to dispense with the substantial body that gives them form. When reminded that the Princess of Cleve is "too Grave," Nemours celebrates that gravity, for he glories in his ability to "laugh with this, and try with that, and veer with every gust of Passion" (I.iii.16–17). He expresses his greatest regret in the play when two simulta-

neous assignations force him to employ Bellamore as a fac-
totum: "Hell! can't I be in two places at once? Heark thee, give
her this, and this, and this, and when thou bitest her with a
parting blow, sigh out Nemours" (IV.i.264–66). A staging as
gross as the play would make the enthusiasm of Nemours' in-
structions require him to employ a third self.

There runs throughout the play, in fact, an imagery of
dream and fantasy which suggests that Nemours' polymorphous desires can never find complete physical satisfaction.
The song that opens the play explains that

> All other Blessings are but Toyes
> To his that in his sleep enjoyes,
> Who in his Fancy can possess
> The object of his Happiness.
>   (I.i.4–7)

Attempting to convince Tournon of the limitlessness of his
desire, Nemours pictures himself "with all the heat and
vigorous Inspiration of an unflesh'd Lover" (I.ii.47–48); later
he states that the "Extravagance of Pleasure" belongs as much
to sleep as to substantial reality: "Thus wou'd I have Time
rowl still all in these lovely Extreams, the Corruption of
Reason being the Generation of Wit; and the Spirit of Wit lying
in the Extravagance of Pleasure: Nay, the two nearest ways to
enter the Closet of the Gods . . . are Fury and Sleep— Therefore
the Fury of Wine and Fury of Women possess me waking and
sleeping" (III.i.125–30). Such imagery indicates that Nemours
seeks a rapture through which he can transcend the fleshly
world that obsesses him: "Sleep" and "Fancy" define an
"unflesh'd" realm where Nemours might surpass the mundane reality that otherwise binds him. The very flesh that so
moves the rake imprisons him; like Donne, Nemours wishes
to transcend his body, though Nemours' ecstasy embodies a
very different conception of love, a very different relationship
to God. The ultimate explanation for Nemours' incredible excess lies precisely here, in his struggle to escape from the
physical world that constitutes at once both his prison and the
essential source of his pleasure. The rake fulfills himself only
in an "Inspiration, Extasie, and Transport . . . that make men
mad" (IV.i.183–84), that drive them out of themselves.

Few Restoration comedies capture so well the extent of the rake's obsessions, or explore the reasons for them; and few so well understand how absolutely destructive of others these obsessions can be. Nemours possesses no sense of responsibility to anything but his own pleasure. He reveals a complete selfishness, born not out of cruelty, but out of a simple inability to see beyond his own desires. Carried away by his overwhelming need for pleasure, the flesh, the rapture that transcends, Nemours remains oblivious to the moral concerns that dictate social realities. Like Horner, Nemours takes pleasure in his aggression: the play pictures him a keen hunter with his nose always "upon another Scent" (III.i.7); part of what attracts him to the Princess, as we have seen, is his expectation of how difficult her gravity will make his conquest:

> Ha! but from Love like hers such daring virtue,
> That like a bleeding Quarry lately chas'd,
> Plunges among the Waves, or turns at Bay,
> What is there to expect.
>   (II.iii.214-17)

At one point the Vidam wonders at Nemours' ability to "outdo Cesar himself in your way" (II.iii.20-21); Nemours, the allusion indicates, conquers women, glorying in the satisfaction of his aggression.

Yet, like Horner again, Nemours never forgets the sexual pleasure that his aggression serves; like Horner he strikes a balance between these forms of pleasure that allows him to express, in a postcoital conversation with Tournon, a genuine sensual appreciation of women:

> *Tour.* Undone, undone! will your sinful Grace never give
>   over, will you neer leave Ruining of Bodies and Damning
>   of Souls—cou'd you imagine that I came for this? What
>   have you done?
> *Nem.* No harm, pretty Rogue, no harm, nay, prithee leave
>   blubbering.
> *Tour.* 'Tis blubbering now, plain blubbering, but before
>   you had your will 'twas another tone; why Madam do
>   you wast those precious Tears, each falling drop shines
>   like an Orient Pearl, and Sets a Gaity on a Face of
>   Sorrow.

Nem. Thou are certainly the pleasantest of Womankind,
   and I am the happiest of Men; dear delightful Rogue,
   let's have another Main like a winning Gamester, I long
   to make it t'other hundred Pound.

                                          (I.ii.1–13)

A master at manipulating the language of romantic cliché—the
movement from "precious Tears" to "blubbering" strikingly
reveals the idealization of women that the urgency of passion
forces him to imitate—Nemours confounds women no more
than he must to enjoy them. Tournon has genuinely pleased
him, and having achieved his aim, he thinks only of the further
pleasure they might share.

The extent to which the play censures this mingled sexual
and aggressive pleasure can be measured by the demonic
imagery that attaches itself to Nemours. Associated
throughout the play with the devil, Nemours boasts that "the
Devil and I [are] as great as ever" (II.iii.273); and Marguerite
angrily screams "Tell him he is a Fiend, Devil, Devil, Devil"
(III.i.105). As in Otway, the rhetoric of sexual demonism remains, though it has been stripped of its ability, for the most
part, to compel more than an aesthetic belief; in both *Venice
Preserv'd* and *The Princess of Cleve*, the language of sexual
demonism exists primarily as an expression of extreme emotional frustration. In Lee's hands, in fact, the details of demonic sexuality become objects of ridicule, undermined by
Nemours' comic exaggeration. When Marguerite enters
masked to try Nemours' fidelity—no more hopeless a task—
she asks if he fears that "you shou'd have pick'd up a Devil Incarnate?" (III.i.50); when he confesses his indifference, she
asks if he could "find in your heart to ingender with a damn'd
Spirit?" (58–59):

Nem. Yes marry cou'd I, for . . . I have long'd any time
   this seven years to be the Father of a Succubus—
Marg. Fiend, and no Man—
Nem. Besides, Madam, don't you think a feat Devil of
   yours and my begetting, wou'd be a prettier sight in a
   House, than a Monkey or a Squirrel? Gad I'd hang Bells
   about his neck, and make my Valet spruce up his Brush
   Tail ev'ry Morning as duly as he comb'd my head.
                                          (60–67)

Nemours' contempt for such superstitions expresses itself in his vainglorious acceptance of demonic paternity ("I have long'd . . . to be the Father of a Succubus") and in the hilarious portrait of their "feat Devil" with his "Brush Tail" and "Bells about his neck." This domesticated spirit, no more frightening than a pet monkey or squirrel, asks us to laugh with Nemours, not at him, to share with him a joke directed against an outmoded language that expresses only Marguerite's violent passion and disappointment. Though J. M. Armistead feels that the play's demonic language adds an "undercurrent of seriousness" to the action,[36] this occult vocabulary is consistently undercut not only by Nemours' contempt for Marguerite's hysterical exaggerations, but by the ridiculousness of Poltrot and St. Andre, the other two characters who employ demonic allusions. In Act III, scene ii, these two buffoons accuse their wives of being witches, not realizing that their wives are the very women they are trying to seduce. The charges of Poltrot and St. Andre—that their wives have "Tets in the wrong place" and employ a "Broom-staff" in order to fly—are not only patently false, but are further undermined by the foolishness of the two husbands. It is difficult to take seriously a demonic vocabulary used primarily by witwouds, and Lee has not written a play in which Nemours' blasphemous mocking of the powers of God and Satan will return to haunt him; unlike Tirso de Molina's original Don Juan play, *El Burlador de Sevilla y Convidado de Piedra* (1617–18), or Shadwell's tragic imitation, *The Libertine* (1675), no devils here present themselves at the play's conclusion to drag the damned hero off to hell.

The end of Lee's play, in fact, provides one of the most self-conscious and cynical conclusions in all of Restoration comedy; again the playwright succeeds in transcending the merely conventional, in ridiculing the normal terms of Restoration comedy even while depending on them. The first part of Nemours' final speech of repentance, in which he transforms himself utterly from raging lover to satisfied husband, represents the convention: "For my part, the Death of the Prince of Cleve, upon second thoughts, has so truly wrought a change in me, as nothing else but a Miracle cou'd—For first I see, and loath my Debaucheries—Next, while I am in Health, I am re-

solv'd to give satisfaction to all I have wrong'd; and first to this
Lady, whom I will make my Wife before all this Company e'er
we part'' (V.iii.294–99). Normally, of course, questioning the
psychological justness of such a repentance misses the point;
the rake's fifth-act conversion necessarily undercuts the libertine sentiments that he boasts during the first four acts. Yet
even Robert Hume, who has long argued that Restoration comedy presents rakes within a conventional movement from affected libertinism to marriage, expresses a disinclination to
take Nemours seriously here.[37] After all, not fifty lines before
this speech of repentance, Nemours had boasted that he would
bed the Princess in "eighteen months three weeks hence, at
half an hour past two in the Morning" (255–56) and had de-
lighted in the coming battle with Marguerite, in which he
would prove that "I know the Souls of / Women better than
they know themselves" (258–59); his repentance comes so
quickly on the heels of his boasting that it is difficult to understand just when he had time to discover "second thoughts."
     The final lines of Nemours' speech indicate even more di-
rectly Lee's cynical inclusion of the conventional speech of
repentance:

> This, I hope, whenever I dye, will convince the World of the
> Ingenuity of my Repentance, because I had the power to go on.
> He well Repents that will not, Sin, yet can,
> But Death bed Sorrow rarely shows the Man.
>
>   (299–303)

As Robert Hume and J. M. Armistead argue, Nemours' final
couplet clearly refers to the death-bed repentance of the earl of
Rochester, ridiculing the significance of so convenient a repentance.[38] Yet this couplet also satirizes Nemours' own transformation, for the rake's fifth-act conversion functions as the
dramatic equivalent of Rochester's final change of heart. Like
Burnet's popular account of Rochester's conversion, the rake's
conventional repentance provides an ideal moral exemplar that
defines a structural formula of celebration and deflation so
much a part of Restoration reactions to the ambiguous freedom
of the rake's sexual license. Nemours, of course, "dies" with
the conclusion of the play that his words signal; like Roches-

ter, he desires to repent when he can no longer sin. Throughout the play Lee has linked Nemours with Rochester; in this
final couplet he completes that identification by suggesting
that neither can earn the repentance they so opportunely
claim. In doing so Lee undercuts the conventional ending of
Restoration comedy, cynically denying the possibility of
reform for a libertine so completely defined by his lust for sexual pleasure.

IV

The movement from *The Country-Wife* and *The Princess
of Cleve* to *The Man of Mode*, from Horner and Nemours to
Dorimant, introduces us to a very different rake. However vile
we judge Horner and Nemours, they possess an exuberance, a
comic ebullience, that in the theatre must prove infectious;
whatever their moral flaws, we remove them from our midst at
our peril: as Falstaff warns Hal, "Banish plump Jack, and
banish all the world." Even Robert Hume, who insists that
Nemours is a "ruttish liar" and "scabrous swine," must admit
that while Nemours may be a "monster," he is "a glamorous
and successful one. Nemours has wit, gaiety, brains, and exuberant energy."[39] In Etherege's play, among the males only Sir
Fopling projects a similiar élan, and he, of course, plays the
fool and comic butt from the start. Dorimant is certainly not
dull or without vitality—far from it—but he possesses an aloof-
ness, a certain frigidity, not apparent in Horner and Nemours,
however much the rakes of Wycherley and Lee plot in secret or
masquerade in public.

Etherege's first rakes—Sir Frederick Frollick, Courtall, and
Freeman—certainly reflect all the prodigality of character and
warmth of a Horner or Nemours. Sir Frederick, in fact, is a reg-
ular hooligan, roaring drunk through the streets, breaking
heads and windows and instruments. Such vulgar pleasures
have little relation to Dorimant, a much more sophisticated
and elegant presence than his roistering predecessor. The difference, however, is not simply one of style: Dorimant's
reserve points to a substantial difference in his appreciation of
the "pleasures" essential to the rake's identity.

Dorimant uses the term early in Act I, when discussing
with Medley his plan to break with Loveit: "Next to the com-

ing to a good understanding with a new Mistress, I love a quarrel with an old one; but the Devils in't, there has been such a calm in my affairs of late, I have not had the pleasure of making a Woman so much as break her Fan, to be sullen, or forswear her self these three days."[40] Dorimant's explanation begins by establishing a hierarchy that subordinates aggression ("a quarrel with an old one") to sensuality ("a good understanding with a new Mistress"), but in the rest of the speech he speaks only of his joy in tormenting women. The "pleasure" that Dorimant laments here has nothing to do with the satisfaction of his sexual desires, but with his current inability to demonstrate his superiority by triumphing over a woman. While the most notorious symbol of Horner's rampant sexuality is the china scene and his admission that he has relinquished all his china, spent himself on behalf of the ladies, Dorimant's success has taken on a destructive edge, for its symbols are the broken fans of the women he has enraged. The broken fan alluded to in this speech becomes the mark of his triumph as he baits Loveit in Act II, scene ii, with the admission that he has pursued a Mask at the playhouse:

> Loveit. And dare you own it to my Face? Hell and
> Furies [Tears her Fan in pieces.
> Dor. Spare your Fan, Madam, you are growing hot, and
> will want it to cool you.
>
> (163–66)

Dorimant's pleasure in destruction takes on added meaning in the first act when the shoemaker asks him, "Why shou'd not you write your own Commentaries as well as Caesar?" (280–81). Nemours is compared to Caesar in *The Princess of Cleve*, but in Etherege's play the image of the battlefield plays a more important role in defining the action of the comedy. The entire first act, of course, recalls the arming of the epic hero: Dorimant's meticulous attention to dress, particularly his desire to cultivate a look that denies the care he takes, reveals a man girding himself for a sexual combat that resembles an actual state of war. Dorimant's opponents, moreover, are specifically the women he has conquered (Loveit, Molly the whore), is about to conquer (Bellinda), or hopes to conquer (Harriet, Emilia). While Horner directs most of his aggression against men, Dorimant chooses women as the occasion for his triumphs. Horner's skill in separating the objects of his lust and aggression is not at all visible in Dorimant.

The joyous sexuality of both Horner and Nemours depends on their ability to maintain an equilibrium between their appetites for lust and power; *The Man of Mode* proves the fragility of that balance. In Dorimant we discover a libertine whose lust for power begins to overwhelm his lust for physical pleasure. Etherege's play portrays a rake who satisfies his aggression only at the expense of his sexuality; for Dorimant sexual satisfaction is not necessarily an end in itself, merely the seal of his success as a conqueror. His most vulnerable moment in the play involves not his inability to carry out a seduction, but his failure to humiliate Loveit publicly:

> *Med.* Would you had brought some more of your Friends,
>   *Dorimant*, to have been Witnesses of Sir *Foplings*
>   disgrace and your Triumph—
> *Dor.* 'Twere unreasonable to desire you not to laugh at me;
>   but pray do not expose me to the Town this day or two.
> *Med.* By that time you hope to have regain'd your Credit?
> *Dor.* I know she hates *Fopling*, . . . had it not been
>   for some powerful Considerations which will be remov'd
>   to morrow morning, I had made her pluck off this
>   mask, and shew the passion that lyes panting under.
>   (III.iii.325–37)

At stake here is Dorimant's reputation as a conqueror. He fails to "Triumph," thus calling into question his ability to dominate his women. His vow of "revenge" (360), his desire to make Loveit pay for her success ("*Loveit to her cost shall find, / I fathom all the depths of Womankind*" [361–62]), his need to brutalize her ("pluck off this mask, and shew the passion that lyes panting under")—all characterize a rake whose pleasure represents primarily an exercise in power. Horner may have no difficulty in presenting himself to the world as a eunuch, but for Dorimant such a strategy remains unthinkable because it would compromise the public image of a conqueror that he strives to realize. Horner finds satisfaction in the secret consummation of his pleasures; the aggressive nature of Dorimant's desires demands public acknowledgement. Dorimant has subordinated sensuality to aggression, discovering in sexual pursuit the triumph of the will and celebration of the ego. Yet Dorimant is certainly not indifferent to sexual pleasure. When Medley in Act I waxes eloquent over Harriet's charms, Dorimant exclaims, "Flesh and blood cannot hear this, and not long to know her" (147–48). Later in the play, while paying court to Harriet, he leaves her when his appointment with Bellinda draws near· "I am not so foppishly in love here to forget; I am flesh and blood yet" (IV.i.349–50). But even his affair with Bellinda hints at the relative coolness of his sexual passions. For all the vigor and wit that Dorimant brings to her seduction, the consummation of their affair realizes very little of his passion. The vulgar stage direction that indicates his success—"Handy tying up Linnen" (IV.ii)— provides only a sense of anticlimax and none of the enthusiastic eroticism that figures like Horner or Nemours bring out of their bedchamber. Dorimant never expresses the overwhelming sensuality that drives a rake like Nemours; not for Dorimant are Nemours' "transport[s] of Imagination [that] shall carry me in my sleep to thy Bed, and I'll wake in the Act" (IV.i.26–27). In spite of his numerous mistresses and the time and energy that he spends in pursuit of women, Dorimant remains a figure for whom sexual pleasure means very little.

In *The Country-Wife*, the penultimate scene, the Banquet of Sense, suggested a number of values that the conventional comic resolution could not encompass; thus the parodic nature of that resolution. In *The Man of Mode* the conventional conclusion, signaled by the marriage of Young Bellair and Emilia and Dorimant's wooing of Harriet, is juxtaposed to Dorimant's attempt to bend Loveit to his will during their long scene in the Mail. His success in triumphing over her remains as essential to the play as the winning of Harriet, for Loveit's final contemptuous dismissal of Sir Fopling allows Dorimant to "clear" "that business," proving his power over women when Medley celebrates him at the play's conclusion: "*Dorimant!* I pronounce thy reputation clear—and henceforward when I would know any thing of woman, I will consult no other Oracle" (V.ii.400–402).

In demonstrating that he "*fathoms[s] all the depths of Womankind*," Dorimant asserts his knowledge not just of the nature of women, but of how to exploit their passions to satisfy his "pleasures." Though Loveit delivers her charge in anger, this does not undermine the truth of her assertion that Dorimant takes "more pleasure in the ruine of a womans reputation than in the indearments of her love" (V.i.193–94). *The Man of Mode* redefines our understanding of what "pleasure" can mean for the Hobbesian rake. Pleasure, as Loveit's charge reveals, no longer possesses an essentially sexual connotation. When Sir Jaspar explained that Horner's business was pleasure, the audience had little doubt that such pleasure was sexual. Dorimant, however, subordinates his sexuality ("the indearments of . . . love") to his aggression ("the ruine of a . . . reputation"). What most motivates Dorimant, as Loveit claims, is his "pride of late in using me ill, that the Town may know the power you have over me" (V.i.173–74). "Pride" and "power" drive him to demand "publick satisfaction for the wrong I have done you!" (243–44). Dorimant triumphs only when he humiliates his women, dominating, not enjoying, the female Other.

The perennial problem of the play's conclusion, the persistent critical hesitation about Dorimant and Harriet's relationship, stems from our recognition, reinforced by the preceding scene with Loveit, that this pride in power makes Dorimant a suspect mate. For Dorimant the bedroom has become a battlefield; it no longer represents a vision of rapture and frenzy, pleasure and soft repose, but of a grim struggle to assert one's superiority over one's partner.

V

The fate of Harriet and Dorimant necessarily raises the problem of the rake's relationship to marriage. Most Restoration comedies, of course, hardly encourage the audience to confront such problems: the comic resolution assumes the rake's comfortable conversion to married life and the marital bliss that the happy couple shall share ever after. There are, however, a substantial number of plays written during the Restoration and early eighteenth century that either question the comforting illusions of the conventional resolution—the three I have examined in this chapter fall into this category—or actually deal with the rake after he has dwindled into a husband. Dryden's *Marriage A-la-Mode* (1673) is only the most famous of a group of Restoration comedies that portray the rake after his domestication,[41] and its opening song emphasizes the importance of pleasure in the rake's response to marriage: "But our Marriage is dead, when the Pleasure is fled: / 'Twas Pleasure first made it an Oath."[42] In considering Otway's *Friendship in Fashion* (1678) we can explore just how a Hobbesian rake responds to this death of pleasure and, through this response, discern more fully the various potentialities of the rake's character.

For a rake devoted primarily to sexual pleasure, the most problematic feature of marriage is its limitation on the variety of women he can enjoy and the inevitable sexual boredom that results from such deprivation. In Colley Cibber's *The Careless Husband* (1704), Sir Charles Easy provides one of the most amusing statements of this problem:

So! the Day is come again—Life but rises to another Stage, and the same dull Journey is before us—How like Children do we judge of Happiness! When I was stinted in my Fortune, almost every thing was a Pleasure to me. . . . now Fortune's in my hand, she's as insipid as an old Acquaintance—It's mighty silly, Faith—Just the same thing by my Wife too; I am told she's extreamly handsom—nay, and I have heard a great many People say she is certainly the best Woman in the World—why, I don't know but she may; yet I could never find that her Person, or good Qualities, gave me any Concern —In my Eye the Woman has no more Charms than my Mother.[43]

Sir Charles's lament reveals a perfectly well-bred gentleman. He understands that the difficulties of marriage resemble most other problems we face in this "dull Journey" of life: expectation provides the spice, and a wife, like a fortune, loses allure once possessed. Melancholy, not rancor, characterizes his speech; he spends no time blaming his wife and directs toward her little of his frustration. The admission that she has "no more Charms than my Mother" stems not from any desire to hurt her, but merely from the profound sense of his utter sexual indifference: nothing acts as a surer antidote to desire than the perception that one's wife resembles one's mother.

Goodvile, the married rake of Otway's comedy, voices a similar complaint in the opening scene of his play. Truman, his ostensible friend, has rallied Goodvile by referring to him as "Matrimony" and laughing because when Goodvile had "hardly been married Ten Days, . . . he left his Wife to go home from the Play alone in her Coach, whilst he debaucht me with two Vizors in a Hackney to Supper" (I.28–31). Goodvile responds to Truman's ridicule by exposing a self-indulgent acceptance of the fetters of matrimony, arguing that even a poor dull wife may occasionally provide some sexual satisfaction: "Oh there are pleasures you dream not of: he is onely confin'd by [marriage] that will be so: A man may make his Condition as easie as he pleases. —Mine is such a fond wanton Ape, I never come home, but she entertains me with fresh kindness: and *Jack* when I have been hunting for Game with you, and miss'd of an Opportunity, stops a Gap well enough" (I.72–78). Goodvile, like Sir Charles Easy, finds marriage an "easie" yoke; though their wives provide little sexual excitement, they can "stop a Gap well enough" in the absence of more novel pleasures. Both Goodvile and Sir Charles take their wives for granted, not only sexually, but by assuming their ignorance and pliability. Goodvile sees his wife as a "fond wanton Ape," a woman he indulges with little freedoms so that he can enjoy larger ones: "I allow her for my own sake what freedom she pleases" (I.65–66). Both rakes value themselves so highly that they underestimate their wives. Sir Charles wonders if his wife's "continual good Humour" indicates her failure to recognize his infidelities (I.i.150–51). Mrs. Goodvile recognizes the same attitude in her husband: "I laugh though to think what an easie fool he believes me; he thinks me the most contented, innocent, harmless Turtle breathing, the very pattern of patience" (II.28–30). Both rakes suffer from their good opinions of themselves: Goodvile, according to his wife, is "as blind with love as his own good opinion of himself has made him" (II.32–33).

Sexual boredom, and the self-indulgent assumption of their own superiority to their wives, are all, however, that Sir Charles and Mr. Goodvile share. To a large degree what critics have labeled Cibber's sentimentality stems from the simplicity of his conception of the rake. Cibber removes, or casually reforms, the rake's most dangerous qualities—his aggression and love of conquest—leaving a well-bred but perfectly respectable and harmless hero in his stead. His characters, as he boasts in the Prologue to *The Careless Husband*, "in Wit are often seen t'abound / And yet have some weak Part, where Folly's found: / For Follies sprout like Weeds, highest in Fruitful Ground" (23–25). Cibber assumes the essential goodness of his rakes; their faults—which merely testify to their potential—can, like weeds, be easily rooted out. Thus, once Sir Charles discovers that his wife is not the silly household dove he assumed, he laments his poor behavior and finds in her precisely the excitement he missed before: "In all my past Experience of the Sex, I found ev'n among the better sort so much of Folly, Pride, Malice, Passion, and irresolute Desire, that I concluded thee but of the foremost Rank, and therefore scarce worthy my Concern; but thou hast stirr'd me with so severe a Proof of thy exalted Virtue, it gives me Wonder equal to my Love" (V.vii.310–14). Sir Charles has learned to reevaluate women, his wife in particular; and the "Wonder" he now enjoys, Cibber's resolution assumes, will remove all the boredom that disfigured their "first marriage."

Otway's play refuses to indulge such pleasant illusions, for Otway possesses a much more complex understanding of the motivations that drive the Hobbesian rake in his pursuit of pleasure: Otway never pretends that "Virtue" can create a "Wonder" sufficient to satisfy the rake's appetite for pleasure and power. *Friendship in Fashion* begins by assuming the primacy of the rake's desire for physical pleasure, just as it begins by pretending that the three male rakes—Goodvile, Truman, and Valentine—are all good friends united by their passion for women. Like Congreve's more famous *The Way of the World*, however, Otway's play gradually reveals that the appearance of friendship belies a state of war: Goodvile, far from a concerned kinsman anxious to marry his cousin Victoria to his friend Truman, has already enjoyed Victoria's favors and seeks to use Truman as a convenient husband for a cast-off mistress. Goodvile also plans to seduce Camillia, Valentine's object of pursuit, and when she reminds him that "*Valentine* you know is your Friend," Goodvile's response illuminates the values that guide his conduct: "I grant it, he is so; A Friend is a thing I love to eat and drink and laugh withall: Nay more, I would on a good occasion lose my life for my

Friend; but not my pleasure" (III.466-70). "Pleasure," of course, dominates all, and the play by degrees exposes not simply the true relations between Goodvile and his "Friends," but the true pleasure that Goodvile pursues.

Goodvile's pleasure seems at first to demand primarily a sexual satisfaction. Bored physically with his wife—"the name of a Wife to a man in love is worse then cold water in a Feaver: 'Tis enough to strike the Distemper to my heart and kill me quite" (III.462-65)—Goodvile lusts after the "lovely kind yielding *Camillia!*" His anticipation of their rendezvous occasions a genuine burst of erotic longing: "How I long for the happy hour! Swelling burning breasts, dying eyes, balmy lips, trembling joints, millions of kisses and unspeakable joys wait for me" (III.661-64). After their assignation he raves about the "feast of delight" he has had: "Surely she was born only to make me happy! her naturall and unexperienced Tenderness exceeded practis'd Charms: —Dear blest lovely *Camillia*, oh! my Joys!" (IV.113-16).

Goodvile's raptures here over the "Joys" he has experienced mark a crucial revelation in the play, for precisely at the moment in which Goodvile most explicitly celebrates sexual pleasure, we discover his complete ignorance of that pleasure, his inability truly to appreciate the nuances of sexual experience. Camillia, of course, had no intention of meeting Goodvile in the garden: the old and affected Lady Squeamish, and not Camillia, laid the table for his "feast of delights," and Goodvile simply could not tell the difference. The very extravagance of his erotic language betrays his utter insensitivity to erotic pleasure, for, as he himself admits, "Have I been mumbling an Old *Kite* all this while instead of my Young *Partridge?* a Pox o' my depraved palate that could distinguish no better" (IV.122-24). Goodvile's inability to distinguish between a tasty virgin and stale leftovers, between "naturall and unexperienced Tenderness" and "practis'd Charms," points to his essential indifference to sexual pleasure. Though Goodvile may think he responds to the sexual promise of women, what truly drives him is a lust for conquest. In cursing Lady Squeamish he cries, "A Pox on the pleasures" (IV.128), revealing a hatred for the sensual world that supposedly motivates him. Near the end of Act IV Victoria asks him if he may not wish to return to the wife ''who has been so Dear to you?'' (653); his nasty response, ''I will sooner return to my Vomit'' (655), suggests a disgust and revulsion not simply with a wife who has betrayed him, but with sexual pleasure itself.

If Otway's play gradually reveals the state of war that underlies the apparent friendship between the three male rakes, it also reveals the state of war that underlies Goodvile's relations to women. The play demonstrates that the rake who too grossly subordinates sexual to aggressive pleasure, far from responding primarily to a love of or need for women, hates the sex that he so obsessively pursues. In the final two acts Goodvile proves himself a man engaged in combat not just with other men—on two different occasions he draws his sword on Truman—but with the women he supposedly adores. Goodvile may still pretend to worship women, as when he tells Victoria ''my good Angel is like Thee, and whensoe'r I err must meet me in thy shape. And with such softness smile and direct me'' (V.23-25); but too often he fails to disguise the contempt he really feels. Victoria, when he doesn't need an ally so desperately, is ''a worse Omen then a Hare in a Journey,'' a mere ''Fubb'' (III.658-60). Again and again in the final two acts he exposes his hatred of women in outbursts that recall the misogyny of Wycherley's Pinchwife: ''Shame and Infamy light upon the whole Sex! may the best of 'em be ever suspected, and the most cautious always betray'd'' (IV.168-70); ''I pronounce there is no Trust nor Faith in the Sex. By Heav'n in every condition they are all Jilts, all false from the Bawd to the Babe'' (V.704-7). Freed from the necessity of diguising his true sentiments, Goodvile's language becomes increasingly violent, expressing at every turn his contempt for women. Confronted by his wife with proof of his infidelities, he doesn't even bother to hide the naked power that determines their relationship: ''Well, if you will have it so, Madam, *Victoria* has been my Mistress, is my Mistress, and shall be my Mistress, and what a Pox would you have more? and so God b'ye to you'' (IV.354-57). Baffled by his failure to overcome her, he storms off the stage in a fit of rage: ''Dear raw Head and bloody Bones be patient a little: —See see you Beagles, Game for you, fresh

Game; that great Towser has started it already, on, on, on halloo, halloo, halloo. [*Thrusts 'em at his Wife, and Exit*" (IV.404-7).

As the play develops, the other characters, particularly the women, become increasingly aware of the true grounds of their relationship to Goodvile. The wise Camillia, of course, recognized his aggressive lust from the moment of his first advances: "I cannot but laugh to think, how easily he swallow'd the cheat: He could not be more transported at possession, then he was with expectation, and he went away in a greater Triumph then if he had conquer'd the *Indies*" (III.533-36). "Possession," the sexual act itself, she realizes, contains few charms for a rake who responds primarily to a "triumph" over women for which sexual consummation is but the proof. Goodvile, Valentine claims, "never made Love but to delude" (III.529), and even the absurd Lady Squeamish recognizes this when she compares Goodvile to Theseus and "the false *Aeneas.*" Mrs. Goodvile demonstrates her perception of the state of war that defines her husband's relations to women when she confronts him in the final scene by crying, "So, now begins the Battle" (V.558). And it is Victoria's recognition of this truth that leads to her extraordinary betrayal of Goodvile and her expressions of solidarity with the wife who also suffers under his preoccupation with aggression and conquest: "Oh Love! Unhappy Women's Curse, and Men's slight Game to pass their idle time at: I find too in my self the Common companion of Infamy, Malice. Has *Goodvile*'s Wife ever wrong'd me? Never. Why then should I conspire to betray her? No, let my Revenge light wholly on that false perjur'd Man; as he has deceiv'd and ruin'd me, I'le play false with him" (V.1-8).

The final act reveals just how far we have come from Horner's Banquet of Sense in *The Country-Wife*. Martial imagery dominates the final action of the play, as Goodvile's hatred and aggression express themselves in his desire to "do speedy execution upon" the "Butterflies" who carouse through his house, and in the vision of his two prostitutes triumphing over his wife: "I'l catch her in [Truman's] very Arms, then civilly Discard her, Bagg and Baggage, whilst you my dainty Doxies take possession of her Priviledges, and enter the Territories with Colours flying" (511-14). At the conclusion Mrs. Goodvile exits in a rage, and even Goodvile's attempts to patch his quarrels with Truman and Valentine provoke little sense of a joyful comic resolution. Goodvile's pleasure has little to do with the erotic raptures of Horner and Nemours, or even with the cold-blooded fascination of Dorimant's regard for women. Goodvile's interest in women springs from his hatred, for women exist for him primarily as objects to be conquered and despised.

VI

Let's wisely manage this last span,
The momentary life of man,
And still in pleasure's circle move,
Giving to our friends the day, and all our nights to love.
Thus, thus, while we are here, let's perfectly live,
And taste all the pleasures that nature can give.
            "Since Death on all lays
                his impartial hand"

For the Hobbesian libertine, "pleasure's circle," celebrated in this song by Etherege or Charles Blount[44] as the chief goal of life, does not represent a simple or static quality. Horner, Nemours, Dorimant, and Goodvile demonstrate the often contradictory impulses that motivate the Hobbesian rake's attempts to satisfy his desires and that determine his relations to women. Though all four share a similar identity, the various ways in which they respond to their aggressive and erotic urges generate very different characters. Though Horner and Nemours manipulate their women in order to satisfy their sexual desires, their aggression remains subservient to their sensuality; aggressive in the service of their lusts, they nonetheless find fulfillment primarily in the sexual delights that crown their triumphs, not in those triumphs themselves. Confirmed sensualists, they would agree with the great eighteenth-century lover Casanova, that "cultivating whatever gave pleasure to my senses was always the chief business of my life; I have never found any occupation more important. Feeling that I was born for the sex opposite to mine, I have always loved it and done all that I could to make myself loved by it."[45] Horner and Nemours use the term "love" —if they use it at all—much more cynically than Casanova, but their delight in sexual enjoyment is intense and unfeigned.

In Dorimant, however, we find a rake who has begun to value his aggression more than his sensuality, and in Goodvile we discover almost the antithesis of Horner and Nemours, for Goodvile values eroticism primarily for its participation in the pleasures of conquest. Another eighteenth-century "lover," the Marquis de Sade, speaks for Goodvile when his Count de Gernande explains to the hapless Justine—the eternal female victim—that "the two sexes do not at all sort agreeably with each other":

> It is natural that individuals of both sexes labor at nothing but to procure [happiness] for themselves, [and] the weaker must reconcile herself to distilling from her submissiveness the only dose of happiness she can possibly hope to cull, and the stronger must strive after his by whatever oppressive methods he is pleased to employ, since it is proven that the mighty's sole happiness is yielded him by the exercise of his strong faculties, by, that is to say, the most thoroughgoing tyranny; thus, that happiness the two sexes cannot find with each other they will find, one in blind obedience, the other in the most energetic expression of his domination.[46]

For Goodvile, "pleasure's circle" defines an arena in which supremacy, rather than sensual delight, is the true prize. Goodvile despises the women he would enjoy, for his pleasure lies not in the sexual ecstasy women can give, but in the humiliation he can make them suffer.

CHAPTER 3

The Philosophical Libertine: "Artist in the Science of Voluptuousness"

I

Absent from thee, I languish still;
Then ask me not, when I return?
The straying fool 'twill plainly kill
To wish all day, all night to mourn.

Dear! from thine arms then let me fly,
That my fantastic mind may prove
The torments it deserves to try
That tears my fixed heart from my love.

—Rochester, "A Song"

I have frequently alluded to Rochester because, as many of his contemporaries acknowledged, his "fantastic mind" seems an ideal reflection of the libertinism current at the court of Charles II during the 1660s and 1670s. Rochester's poems and letters document the contradictory desires that define and impel the Hobbesian libertine-rake. The tension between Rochester's love of women and contempt for, even fear of, them, between his obsession with sensual pleasure and loathing of the perversity of corrupt sexuality, between, in the short song I have quoted from above, his "fixed heart" and "straying" nature, all point to the volatile character of the Hobbesian rake and the complexity of the "pleasure" he would enjoy. Rochester's acute self-consciousness about the contradictions that divide him from himself, his feeling, as he writes in a letter to his wife, that "I myself have a sence of

what the methods of my Life seeme soe utterly to contra-
dict,''[1] makes him a perfect vehicle for understanding those
first decades of the Restoration. This ''wildest and most fan-
tastical odd man alive''[2]—the description, of course, is his own
—seems to sum up, in his years of drunken debauch and final
conversion, in his apparently sincere regard for his wife and
multitudinous love affairs, the complexity of the rakish personality portrayed on the stage by figures as diverse as Horner
and Nemours, Dorimant and Goodvile.

Rochester, however, exemplifies only one particular strain
of libertinism, and to place him among other libertines—such
as the French philosopher Gassendi, the man of the world
Saint-Évremond, or the diplomat and intellectual Sir William
Temple—illustrates just how varied were seventeenth-century
interpretations of the libertine philosophy. Indeed, until the
second half of the century the term *libertine* meant ''first and
foremost a man who refused to accept current beliefs and desired to free himself especially from the bonds of Christian
doctrine.''[3] Eventually the illogical connection between free-
thinking and free living overturned the philosophical significance of the term and linked libertinism with the debauchee
and profligate. Though Rochester's species of libertinism was
not restricted to the court of Charles II, rather different conceptions of the pleasures that a libertine might pursue characterize the last two decades of the seventeeth century in
England.

Central to this ''philosophical libertinism'' was the rehabilitation of Epicurus that probably began in 1647 with Gassendi's publication of his apology for the Greek philosopher,
De vita et moribus Epicuri libri octo.[4] Though commentators differed in their interpretations of how to define his
voluptas, most agreed that Epicurus' pursuit of happiness involved the creation of a refined art of living that brought into
harmony reason and desire. The effect that Epicurus had on
definitions of the pleasure that so concerned the rake can be
seen in *The Oracles of Reason* (1693), by Charles Blount and
Charles Gildon. This work marks a good place to begin our
reconsideration of the rake's devotion to pleasure, for Blount
corresponded with Rochester during the last years of the earl's
life, attempting to convince the debauched peer that ''to

believe an immortality of the soul without its due rewards and
punishments is altogether as irrational and useless as to
believe the soul itself to be mortal."[5] The section of *The
Oracles of Reason* entitled "That felicity consists generally in
Pleasure" is composed almost entirely of a long quote from
Epicurus that ends with the following distinction between two
different types of pleasure:

> That Pleasure wherein consists Felicity is Indolence of Body and
> tranquility of Mind. There being two kinds of Pleasure, one in sta-
> tion or rest, which is a placibility, calmness and vanity, or immun-
> ity from trouble and grief: The other in motion, which consists in a
> sweet movement, as in gladness, mirth, or whatever moves the
> sense delightfully with a kind of sweetness and titilation, as to eat
> and drink out of hunger and thirst: It may be demanded whether, in
> both, or in either, and in which consists Felicity? We say that
> Pleasure wherein Felicity consists, is of the first kind, the stable, or
> that which is in station, and so can be no other than indolence of
> Body, and tranquility of Mind.[6]

The use of Epicurus here clearly indicates the inferiority of
those pleasures that motivate the Hobbesian rake. The rake's
frenetic search for satisfaction, whether sexual or aggressive,
partakes of Epicurus' second type of pleasure, that of "motion," of "sweet movement," of "titilation" and sensual
delights. Epicurus recognizes the appetites, like "hunger and
thirst," that help explain the frenzied obsession with sexual
pleasure that characterizes the short and intense life of Rochester, who, in spite of his "fixed heart," asks only that his
lover "from thine arms . . . let me fly." The extraordinary activity of the Hobbesian rakes examined in the last chapter, the
sense of their ceaseless movement from one mistress to the
next, one conquest to another, reflects that pleasure which implicitly rejects "Indolence of Body and tranquility of Mind."
Nemours' lust for "Inspiration, Extasie, and Transport, all
these bewitching Joys that make men mad" (IV.i.183–84),
almost parodies the "sweet movement" that defines Epicurus'
second type of pleasure.

While Rochester emerges as the historical figure who epitomizes the career of the Hobbesian rake, Sir William Temple
reflects the philosophy of the philosophical libertine. After

leaving public life in 1681, Temple retired to his home at
Sheen, later Moor Park, to cultivate that "tranquility of
Mind" recommended by Epicurus. Temple's essay "Upon the
Gardens of Epicurus; or, Of Gardening, in the Year 1685"
makes explicit his debt to Epicurus and his determination to
eschew a "public business the most contrary of all others to
that tranquility of mind, which they [all the different sects of
philosophers] esteemed and taught to be the only true felicity
of man." In this essay Temple tries to accommodate both "the
Stoics and Epicureans," arguing that

> the Stoics would have [happiness] to consist in virtue, and the
> Epicureans in pleasure; yet the most reasonable of the Stoics made
> the pleasure of virtue to be the greatest happiness; and the best of
> the Epicureans made the greatest pleasure to consist in virtue; and
> the difference between these two seems not easily discovered. All
> agreed the greatest temper, if not the total subduing of passion, and
> exercise of reason, to be the state of the greatest felicity.

"True pleasure," Temple continues, resides "in temperance,
rather than in satisfying the senses."[7]
    The writings of Saint-Évremond probably draw most
clearly the distinction between the different types of pleasure
that impel Hobbesian and philosphical libertines. Saint-
Évremond does not go as far as Temple in praising "temperance" over "satisfying the senses," for he recognizes the importance of sensual delights. Saint-Évremond argues instead
that we must "endeavour only to enjoy them with modera-
tion; and rest persuaded that it is an error to condemn *Pleasures as Pleasures*, and not as they are *unjust and unlawful*. In
truth, let them be never so innocent, the *excess is always
criminal*, and tends not only to our *disgrace*, but to our *dissatisfaction*."[8] He emphasizes that "we must use things in such
sort, as that we may be without them, we must be their
Masters, and not their *Slaves*; we must not grow impatient for
'em, nor be cast down for their loss; lets enjoy 'em peaceably,
when *occasion* is offered, and not pursue 'em with disquiet and
turmoil."[9] Here we see again the crucial distinction between
the frenzied pursuit of pleasure and its calm enjoyment, between a restless and ultimately futile motion and a tranquility
of just appreciation.

For Saint-Évremond the classical figure who best exemplified this proper understanding of pleasure was Petronius Arbiter, "this great *Disciple* of Epicurus."[10] In "The Life of Petronius Arbiter,"[11] Saint-Évremond dramatizes the conflict between Epicurus' two types of pleasure by pitting Petronius against the courtier Tigillinus for the soul of the Roman emperor Nero. In this struggle Tigillinus represents the "gross Debauches" of the Hobbesian rake, while Petronius embodies the "tranquility" of the philosophical libertine. In Saint-Évremond's account of this confrontation, Petronius clearly "surpassed . . . [Tigillinus] in the Science of Pleasures" (p. xi), though the changeable character of their prince inevitably leads to Petronius' defeat and death: "The choice and delicious Pleasures invented by Petronius grated the gross Debauches of Tigillinus . . . [Tigillinus] therefore endeavour'd to possess himself of the Heart of the Prince; and finding himself prevail by degrees, he soon engag'd [Nero] in the foulest Brutalities" (p. ix). Under the influence of Tigillinus and others, Nero "insensibly plung'd into Debauchery, abandon'd himself to his Passions, and became as morose and wicked a Prince, as before he had been pleasant and equitable" (p. vii). Saint-Évremond's idealized account of this tragic court drama allows him to describe at length the types of pleasure valued by the true Epicurean:

[Petronius] took no delight in the brutal Pleasures of Love, like *Messalina*, nor in those of the Table and Drunkenness with *Claudius*; only in a gallant and delicate manner took a relish of both, rather to gratifie his Curiosity than his Senses. In this manner he employ'd a part of the Day in Sleeping, and dedicated the whole Night to Pleasure and Business. His House was the Rendezvous of the better sort of the People of *Rome*: . . . One might then represent him in a continual exercise of Wit in Conversation, in the most charming Pleasures of the Table, publick Sights, Gaming, and in spending his Estate, not like a Prodigal and Debauchee, but like a nice and learned Artist in the Science of Voluptuousness. (Pp. iii–iv)

To a large extent, this vision of the "Artist in the Science of Voluptuousness" shapes the career of the rake on the Restoration stage during the 1680s and 1690s. The Hobbesian rake, of course, does not become extinct, but he begins to share the stage with a more refined version of himself, the ideal gentleman as *honnête homme*.[12] In the comedies of William Congreve, in particular, we can chart the transformation that the rake undergoes as Congreve replaces the Hobbesian libertine with the more refined philosophical libertine outlined above. Congreve himself, as Maximillian Novak notes, appears to have governed his conduct in imitation of the "genteel epicurean . . . as set forth by Sir William Temple and St. Évremond."[13] In a letter to his good friend Joseph Keally, Congreve explains that "Ease and quiet is what I hunt after. If I have not ambition, I have other passions more easily gratified."[14] Congreve's love of retirement and enjoyment of good conversation, fine dining, and a small circle of intimate friends indicate a more refined sensibility than that of Rochester or Etherege, who, like a true Hobbesian rake, happily admits that "I have preferr'd my pleasure to my profit and have followed what was likelier to ruin a fortune already made than make one: play and women. Of the two the Sex is my strongest passion."[15] In a similar fashion, Congreve's rake Valentine displays a devotion to the "Science of Pleasures" when, instead of quoting witty verses from Waller like Etherege's Dorimant, he opens *Love for Love* reading Epictetus, the Stoic philosopher who recommends, according to Valentine, that you "refine your Appetite; learn to live upon Instruction; feast your Mind, and mortifie your Flesh; Read, and take your Nourishment in at your Eyes" (I.i.12–15). Though Valentine and Congreve's other rake-heroes fail to demonstrate consistently quite the degree of asceticism here recommended—Valentine's admonition to "mortifie your Flesh" is followed by his providing money to support his bastards—Congreve struggles in his four comedies to remove the worst excesses of the Hobbesian rake.

While the differences between the Hobbesian and philosophical libertine reflect the changes in society and audience that took place during the quarter-century separating the careers of Horner and Mirabell, they also depend on the logic of Congreve's clear-sighted evaluation of the psychological contours of the Hobbesian rake. More than other Restoration dramatists, Congreve recognizes the destructive potential of the Hobbesian rake; in *The Old Batchelour* and *The Double-Dealer* he focuses on the tension between this rake's lust for the pleasures of sensuality and conquest, dramatizing how this tension can lead to a devastation that threatens both the rake and his society. Yet Congreve also recognizes the value of the rake's tremendous energy and power, and in *The Double-Dealer, Love for Love,* and *The Way of the World* he works to preserve that vitality for society; in the figures of Mellefont, Valentine, and Mirabell, Congreve attempts to redefine the rake-hero by controlling his predilection for disorder and misrule. Though Congreve does not completely succeed in socializing the rake's sexual energies and taming the rake's aggressive passions, in representing the psychological profiles of Hobbesian and philosophical libertinism, his four plays reveal the sexual and aggressive conflicts that divide both the individual and his society; and they explore the relationship of sexual license to social order.

II

In many ways Congreve's first comedy, *The Old Batchelour* (1693), is a conventional Restoration comedy dependent on the exploitation of stock characters and situations. Congreve crowds his stage with a melange of familiar character types: two rakes (Bellmour and Vainlove), two witty virgins (Belinda and Araminta), two tricky servants (Setter and Lucy), a *miles gloriosus* (Captain Bluffe), a cuckolded cit (Fondlewife), a booby knight (Sir Joseph Wittoll), and a superannuated rake (Heartwell). Yet Congreve uses these conventional types for quite unconventional ends. *The Old Batchelour* demonstrates, in a fashion unlike any other Restoraton comedy, the unhealthy complexion of the Hobbesian rake who would subordinate sexual to aggressive pleasure. Congreve dramatizes the perverseness of such a figure by revealing the impotence to which the rake can reduce himself when he no longer responds to his sexual needs. Concerned only with the gratification of his ego, such a rake displays a surprising indifference to the sexual pleasure that is normally his primary concern.

Impotence, in fact, provides the major sexual focus of *The Old Batchelour.* In the first scene, Sharper, one of the play's wits, alludes to the central problem of the play for the old bachelor of the title, Heartwell. Though Heartwell pretends to slight women, he nonetheless harbors a passion for Sylvia that Sharper suggests Heartwell cannot really fulfill. Heartwell's sexual powers, Sharper reminds him, will only allow him to "Mouth a little . . . I think that's all thou art fit for now" (I.i.227–28). Heartwell's foolish infatuation with Sylvia leads him to mistake his powers by driving a sickly and failing lust beyond itself, for in his frantic search for sexual pleasure the Hobbesian rake plays essentially a young man's game. Etherege, in a letter to his old friend William Jephson, admits as much when he remarks that "I am sorry to hear you complain of an Ebb at your years. It makes me open my Eyes, and trust me it is a sad prospect a man has after fifty. No more Spring tydes of Love are to be expected. Yet I will endeavour to be as wise in this point as Anacreon was and cherish the spark that remains, now I can blaze no longer."[16] Heartwell possesses hardly even a "spark" of his youth and the clearest proof of this lies in the song that introduces his wooing of Sylvia in Act III, scene ii:

I
As *Amoret* and *Thyrsis*, lay
Melting the Hours, in gentle Play;
Joining Faces, mingling Kisses,
And exchanging harmless Blisses:
He trembling, cry'd, with eager haste,
O let me feed as well as taste,
I die, if I'm not wholly blest.

II
The fearful Nymph reply'd—*Forbear;*
I cannot, dare not, must not hear:
Dearest Thyrsis, *do not move me,*
Do not—do not—if you Love me
O let me—still the Sheperd said;
But while she fond Resistance made,
The hasty Joy, in strugling fled.

III
Vex'd at the Pleasure she had miss'd,
She frown'd and blush'd, then sigh'd and kiss'd,
And seem'd to moan, in sullen Cooing,
The sad miscarriage of their Wooing:
But vain alas! were all her Charms;
For *Thyrsis* deaf to Loves allarms,
Baffled and senseless, tir'd her Arms.

(1–24)

Heartwell, like Thyrsis, desires to "feed as well as taste," though as Sharper's complementary image states, he can but "Mouth a little." The song emphasizes his infirmity in the premature ejaculation that leaves Thyrsis "Baffled and senseless" and Amoret "Vex'd at the Pleasure she had miss'd." The song belongs to a recognizable genre of "imperfect enjoyment" poems that had its roots in Ovid and Petronius.[17] Though based on a rather narrowly defined subject, such poems demonstrate a wide range of dramatic possibilities. Etherege, for example, in imitating Charles Beys' "La Iovissance Imparfaite. Caprice," uses his failure to turn a very pretty compliment to his mistress—"You'd been more happy had you been less fair"[18]—while Rochester, with his characteristic complexity, finds in it an occasion to curse his inability to control his own desires, turning on his prick as that "Worst part of me, and henceforth hated most."[19] For Congreve the song provides a perfect representation of Heartwell's impotence; as Heartwell and Sylvia listen to the song, and enjoy the "*Dance of Antick*" that accompanies it, we see how powerless Heartwell's impotence has rendered him in the hands of the scheming Sylvia, who needs a husband to shore up her faded reputation. Heartwell follows the performance by claiming "why 'twas I Sung and Danc'd; I gave Musick to the Voice, and Life to their Measures—Look you here *Sylvia*, here are Songs and Dances, Poetry and Musick—hark! (*pulling out a Purse and chinking It*)" (32–35). Heartwell attempts to replace sexual vitality with economic power, and only the machinations of the play's hero save Heartwell from the consequences of his impotent folly.

Unlike Heartwell, Fondlewife—whose name suggests the extent of his powers—cannot avoid the consequences of his folly; and through the tender offices of Bellmour, Fondlewife suffers the fate of all inadequate husbands. As Fondlewife himself recognizes, his wife is "young and vigorous, and I am Old and impotent," and he can only lament the desires that drove him to such a pass: "Why didst thee marry *Isaac*? —Because she was beautiful and tempting, and because I was obstinate and doating; so that my inclination was (and is still) greater than my power" (IV.i.51–55). In spite of all Fondlewife's threats and bullying, his wife Laetitia will look elsewhere for what her husband cannot provide; and Fondlewife lives to prove the truth of his servant's prophecy that an insufficient

husband betrays "the vanity of taking a fine House, and yet . . .
[is] forced to let Lodgings, to help pay the Rent" (IV.i.42–44).
Congreve attempts nothing unusual with either Heartwell
or Fondlewife, for both figures remain stock Restoration victims. Yet together they provide a context within which we
come to understand the precise nature of Vainlove's libertine
impotence. At first glance it is difficult to see what impotence
has to do with Vainlove, ostensibly a perfect image of the rake-
hero. Young, vigorous, witty, attractive to women and attracted by them, he seems the last character in the play for
whom impotence would be a concern.

Yet Vainlove is impotent, as his name suggests, and Congreve's triumph lies in his ability to recognize the sterility to
which the Hobbesian rake can reduce himself. Vainlove's
impotence lies not in his inability to perform but in his indifference to performance. While he begins the intrigue with Fondlewife's Laetitia and sets in motion her desires and deceit, it
is Bellmour to whom he turns for its consummation. Vainlove
and Bellmour are perfectly matched, for, as Vainlove tells Bellmour early in the play, "my Temper quits an Amour, just
where thine takes it up" (I.i.77–78). Vainlove quits an amour
precisely when he has brought it to fruition, for all his interest
lies in the social manipulation involved in the love game. Just
when the moment is ripe Vainlove loses his passion, for, as his
friends note, he has little interest in enjoying the passions he
raises:

> *Sharper.* You *Bellmour* are bound in gratitude to stickle for
>   him; you with pleasure reap that fruit, which he takes
>   pains to sow: he does the drudgery in the Mine, and you
>   stamp your image on the Gold.
> *Bellmour.* He's of another opinion, and says I do the
>   drudgery in the Mine; well, we have each our share of
>   sport, and each that which he likes best; 'tis his diver-
>   sion to Set, 'tis mine to Cover the Partridge.
>   (I.i.218–25)

Though the sexual pun on the word "stickle"—to stand up
for[20]—remains the crudest indication in this exchange of Vainlove's sexual behavior, or lack of it, the metaphor of the hunt
possesses the most resonance in the world of the play, for it
demonstrates the relationship of men to women, the predatory

nature of men's desires and their attempts to enforce their will on female prey. As Bellmour's use of the metaphor suggests, however, Vainlove demonstrates an interest only in tracking the game, not in its capture. Vainlove himself tells us that he enjoys "continually starting of Hares for [Bellmour] to Course" (I.i.75-76), and as the play progresses we come to see the futility of a passion severed from its object.

Even a casual survey of Restoration drama and poetry reveals that in itself Vainlove's obsession with the chase manifests nothing unusual. In Otway's *Friendship in Fashion*, for instance, Camillia uses the identical metaphor to accuse Valentine of "hunt[ing] more for the love of the sport, then for the sake of the prey" (II.175-76). Charles Sackville's "The Antiquated Coquette," in fact, assumes that the male pursuit of a female victim represents an essential and natural part of the love game:

> But nature's turn'd when women woo—
> We hate in them what we should do;
> Desire's asleep and cannot wake
> When women such advances make:
> Both time and charms thus Phyllis wastes,
> Since each must surfeit ere he tastes.[21]

Using the same metaphor of sexual appetite that we find in Congreve's play, Sackville assumes the necessity and propriety of male aggression and female passivity. Behind all such metaphors lies the perception, which holds true both for men and women, that

> There is not half so warm a fire
> In fruition as desire.
> When we have got the fruit of pain,
> Possession makes us poor again.
> Expected form and shape unknown,
> Whets and makes sharpe temptation:
> Sense is too nigardly for bliss,
> And daily pays us with what is.[22]

The anonymous author of these lines recognizes a truth that explains, at least to some degree, why both men and women accept the arbitrary terms of the love game: its stimulation of desire benefits both sexes, though the rigid roles both have to play diminish them as well.

Vainlove has learned to play this game too well; entangled by "desire" and "temptation," he refuses ever to bring his passion to "fruition," to take "possession" of what he woos. The pursuit of an "unwilling" female that should function as a pleasing spur to desire has engrossed all his attention, and he mistakes the road to bliss for bliss itself. Thus, his affair with Araminta continually founders on the barriers that he has created against women: happy in his pursuit, the least sign of interest by Araminta disgusts him, sending him off in the opposite direction. Vainlove finds most satisfaction only when least assured of success: "By Heav'n there's not a Woman, will give a Man the pleasure of a chase: My sport is always balkt or cut short—I stumble ore the Game I would pursue. —'Tis dull and unnatural to have a Hare run full in the Hounds Mouth; and would distaste the keenest Hunter—I would have overtaken, not have met my Game" (IV.i.175–80).

Such behavior, the play insists, is a form of impotence, for Sharper's judgment of Vainlove's desires—"Thou hast a sickly peevish Appetite; only chew Love and cannot digest it" (IV.i.172–73)—bears a striking resemblance to Sharper's earlier judgment of Heartwell's ability only to "Mouth a little." While Heartwell's impotence manifests his physical weakness, Vainlove's failure is psychological: his desires are perverse precisely because they can achieve no true fulfillment. He is, as Lucy remarks, "a Mumper in Love, lies Canting at the Gate; but never dare presume to enter the House" (III.i. 193–94). The truth of this observation, expressed in a metaphor that relates Vainlove's impotence to Fondlewife's, marks the play's conclusion. Convinced that Araminta had not, in fact, responded to his advances, Vainlove again raises the pursuit and proposes marriage. Araminta hesitates, however, for as Bellmour realizes, "she dares not consent, for fear he shou'd recant" (V.ii.175–76). Their affair concludes thus unresolved, suggesting the impossibility of any consummation because consummation is what Vainlove most abhors. In Vainlove we search in vain for the sensualist or the lover of easy delights. He employs his passion and vitality only in the service of his desire for conquest and preeminence.

Vainlove emerges from *The Old Batchelour* a ridiculous figure, unable to overcome his "sickly peevish Appetite" or to influence significantly the comic action; the play's conclusion, after all, depends on Bellmour's ability to dominate the comic world and direct events to their proper resolution. Bellmour hopes that his own marriage to Belinda will "get you [Vainlove] an Appetite to see us fall to before ye" (V.ii.177–78), but Vainlove's fastidious temper suggests that Horner's taste for "falling on briskly" will always remain beyond the impotent libertine. The contrast between Horner and Vainlove indicates the enfeeblement of the libertine ideal that results from a loss of sexual appetite. When Bellmour and Vainlove first visit Belinda and Araminta, they accompany their wooing with a song that reveals the psychology of the love game:

> Men will admire, adore and die,
> While wishing at your Feet they lie:
> But admitting their Embraces,
> Wakes 'em from the golden Dream;
> Nothing's new besides our Faces,
> Every Woman is the same.
> (II.ii.197–202)

The song's reference to the "golden Dream" that women represent testifies chiefly to the price that women pay for allowing themselves to become objects of false adoration; they can never, obviously, live up to the illusions they are forced to maintain. But Congreve's play reveals too the price that men pay for believing such illusions, for, as James Thompson notes, the song's embodiment of "both romance and cynicism . . . manages to convey all that is desired in the play, at the same time that it admits that desire cannot be fulfilled. The uneasy stasis which the song recommends is matched by the irresolution with which the play ends."[23] Vainlove, more than any other character in the play, is a prisoner of the "golden Dream" that he pursues but never possesses. For Vainlove "Every Woman is the same," simply an excuse for a pursuit that can never end.

III
In the figure of Vainlove, Congreve reduces to comic absurdity the subversive potential of a Dorimant; the immense

energy of the Hobbesian libertine becomes severed from its object and spends itself in a furious but ultimately futile motion. In *The Double-Dealer* (1693), however, Congreve reveals the destructive potential of the increased aggression that accompanies this indifference to sexual satisfaction. In the figure of Maskwell, Congreve portrays the Hobbesian libertine's love of devastation with a dramatic clarity and force that has both fascinated and puzzled critics. Brian Corman, for instance, in order to account for Maskwell's evil, a force which Corman considers "alien to Restoration comedy," theorizes that *The Double-Dealer* mixes the wit-intrigue comedy of Fletcher with the humour-cheat comedy of Jonson; in such a scheme Maskwell becomes a "descendant of the rogue-hero of punitive comedy," while Mellefont is a "variation on the rake-hero of Restoration comedy." B. Eugene McCarthy tries to explain the dramatic importance of Maskwell and Lady Touchwood by citing Northrop Frye's discussion in *Anatomy of Criticism* of types of comedy in which the blocking characters achieve a primacy denied the nominal hero and heroine.[24]

Such explanations of Maskwell's presence are certainly ingenious, but John Traugott seems to understand more precisely the issues involved when he notes that in *The Double-Dealer* Congreve hits on the "simple expedient . . . of splitting the rake-figure between his nasty and attractive qualities."[25] Both Mellefont and Maskwell represent aspects of the traditional rake-hero, and Maskwell's extraordinary presence stems only from the severity of his definition; all other qualities filtered out, he dramatizes the naked aggression and will to power that make up one strand of the Hobbesian rake's character. His evil is not alien to Restoration comedy, but a quality previously gilded over by the rake's more attractive virtues—his sexual vitality, high spirits, and charming wit. As such Maskwell's character stands as a revelation of one aspect of the Hobbesian libertine's true personality, much as Satan's assumed forms in Milton's *Paradise Lost*—cormorant, toad, snake—represent not the progressive corruption of his being, but revelations of what he has always been.

Critics find *The Double-Dealer* unusual because the action of Restoration comedy typically depends on the exposure of fools, not villains. Restoration dramatic theory, according to

John Dennis, assumed that tragedy deals with "the pernicious outragious Passions and the abominable monstrous Crimes," while comedy "endeavours to correct the Follies and Errors, and epidemick Vices."[26] In his highly influential *Lectures on Rhetoric and Belles Lettres* (1783), Hugh Blair sums up over a century of dramatic theory when he explains that

> Comedy is sufficiently discriminated from Tragedy, by its general spirit and strain. While pity and terror, and the other strong passions, form the province of the latter, the chief, or rather sole instrument of the former, is ridicule. Comedy proposes for its object, neither the great sufferings nor the great crimes of men; but their follies and slighter vices, those parts of their character, which raise in beholders a sense of impropriety, which expose them to be censured, and laughed at by others, or which render them troublesome in civil society.[27]

Though *The Double-Dealer* presents a host of fools for us to ridicule, Maskwell's "abominable monstrous Crimes" seem distinctly out of place in the Restoration comic world. The extravagance of his evil even, as I suggest above, takes on demonic dimensions as he gradually reveals his character. During their first meeting, Lady Touchwood damns Maskwell as an "Insolent Devil," threatening him with "Eternal Fire" (I.i.321–22). By the fifth act, when he has discovered that "to go naked is the best disguise" (V.i.101), Maskwell doesn't hesitate to reveal himself as the satanic serpent: "Why, *qui vult decipi decipiatur.* —'Tis no fault of mine, I have told 'em in plain terms, how easie 'tis for me to cheat 'em; and if they will not hear the Serpent's hiss, they must be stung into experience" (262–65).

Aubrey Williams, in fact, has demonstrated the magnitude of the demonic imagery that defines both Maskwell and Lady Touchwood: "The repeated association of Maskwell with 'Hell' and 'Damnation,' along with all the occasions when Lady Touchwood not only is specifically categorized as a 'Witch' but also is said to be 'possess'd,' would have been, to a contemporary audience, more than casual reminders of an ancient Adversary and of the human agents he might enter and subdue to his purposes."[28] More than any other Restoration comedy we have considered, *The Double-Dealer* depends on a

demonic context to expose the malignant desires that can motivate the rake. Yet in spite of the satanic references that signify the depths of Maskwell's iniquity, little of the language of
demonic sexuality clings to him. Though Maskwell's "possession" of Lady Touchwood bears an explicitly sexual significance, Congreve does not present Maskwell as primarily a
sexual monster. Like Iago, Maskwell achieves his success by
manipulating the sexual passions and fears of others, but
neither character seems motivated primarily by their sexual
desires. Maskwell involves himself with Lady Touchwood and
intrigues for possession of Cynthia not for erotic pleasures, but
to make himself master of the estate, to raise himself, as Lady
Touchwood complains, above "the nature of a Servant . . . [to]
Lord of all, of me, and of my Lord" (I.i.348–49). The rake most
emphatically linked to the devil is the least erotic of all rakes
examined so far, for his sexuality has been engrossed by his
lust for destruction, displaced into the service of his ambition
and aggression.

Maskwell hardly pretends that sexual pursuit or satisfaction represents his chief good. For all his sexual intrigue, he is
not a passionate man. Lady Touchwood complains early in the
play that he is "a sedate, a thinking Villain, whose Black Blood
runs temperately bad" (I.i.328–29), and Maskwell himself reveals that social chaos, and not sexual delights, move his mind
most profoundly: "One Minute, gives Invention to Destroy, /
What, to Rebuild, will a whole Age Employ" (I.i.421–22). In
his first extended soliloquy Maskwell reiterates these sentiments even more forcefully. Though he begins by excusing
his crimes as the effect of his love for Mellefont's Cynthia, his
speech exposes his true relish only when it turns to the subject
of manipulation:

Well for Wisdom and Honesty, give me Cunning and Hypocrisie;
oh, 'tis such a pleasure, to angle for fair-faced Fools! then that
hungry Gudgeon Credulity, will bite at any thing—Why, let me see,
I have the same Face, the same Words and Accents, when I speak
what I do think; and when I speak what I do not think—the very
same—and dear dissimulation is the only Art, not to be known from
Nature.

(II.i.457–64)

The sexual overtones of this passage, its references to appetite, "hungry Gudgeon," "pleasure," and the objects of his attention, "dear dissimulation" and "fair-faced Fools," reveal to the audience that Maskwell's eroticism has been absorbed by his aggression; the pleasures of sex itself arise primarily from their participation in the satisfactions of aggression and power. He "angles" to satisfy his desires for social domination and the extension of his ego, not to fulfill his lust.

In a later soliloquy Maskwell does speak of the pleasures that he once received as Lady Touchwood's lover; he has, however, "lost all Appetite to her," and he suggests that now only dissimulation affords true satisfaction: "She has a damn'd penetrating head, and knows how to interpret a Coldness the right way; therefore I must dissemble Ardour and Ecstasie, that's resolv'd: How easily and pleasantly is that dissembled before Fruition!" (III.i.175–84). Maskwell's admission here that he can take as much pleasure in dissembling ardor as in actually experiencing it reflects his kinship to Vainlove: for both, the game is the thing. In the right context, of course, Maskwell's admission might even be comic, for there is something amusing about the disparity between the excess of the performance and the emotional indifference of the player. In *The Double-Dealer*, however, Congreve portrays such behavior as perverse because it reveals the darker side of human nature, its capacity for evil and senseless destruction. Maskwell incarnates the destructive potential that we first discovered in Horner. The Hobbesian rake now stands completely outside the pale of society; his pleasure arises only from his success in bending the conventions of that society to his destructive will.[29]

Congreve's division of the rake-hero, however, stems not simply from his desire to portray the absurdity and horror to which such a figure can reduce himself, but also to determine what is valuable in the rake. Mellefont, in *The Double-Dealer*, stands forth as Congreve's initial attempt to redefine the libertine by removing the dross and examining the gold that shines beneath. Purged of the aggression that his alter ego now bears, Mellefont moves through the play as a perfect gentleman, a man perfectly in control of his sexual desires because they are

not linked to an outsized desire to conquer. Indeed, Mellefont's apparent chastity may even lead us to question his relationship to the rake tradition, for, unlike *Love for Love* and
The Way of the World, this play never refers to the hero's past
sexual indiscretions. The play opens with Mellefont's settled
conviction that matrimony is what he most desires, and his
object throughout the play is simply to remove the barriers
that stand between Cynthia and himself. Though such an
outlook expresses itself through the metaphor of the chase, in
The Double-Dealer that metaphor takes on an entirely new
signficance. Now, as Cynthia notes, "we Hunt in Couples
where we both pursue the same Game," and Mellefont is not
far behind in insisting that "Marriage is the Game that we
Hunt" (IV.i.16–20). The hunt no longer implies a predatory
relationship between men and women, but a mutual activity
in which neither is the prey. In an earlier meeting the two
speak of marriage as a game of cards or bowls, but again the
point is made that in such a game neither stands to lose:

> *Cynthia.* Still it is a Game, and Consequently one of us
>   must be a Loser.
> *Mellefont.* Not at all; only a Friendly Tryal of Skill, and
>   the Winnings to be Shared between us.
>
>   (II.i.168–71)

Mellefont has little interest in the pursuit, for he insists that
marriage represents a way to unite two lovers and resolve the
tensions that divide the two sexes. Throughout the play his
sexual desires remain securely limited by the conventions of
society. While his impulsive wish to elope with Cynthia gives
evidence of his high spirits and sexual vitality, he has apparently little difficulty in accommodating his personal desires
to the needs of society. Mellefont, as the play's conclusion affirms, is the true heir of Lord Touchwood, the legitimate
master of the estate.

Yet for all his undeniable virtues, Mellefont emerges in the
course of the play as a passive figure; for all his wit, discern-
ment, and judicious reasoning, he appears curiously inept.
Whether one believes, with Aubrey Williams, that the play
reveals a world governed by Divine Providence or, with B.

Eugene McCarthy, that the truly significant force in the play is Chance and the probability of accident, Mellefont is clearly unable to affect the outcome of events.[30] Except for setting Careless on the trail of Lady Plyant, Mellefont initiates not a single action in the play; all his other activities are suggested and set in motion by Maskwell, and all lead inexorably to Mellefont's doom. Congreve's remarks on Mellefont in the dedication to Charles Mountague recognize this problem without really solving it. While Congreve's insistence that not "every Man [is] a Gull and a Fool that is deceiv'd" makes much sense, it does not absolve Mellefont from his inability to protect his own interests. The helping hand of Providence or Chance is a recognized part of the action of comedy, but the hero must as least not hinder the happy outcome we all anticipate.

Even the terms of the comic action itself find Mellefont insufficient. At the beginning of Act IV, Cynthia enters into an agreement with Mellfont that establishes his responsibility to "demonstrate his Wit" by foiling Lady Touchwood:

> *Cynthia.* Here then, I give you my promise, in spight of
> Duty, any temptation of Wealth, your inconstancy, or
> my own inclination to change—
> *Mellefont.* To run most wilfully and unreasonably away
> with me this moment and be Married.
> *Cynthia.* Hold—Never to Marry any Body else.
> *Mellefont.* That's but a kind of Negative Consent.—Why,
> you won't baulk the Frollick?
> *Cynthia.* If you had not been so assured of your own
> Conduct I would not—But 'tis but reasonable that since
> I consent to like a Man without the vile Consideration
> of Money, He should give me a very evident demon-
> stration of his Wit: Therefore let me see you undermine
> my Lady *Touchwood*, as you boasted.
> (IV.i.35–48)

Shorn of his aggression, however, Mellefont is simply incapable of dealing with the powerful evil with which Maskwell challenges society; Maskwell controls Mellefont as adroitly as he controls the less discerning members of society, leading his alter ego as easily as a child. Only Cynthia's quick thinking allows Lord Touchwood to penetrate the intricacies of Mask-well's plot; Mellefont remains a dupe almost until the denouement.

In dividing the Hobbesian rake, Congreve succeeds in creating a figure who no longer threatens social order but who also proves powerless to preserve it when it is threatened. The play reveals that the rake's aggression remains too closely allied to his virtues to be easily removed; to do away with his aggressive nature is to remove what in many ways marks his most valuable offering to society. In distinguishing between the primary elements of the rake's personality, I have often spoken as if the rake's aggression and eroticism embodied two very different aspects of his identity. In the figure of Mellefont, Congreve clearly reveals the interconnectedness of the rake's two passions, the interdependence of his aggression and sensuality. In eliminating the rake's aggression, Congreve compromises the vitality and power that make the rake a "heroic" figure. Anthony Gosse has spoken of the dramatic problem this raises when he notes how careful Congreve must be not to let the evil of Maskwell and Lady Touchwood overwhelm the comedy in *The Double-Dealer;*[31] and this recognition makes us aware that for all his undeniable evil, Maskwell is the most compelling character in the play. If Maskwell and Mellefont are alter egos, Mellefont describes the weaker self, the pale shadow who lacks the vigor and authority he should possess to define the center of the comic world.

IV

In Congreve's third play, *Love for Love* (1695), we return to the "normal" comic world of Restoration drama; no characters reveal the depths of evil represented by Maskwell or Lady Touchwood. Yet the absence of their satanic passion for destruction does not mean that the comic realm possesses an order or discipline indicative of a well-regulated society, for *Love for Love* presents Congreve's most grotesque vision of a society lost in illusion, affectation, and corruption.[32] What dominates this play is not evil but madness, not malice but affectation, not a rage for destruction but an inability to distinguish properly between illusion and reality. Valentine suggests

the disorder into which society has fallen when he notes that
"I know no effectual Difference between continued Affectation and Reality" (III.i.40-41). His disguise as the mad
"Truth" in Act IV, of course, constitutes the most prominent
image of the insanity that characterizes the play, but other
images of madness consistently draw our attention to a society out of balance. Utterly bewildered by the unreasonable
behavior of a polite society he has returned to after three years
at sea, Ben complains, "All mad, I think—Flesh, I believe
all the *Calentures* of the Sea are come ashore, for my part"
(IV.i.356-57). In Ben's view this delirium comes to affect just
about everyone: Miss Prue, his intended; Mrs. Frail ("she's
mad, poor Young Woman, Love has turn'd her senses, her
Brain is quite overset" [IV.i.403-4]); his father; his brother;
even Angelica. Foresight, unable to understand Tattle's "Mystery," asks for "Mercy on us, what do these Lunacies portend?
Alas! he's Mad, Child, stark Wild" (V.i.302-3); his daughter's
outrageous desires for a husband lead him to think "the Girl's
influenc'd too" (313).

In Middleton's *A Mad World, My Masters* the "mad world"
contains a comic exhilaration and vitality that describes a real
value for society. In Congreve's play this madness is hardly
therapeutic, displaying not primarily an energy society must
embrace—although in Valentine's affected madness there lies
truth—but an ungoverned passion that makes people unable to
come to grips with the basic problems that frustrate them. The
madness of *Love for Love* calls into question the most fundamental institution and relationships that define civilized
society: marriage, and the bond between man and wife, parents
and their children. In this "world upside down" marriage functions not as the mechanism that structures proper relations between men and women, but as a monstrous coupling that leads
to the propagation of a system of irresponsibility and selfishness. The institution that in almost all Restoration comedies
represents society's most powerful attempt to order itself and
its members here becomes an unnatural arrangement that
undermines people's attempts to locate themselves in a
Hobbesian state of nature.

Sir Sampson's attempt to disinherit his own son represents
the most blatant manifestation of this madness. Sir Sampson,

when he first confronts Valentine in Act II, refuses to recognize
Valentine's "damn'd *Tyburn* face" as his own son's:

> *Sir Sampson.* You, Sir; and you Sir: —Why, who are you
>   Sir?
> *Valentine.* Your Son, Sir.
> *Sir Sampson.* That's more than I know, Sir, and I
>   believe not.
>
>   (II.i.314–16)

When Valentine complains of his father's "Barbarity and Unnatural Usage," Sir Sampson simply disclaims any responsibility for the individual he has brought into the world:

> *Sir Sampson.* Excuse! Impudence! why Sirrah, mayn't I do
>   what I please? Are not you my Slave? Did not I beget
>   you? And might not I have chosen whether I would have
>   begot you or no? Ouns who are you? Whence came you?
>   What brought you into the World? How came you here,
>   Sir? Here, to stand here, upon those two Leggs, and look
>   erect with that audacious face, hah? Answer me that? Did
>   you come a Voluntier into the World? Or did I beat up
>   for you with the lawful Authority of a Parent, and press
>   you to the service?
> *Valentine.* I know no more why I came, than you do
>   why you call'd me. But here I am, and if you don't mean
>   to provide for me, I desire you wou'd leave me as you
>   found me.
> *Sir Sampson.* With all my heart: Come, Uncase, Strip, and
>   go naked out of the World as you came into't.
>
>   (323–38)

Sir Sampson's logic defines children as slaves or soldiers,
wholly in the service of the "lawful Authority of a Parent."
Law, not affection or love, rules such a relationship, for Sir
Sampson's power stems from the simple fact that "Did not I
beget you?" Sir Sampson's extraordinary desire to turn his son
out-of-doors naked, to refuse any responsibility for what he has
created, reveals that relations between parents and children
describe a state of war, not of affection or mutual obligation.
Sir Sampson's indifference to his son indicates the bestial
nature of this society: Sir Sampson wishes he were a Bear,

"that my Cubs might have liv'd upon sucking their Paws;
Nature has been provident only to Bears and Spiders; the one
has its Nutriment in his own hands; and t'other spins his
Habitation out of his Entrails" (390–93). In this image society
can no longer nourish its members; all must depend on themselves, for their world no longer joins individuals into a larger
community. All exist in a state of nature in which even the
most personal bonds no longer make any sense. Honest, if
foolish, Ben describes just such a world when he answers
Mrs. Frail's charge that "were you this undutiful and graceless Wretch to your Father?": "Then why was he so graceless first, —if I am undutiful and Graceless, why did he beget
me so? I did not get my self" (IV.i. 388–91). Ben did not, of
course, beget himself, but confronted by a father who relishes
his power to deny his sons even "the Prospect of an Estate,"
Ben, like his brother Valentine, is figuratively left without a
father, a begetter. As Valentine points out when Sir Sampson
asks if he could "hope to prosper" after cheating his father,
"Indeed, I thought, Sir, when the Father endeavoured to undoe
the Son, it was a reasonable return of Nature" (V.i.511–12).

This disintegration of the bond between parents and children leads to the play's frightening depiction of marriage. Restoration comedy, of course, fairly bristles with rakish denunciations of the married state: Ben's nautical descriptions of
marriage as being "Portbound," of a husband as a man with
"his feet in the Bilboes" or a "Gally-slave" (III.i.311–16), participate in this conventional understanding of marriage as a
prison and unnatural limitation on the individual's freedom.
Tattle's attempts to free himself from the persistent Miss Prue
echo this same complaint: "No, no, to marry, is to be a Child
again, and play with the same Rattle always: O fie, marrying is
a paw thing" (V.i.245–47). Yet Congreve's play goes far
beyond such conventional, and easily reformed, sentiments.
When Sir Sampson asks his supposedly mad son, "Why did I
ever marry," Valentine in his role as Truth explains

> Because thou wer't a Monster; old Boy: —The two
> greatest Monsters in the World are a Man and a Woman;
> what's thy Opinion?
> *Sir Sampson.* Why, my Opinion is, that those two Mon-

sters join'd together, make yet a greater, that's a Man
and his Wife.
Valentine. A ha! Old Truepenny, say'st thou so? thou hast
    nick'd it.

(IV.i.261-69)

These images of marriage, naturally, rebuke those who utter
them: Ben is the rude "Sea-Lover" unfit for civil society;
Tattle, the would-be rake who fears the sex he tries to court;
Sir Sampson, the unnatural monster he has made himself by
refusing to acknowledge his responsibility to the children he
has engendered. But Valentine as the mad Truth correctly
understands what these individuals have made of themselves,
marriage, and the society they inhabit. In his humorous community, the union of Tattle and Mrs. Frail exemplifies the corruption and meaningless of marriage: "But this is the most
cruel thing, to marry one does not know how, nor why, nor
wherefore" (V.i.458-59).

Implicated as well in the madness that deforms marriage,
and the relations between children and parents, are characters'
expressions of their sexuality. Congreve's first two plays certainly provide numerous examples of the sexual grotesque: the
impotence of Vainlove and Heartwell in *The Old Batchelour*
and the enforced captivity of Sir Paul Plyant—"pinion'd Night
after Night for three Years. . . . swath'd in Blankets till I have
even been depriv'd of motion" (IV.i.423-25)—in *The Double-
Dealer* testify to the corrupt sexuality that haunts the social
milieu Congreve portrays. In *Love for Love,* however, we find
by far the most striking expressions of a deformed and unnatural sexuality. The young and the old, the married and the
unmarried—all share a sexual nature that assumes the unhealthy forms determined by the bankruptcy of marriage that
characterizes this society.

Miss Prue, the witless daughter of Foresight's first marriage, indicates most clearly the sexual perversity that infects
this company. As the untutored and innocent country girl,
Miss Prue superficially resembles Margery Pinchwife of Wycherley's *The Country-Wife:* in their natural and ungoverned
passions both characters reveal the powerful sexual desires
that define an essential part of the human personality. Yet

Margery's healthy exuberance seems worlds apart from the immaturity and silliness of Prue. Margery's passions are certainly unsophisticated, but she can emerge from Wycherley's play an attractive and winning woman. Her sexual enthusiasms, her love for Horner's "sweetest breath" and desire to be "treading on your Toe under the Table . . . or rubbing knees with you, and staring in your face, 'till you saw me" (IV.ii.159-61), reveal a frank passion and vitality that almost dominates the play that bears her name: in the final scene she proves almost too much even for Horner to handle. In Miss Prue, however, we find little beyond the callow child, the whining baby who never seems to understand her own desires. Her effusions over the fool Tattle make her ridiculous, for they express not a healthy appetite but her infantile and unformed passions: "Look you here, Madam then, what Mr. *Tattle* has giv'n me— Look you here Cousin, here's a Snuff-box; nay, there's Snuff in't; —here, will you have any—Oh good! how sweet it is—Mr. *Tattle* is all over sweet, his Perruke is sweet, and hs Gloves are sweet. —and his Hankerchief is sweet, pure sweet, sweeter than Roses" (II.i.515-20).

By the end of *The Country-Wife* we feel sorry for Margery, her vitality thwarted by the artificial social world she has come to join; only an eccentric production of the play would fail to portray her as a sympathetic character. Prue, however, does not oppose her world but reflects it; her coarse and unripe desires describe a community that has yet to understand the sexual impulses that motivate it: "For now my Mind is set upon a Man, I will have a Man some way or other. Oh! methinks I'm sick when I think of a Man; and if I can't have one, I wou'd go to sleep all my Life: for when I'm awake, it makes me wish and long, and I don't know for what—And I'd rather be always a sleeping, than sick with thinking" (V.i.306-12). Prue reveals the lack of self-consciousness, the failure to come to terms with her own nature, that characterizes her society.

Prue's ignorance might be forgiven as the fruit of her youth, but in Sir Sampson youth cannot excuse the blindness of dotage. Sir Sampson's pathetic attempts to woo Angelica, his insistence that "I have warm Blood about me yet, I can serve a Lady any way" (V.i.23-24), betray a man unable to recognize his failing sexual powers. Sir Sampson makes himself even more ridiculous than Heartwell, for Sir Sampson struts like a cock-of-the-walk, denies his age, and asserts a passion that has long since decayed:

> Odzooks I'm a Young Man: Odzooks I'm a young Man, and I'll make it appear—Odd, you're devilish Handsom; Faith and Troth, you're very Handsom, and I'm very Young, and very Lusty—Odsbud, Hussy, you know how to chuse, and so do I; —Odd, I think we are very well met; —Give me your Hand, Odd let me kiss it; 'tis as warm and as soft—as what? —Odd, as t'other Hand—give me t'other Hand, and I'll mumble 'em, and kiss 'em till they melt in my Mouth. (V.i.139–48)

To an audience familiar with Heartwell's ability only to "Mouth a little," Sir Sampson's desire to "mumble 'em" strikes a suspicious note: we hardly need Ben's suggeston that his father's "Fire's little better than Tinder" (410) to recognize that Sir Sampson has overstated his qualifications as a husband.

In this play it is hard to respect even Mrs. Foresight's desires to escape an impotent husband. Scandal may have found their "Pleasures . . . too considerable to be forgot" (IV.i. 316–17), but the wandering wife has no memory at all of such joys: even Horner's "Women of Honour" never practiced so determined an affectation.

Against such a mad world, with its perverse understandings of marriage, family, and sex, Valentine must define himself and his relationship to Angelica. Unlike most rakes, Valentine refuses to accept the conventional terms of his society; most rakes, in spite of their discomfort with social restraints, are not revolutionary figures bent on changing the community they inhabit. Rakes normally prefer to manipulate their society in order to fulfill their own desires, rather than to reform it. The Hobbesian rake, in particular, glories in his ability to use his understanding of society's conventions to his advantage. Scandal represents this type of rake, for his portraits of men and women at the end of Act I reveal his cynical knowledge of the base impulses that motivate most people: "And yet there are some set out in their true Colours, both Men and Women. I can shew you Pride, Folly, Affectation, Wantonness, Inconstancy, Covetousness, Dissimulation, Malice, and Ignorance, all in one Piece. Then I can shew you Lying, Foppery, Vanity, Cowardise, Bragging, Lechery, Impotence, and Ugliness in another Piece; and yet one of these is a celebrated Beauty, and t'other a profest Beau'' (626–33). In the course of the play, Scandal uses this knowledge of people to pursue his pleasures: his seduction of Mrs. Foresight demonstrates his willingness to take advantage of the freedom he can secure within the conventional framework of society. As he points out to Mrs. Foresight, ''I am a Jugler, that act by Confederacy; and if you please, we'll put a Trick upon the world'' (III.i.699–701).

Valentine, on the other hand, has few tricks left. He begins the play under a ''forc'd Confinement,'' having lost much of the freedom of action that a rake normally enjoys. Even when this confinement ends, Valentine makes few forays into the larger world: he briefly visits Foresight's house in Act II, but returns to his lodgings early in Act III and does not venture out again until the very end of the play. As Peter Holland recognizes, ''Valentine's chamber is no longer the place from which the rake sallies forth to conquer the world. Instead it is a refuge from a world that is pursuing him for money.''[33] The ceaseless activity that Hobbesian rakes such as Dorimant and Horner enjoy is foreign to Valentine. He possesses, as Scandal notes at the end of Act I, a ''losing hand,'' and through his only trick— his affected madness—he attempts merely to gain some time: ''My seeming Madness has decciv'd my Father, and procur'd me time to think of means to reconcile me to him'' (IV.i. 715–17). Valentine succeeds in delaying his doom, but, as the play's conclusion makes clear, he fails utterly to appease his father.

Yet Valentine's confinement also represents a voluntary withdrawal from the humorous society that he now disdains. We have already examined his reading of Epictetus that opens the play, his determination to ''chew the Cud of Understanding'' and ''mew'' himself up in order to reform. His madness in Act IV allows him to utter the truths he has learned, to ''come to give the World the Lie'' (IV.i.164–65). As Truth he can damn his father's lawyer for wearing black and thus carrying ''his Conscience withoutside'' (168), can ask if the ''Bible saves more Souls in *Westminster-Abby*, or damns more in *Westminster-Hall*'' (176–77), can forecast Foresight's horns because he recognizes there "are Wanton Wives, with their Legs at liberty, and Tame Cuckolds, with Chains about their Necks" (511–13). For all the freedom he enjoys as the Mad Truth, however, Valentine simply cannot escape from or reform the corrupt society that confines him. Like Mellefont, Valentine emerges an essentially passive hero unable to order the misrule that reigns over his comic world. While he proves . his goodness by undergoing Angelica's strict test of his virtue, that virtue proves powerless to transform his society without the intervention of Angelica.

Angelica can move the play to its proper resolution because she, more than any other character, recognizes the truths that her society corrupts. She understands, for instance, the blindness of Foresight's attention to the stars; in Act II she mocks his occult science, with great amusement accusing him of "unlawful Midnight Practices" in which he and the Nurse "Suckle a Young Devil in the Shape of a Tabby-Cat, by turns" (121–22). Her disdain for the rhetoric of demonology reveals an intelligence contemptuous of the "Exaltation of madness" (IV.i.106) that disfigures most of the other characters; Foresight's astrology and demonology represent only the most extreme forms of that madness. Even her apparently whimsical response to Valentine's pursuit stems from her appreciation of how men and women must act if they would escape the insanity of this unnatural society: "Uncertainty and Expectation are the Joys of Life. Security is an insipid thing, and the overtaking and possessing of a Wish, discovers the Folly of the Chase. Never let us know one another better; for the Pleasure of a Masquerade is done, when we come to shew Faces" (IV.i. 786–90). Unlike Cynthia and Mellefont, Angelica recognizes that the tensions between conquest and possession cannot be so easily resolved. Her insistence that the "Uncertainty and Expectation" of the chase should be valued rather than overcome suggests the limitations of the accommodation reached by Cynthia and Mellefont.

Angelica's power manifests itself most completely at the play's conclusion, where she rebukes Sir Sampson for his unnaturalness and reads him his lessons: "Since I have plaid you a Trick, I'll advise you, how you may avoid such another.

Learn to be a good Father, or you'll never get a second Wife''
(570–72). Congreve even places the play's final lines in her
mouth, when she reminds us that ''the Miracle to Day is, that
we find / A Lover true: not that a Woman's kind.'' Without
Angelica's power, Valentine's virtue goes for naught; he plays
Orlando to Angelica's Rosalind, for both here and in *As You
Like It* it falls to the woman to secure a comic resolution that
lies beyond the reach of the men. Like Mellefont, Valentine
maintains his virtue only at the expense of his aggression.

V

The Double-Dealer and *Love for Love* propose inadequate
solutions to the reformation of the Hobbesian libertine. While
they succeed in embracing for society the illusive figure of the
rake, in doing so they fail to gain the vitality that distinguishes
him. The rake, finally, is not a perfect gentleman; and neither
Mellefont nor Valentine, for all their attractiveness, possess
the power that makes the rake a ''heroic'' figure. Congreve
does not make the same mistake when he next attempts to
divide the rake-hero. In Congreve's final play, *The Way of the
World* (1700), Mirabell, for all his virtues, is quite as aggressive, quite as subtle in his ability to manipulate the forms of
society, as Fainall. Mirabell's success in this regard, in fact,
has led a number of critics to question his morality. Such sus-
picions are understandable, for Congreve here makes no attempt to qualify or reduce the libertine's aggressive nature.

Mirabell's plots, of course, do not carry the day without
considerable strain, ingenuity, and flexibility on his part.
Aubrey Williams correctly insists that ''all of the schemes set
forward by this so-called Machiavellian master of convention
and society are shown, in the play itself, as countermined and
frustrated.''[34] Like Horner and Dorimant, however, who also
find their plots frustrated, Mirabell succeeds in spite of such
checks because he responds aggressively to the accidents that,
in a complex society, overturn the best-laid plans. Fainall puts
Mirabell through his paces, but Mirabell recognizes as early as
Act II that even though Fainall may have won the game of
cards that opened the play, in the larger game Fainall does not

hold the necessary trump: "When you are weary of him," he tells Mrs. Fainall, "you know your Remedy" (II.i.277). Though Mirabell did not originally think that her remedy would prove his own, at the last moment his prudent play earlier in the game saves him. While Williams properly argues that this final trump is not "part of some grand strategy," Mirabell has it to hand when he needs it. And though Williams insists that "the play in no way suggests her decision as taken solely on the advice of Mirabell,"[35] Mrs. Fainall clearly states, in response to her mother's vain boast that "'tis plain thou hast inherited thy Mother's prudence," "Thank Mr. *Mirabell*, a Cautious Friend, to whose advice all is owing" (V.i.568–71). Unlike Valentine, Mirabell is not a man playing out a "losing hand."

As Mrs. Fainall's response indicates, Mirabell confronts his society with all the strength and subtlety of a true heir of Horner and Dorimant. Like them, Mirabell possesses a certain knowledge of the ways in which one must operate within society to satisfy one's own desires. When Mirabell tells Mrs. Fainall that "we daily commit disagreeable and dangerous Actions . . . To save that Idol Reputaton" (II.i.265–66), he demonstrates as penetrating an understanding of society as Horner, when Wycherley's rake assures his "Women of Honour" that "Honour, like Beauty now, only depends on the opinion of others" (V.iv.168–69). Mirabell is not a figure to be trifled with, for like his predecessors he knows his own desires and moves purposefully to satisfy them.

Yet there can be little doubt that Mirabell wishes to fulfill his desires within the acceptable limits of society. Though his attempt to trick Lady Wishfort into an engagement with his servant is surely a dastardly scheme, the play does not suggest that Mirabell takes excessive pleasure in his plots or that he pursues them without regard to their moral implications. In his first conversation with Fainall, Mirabell protests that in pretending to court Lady Wishfort he "did as much as Man cou'd, with any reasonable Conscience" (I.i.68–69). The odd phrase "reasonable Conscience" reveals the fine moral line Mirabell would walk. Normally we speak of conscience as an absolute: one either has a conscience or one hasn't. Mirabell's allusion to a "reasonable Conscience," however, demonstrates his recognition that morality is not a simple or absolute quality. Confronted by the chaotic power of Lady Wishfort, whose desires and affectations lead her to transgress the reasonable bounds of society and conscience, a strict virtue will simply prove inadequate. Mirabell's subtle moral sense here parallels that of Steele's Bevil Junior, who, in *The Conscious Lovers* (1722), resolves on a course of "honest dissimulation"[36]—another odd joining of terms—to secure the woman he loves. That Mirabell's "reasonable Conscience" has its moral limits becomes apparent later in his conversation with Fainall: "The Devil's in't, if an old woman is to be flatter'd further, unless a Man shou'd endeavour downright personally to debauch her; and that my Virtue forbad me" (76-79). Mirabell's schemes are unpleasant but necessary, and he possesses a clear sense of just how far he can carry them.

Mirabell's schemes are not ends in themselves, and his pleasures do not arise primarily from his success in manipulating people or establishing his superiority over them. His discussion with Fainall over the card game that opens the play quickly establishes the essential distinction between Fainall and himself:

> *Mirabell.* I'll play on to entertain you.
> *Fainall.* No, I'll give you your Revenge another time, when you are not so indifferent; you are thinking of something else now, and play too negligently; the Coldness of a losing Gamester lessens the Pleasure of the Winner: I'd no more play with a Man that slighted his ill Fortune, than I'd make Love to a Woman who undervalu'd the Loss of her Reputation.
> *Mirabell.* You have a Taste extreamly delicate, and are for refining on your Pleasures.
>
> (I.i.3-12)

For Fainall the game proves valuable only for its demonstration of his superiority. His "Pleasures" arise not primarily from winning, but from his ability to triumph over his adversary; and his movement from the social game of cards to the game of love reveals the inability we discovered in Dorimant and Vainlove to separate aggressive from sexual impulses. Like Dorimant, Fainall finds relations with women satisfying only when he can play the predator.

In Act II Fainall reveals that he understands his relationship to his wife only in terms of conquest:

> *Fainall.* Excellent Creature! Well sure if I shou'd live to be rid of my Wife, I shou'd be a miserable Man.
> *Mrs. Marwood.* Ay!
> *Fainall.* For having only that one Hope, the accomplishment of it, of Consequence must put an end to all my hopes; and what a Wretch is he who must survive his hopes! Nothing remains when that Day comes but to sit down and weep like *Alexander*, when he wanted other Worlds to conquer.
>
> (II.i.109–17)

Though Fainall speaks ironically here, the play strongly suggests that his self-portrait as Alexander contains a large element of truth. The play ends, in fact, with Fainall's destructive fury in full view, for when his main plot misfires he can still take a measure of pleasure and revenge in exposing his wife to public scorn.

> This, my Lady *Wishfort*, must be subscrib'd, or your darling Daughter's turn'd a drift, like a leaky hulk to Sink or Swim, as she and the Current of this Lewd Town can agree. (V.i.441–44)

> You thing that was a Wife, shall smart for this. I will not leave thee where-withall to hide thy Shame; Your Body shall be Naked as your Reputation. (494–97)

Again we find the vocabulary of sexual desire transformed into a language of aggressive lust and destructive power.

This desire for conquest appears even in Fainall's relations with his mistress and confidant, Mrs. Marwood. Their one major scene together, near the beginning of Act II, dramatizes his need to humiliate and inflict pain on even the woman he claims to love. He begins their dialogue by accusing her of being false, of "Infidelity, with loving of another, with love of *Mirabell*" (II.i.151–52). When Mrs. Marwood attempts to defend herself by claiming that her friendship with Lady Wishfort occasioned her betrayal of Mirabell's plot, Fainall contemptuously retorts, "What, was it Conscience then! profess'd a Friendship! O the pious Friendships of the Female Sex!" (165–66); Fainall follows her reply by laughing at her, reminding her that "you are my Wife's Friend too." Fainall, of course, correctly divines the love Mrs. Marwood bears Mirabell and the insincerity of her friendships; one cannot question the truth of his charges. But the brutality of his manner, his quite evident desire to hurt her, leads him far beyond the mere "Reproof" he claims to have intended. Mrs. Marwood, stung to a fury by his venom, recognizes that "you urg'd it with deliberate Malice—'Twas spoke in scorn, and I never will forgive it" (182–83). Even his attempt to apologize manifests his brutal power, as Marwood struggles in his grasp: "Let me go—Break my Hands, do—I'd leave 'em to get loose" (225–26). And the only way he can think to make things up is by reviling his wife; Fainall can express his love only through his hatred: "I'm convinc'd I've done you wrong; and any way, every way will make amends; I'll hate my Wife yet more, Dam her, I'll part with her, rob her of all she's worth, and we'll retire somewhere, any where to another World" (242–46). Neither Marwood nor Fainall can properly claim an audience's sympathy, but their relationship betrays so great a mutual hatred and contempt that their painful moment of intimacy seems almost poignant in its evocation of a relationship based on selfishness and the desire to inflict pain; they emerge, sadly, as a perfect match.[37]

Mirabell's contemptuous reply to Fainall's opening remarks in Act I establishes the philosophical libertine's distance from the Hobbesian libertine. Mirabell's tone implies that such a "Taste" is too "delicate," too "refined," and that it betokens a decadent and perverse palate; the images of a "sickly and peevish Appetite" that previously characterized Vainlove and Maskwell establish the proper context for interpreting Fainall's "Taste extreamly delicate." At the end of Act I, Petulant and Witwoud invite Mirabell and Fainall to accompany them to the park and "be very severe" with the ladies by making them blush. Fainall accepts their invitation, but Mirabell's refusal demonstrates that in this play only the witwouds take pleasure in humiliating women: "Hast not thou then Sense enough to know that thou ought'st to be most asham'd

thy Self, when thou has put another out of Countenance?''
(I.i.533–35). Mirabell's treatment of Mrs. Fainall, his endeav-
ors to protect her reputation and secure her fortune, reveals the
generosity towards women previously seen in Horner.
Like Horner, too, Mirabell possesses a frank and unabashed
understanding of his sexual needs. While he does what he can
to protect his discarded mistress, he never pretends that his
passion for Mrs. Fainall was anything more than physical; nor
does he apologize for having grown tired of her. Unlike Dorimant and Vainlove, Mirabell does not manipulate the clichés
of romantic love in order to ennoble his passion or dupe his
women: Mrs. Fainall may have ''lov'd without Bounds,'' but
Mirabell sees no reason to affect an emotion he did not feel.

Mirabell's behavior towards Mrs. Fainall has excited much
critical comment, for his rejection of her love and decision to
marry her to Fainall bespeaks a cold-bloodedness verging on
the unfeeling. Mirabell's actions again demonstrate the complexity of his moral sense and the fine ethical distinctions with
which he maneuvers within the confines of society. His decision to marry the then widow Languish to Fainall is not taken
without due regard for both his mistress's reputation or Fainall's character: ''I knew *Fainall* to be a Man lavish of his
Morals, an interested and professing Friend, a false and a
designing Lover; yet one whose Wit and outward fair Behavior
have gain'd a Reputation with the Town, enough to make that
Woman stand excus'd, who has suffer'd herself to be won by
his Addresses. A better Man ought not to have been sacrific'd
to the Occasion; a worse had not answer'd to the Purpose''
(II.i.269–76). Mirabell's description of Fainall's character and
Mrs. Languish's predicament suggests Henry James in its intri-
cate subtlety, the sense of an almost perverse refinement of
moral vision at work. His analysis of Fainall moves between a
clear appreciation of his friend's limitations—''lavish of his
Morals,'' ''professing Friend,'' ''false and a designing Lover''—
and a certain understanding of Fainall's value as a husband
whose ''Reputation with the Town'' would excuse that
woman ''who has suffered herself to be won by his Addresses.''
His final estimation of Fainall reinforces our impression of his
ability to set nice ethical limits on his actions: he would not
have sacrificed a ''better Man.''

An audience may feel, of course, that Mirabell should have sacrificed himself, but that is not the way of this world. Congreve recognizes his difficulty in constructing a philosophical libertine aggressive enough to confront Fainall yet decent enough to become the center of a new and better society: frequently his characterizations of Mirabell attempt to unite opposing or even contradictory terms. Fainall unknowingly helps us to judge the man who manipulated him into marriage when he notes that "you are a gallant Man, *Mirabell*; and tho' you may have Cruelty enough, not to satisfie a Lady's longing; you have too much Generosity, not to be tender of her Honour" (I.i.90–92). Fainall's is a perfect formulation for understanding Mirabell's past actions in regard to Mrs. Fainall, for though Mirabell was Cruel "enough, not to satisfie a Lady's longing," he was generous enough "to be tender of her Honour." Moving between the contradictory poles of "Cruelty" and "Generosity," Mirabell attempts to satisfy his own desires while still protecting Mrs. Fainall's reputation. The trouble he undergoes to salvage her honor reveals his generosity; that he cares for himself and his desires appears in his refusal to marry her himself, to be that "better Man."

The play's language articulates Mirabell's moral complexity by moving repeatedly between conflicting poles of judgment and emotion: "a better Man ought not to have been sacrific'd . . . a worse had not answer'd to the Purpose"; "Cruelty enough, not to satisfie a Lady's longing . . . too much Generosity, not to be tender of her Honour." This type of linguistic formulation figures prominently as well in Mirabell's wooing of Millamant, where the pervasive sense of opposition and contradiction demonstrates the difficulty of their attempt to maintain the energy and excitement of courtship even as they dwindle into marriage. The first act presents two examples of this when Fainall snipes at Mirabell:

> *Fainall.* For a passionate Lover, methinks you are a Man somewhat too discerning in the Failings of your Mistress.
> *Mirabell.* And for a discerning Man, somewhat too passionate a Lover; for I like her with all her Faults; nay, like her for her Faults.
>
> (I.i.158–60)

Mirabell desires, of course, to be both the "passionate Lover" and the "discerning Man," to pursue the "golden Dream" and the pleasures it promises, but to recognize as well the illusions that surround and define it. Thus the movement from liking Millamant "with all her Faults" to liking her "for her Faults" represents another attempt to bring into harmony opposing perceptions of his lover.

The similarity of the play's attempt to unite oppositions in both its presentation of the rake and the love game suggests that the redefinition of the rake that occurs in the progression from *The Old Batchelour* to *The Way of the World* generates a corresponding transformation in Congreve's conception of the resolution of the love game. In *The Double-Dealer* Congreve tries to transcend the irresolution of his first play—signaled by the failure of Vainlove and Araminta to commit themselves to marriage—by providing a conventional romantic conclusion in which Lord Touchwood celebrates the "happy ever after" fate of Cynthia and Mellefont: "Let me join your hands. —Unwearied Nights, and wishing Days attend you both; mutual Love, lasting Health, and Circling Joys, tread round each happy Year of your long Lives" (V.i.586–90). Like Duke Senior's concluding lines in *As You Like It*—"Proceed, proceed. We will begin these rites, / As we do trust they'll end, in true delights"—Lord Touchwood's final pronouncement represents the power of the chief judicial authority to bring order to chaos and secure the efficacy of the conventional comic resolution. Mellefont and Cynthia's reformulation of the metaphors of the chase and gaming strengthen this conventional resolution, for the lovers indicate their readiness to marry by attempting to banish the tensions between men and women, courtship and marriage, that define the love game.

Mirabell and Millamant, on the other hand, attempt to unite or merge contraries in order to demonstrate the complexity of the agreement they would reach. Their climactic proviso scene begins with the conventional image of the hunt:

> *Mirabell.* . . . is this pretty Artifice Contriv'd, to Signifie
> that here the Chase must end, and my pursuit be
> Crown'd, for you can fly no further. —
> *Millamant.* Vanity! No—I'll fly and be follow'd to the last
> moment, tho' I am upon the very Verge of Matrimony,

I expect you shou'd solicit me as much as if I were wavering at the grate of a Monastery, with one foot over the threshold. I'll be solicited to the very last, nay and afterwards.

(IV.i.157–65)

The marvellous image of Millamant "wavering at the grate," poised to step either way, to accept either of two contradictory courses of action, captures the tension in opposition that characterizes their relationship. Here Millamant, like Angelica, is not attempting to resolve that tension by redrawing the metaphor of the chase, but to accept and value that tension because it indicates the depths of her attraction to and for Mirabell: "I'll be solicited to the very last, nay and afterwards." Marriage should not signify the end of courtship, the conclusion of the chase, suggests Millamant, who abhors the signs of familiarity in a husband, "the sawcy look of an assured man, Confident of Success" (177–78). Thus her desire to avoid "Names," "as Wife, Spouse, My dear, Joy, Jewel, Love, Sweet heart and the rest of that Nauseous Cant in which Men and their Wives are so fulsomely familiar" (197–99); thus her desire, again expressed in terms of contradiction, to "be as strange as if we had been married a great while; and as well bred as if we were not marri'd at all" (208–9). Mirabell agrees, for if she "may by degrees dwindle into a Wife," he will "not be beyond Measure enlarg'd into a Husband" (226–31). Both recognize the truth best articulated by Angelica in *Love for Love*, that "Security is an insipid thing, and the overtaking and possessing of a Wish, discovers the Folly of the Chase" (IV.i.787–88).

The strain in all these images between opposing or contradictory poles of experience reveals how tentative Mirabell and Millamant must be in trying to satisfy, as Millamant flatly states, their "will and pleasure." The two qualities she values describe, not coincidentally, the two opposing desires that divide the rake; their attempt to unite oppositions ultimately moves to embrace the two chief aspects of the rake himself, to define, in their great proviso scene, a bond that will prevail over the destructive impulses of the rake while securing for society his necessary vitality.

The fragility of the balance they hope to achieve marks the play's conclusion, where, as James Thompson notes, it is the very "tentativeness, the caution, with which they approach their union, in short, it is their very doubt of success which most promises it."[38] The major strain in the play's resolution, of course, stems from the refusal of Fainall and Marwood to join in the final celebratory dance. Like Malvolio's pledge in *Twelfth Night* to "be reveng'd on the whole pack of you," Fainall's promise that "you shall hear of this Sir, be sure you shall" (V.i.560) and Marwood's vow that her resentment "shall have Vent—and to your Confusion, or I'll perish in the attempt" (565–66) strike a discordant note in the comic harmony that should end the play. Though Fainall and Marwood no longer possess the power to undo the accommodation reached by Mirabell and Millamant, their bitterness mars the closure Mirabell attempts to realize.

This remains true in spite of the power that Mirabell displays in trying to set all to rights. Though many critics have assumed Millamant's superiority over Mirabell, she has almost nothing to say during the crucial confrontation with Fainall and Mrs. Marwood that leads to the successful resolution. All depends on Mirabell, who demonstrates the extent of his success not only by saving Mrs. Fainall and placating Lady Wishfort, but also by looking forward to a time when even Fainall himself might be welcomed back into society: "For my part I will Contribute all that in me lies to a Reunion, (*To Mrs. Fainall*) in the mean time, *Madam*, let me before these Witnesses, restore to you this deed of trust. It may be a means well manag'd to make you live Easily together" (615–19).

Mirabell's desire to include even Fainall in the play's comic resolution testifies both to his strength and to his generosity: Mirabell is powerful and virtuous enough neither to fear nor hate his rival. Yet Mirabell cannot, finally, create a harmony that will encompass both Fainall and Mrs. Marwood, nor can he even assure us of the stability of the love he and Millamant share. When she asks if he would "have me give my self to you over again," he replies, "Ay, and over and over again" (594–96). In spite of his evident love, and the exhilarating sexual implications of his response, that response points to the instability of their relationship, the necessity of recognizing, as the song in Act III suggests, that

> Love's but the frailty of the Mind,
> When 'tis not with Ambition join'd;
> A sickly Flame, which if not fed expires;
> And feeding, wasts in Self-consuming Fires.
> (III.i.377–80)

This song, requested by Millamant and sung before her rival, Marwood, insists that love cannot be separated from conquest, that there can be no ideal mediation between the rake's creative pleasure and destructive will.

James Thompson has observed that all of Congreve's comedies possess a tension between song and plot, that "while the comic plot works its way toward love and marriage, the song insists that such a goal is impossible."[39] It is this tension, as much as the absence of Fainall and Marwood, that points to the complexity of the play's resolution. In it Congreve comes as close as possible to retaining the energy of courtship in marriage by redefining the rake's lust for pleasure without sacrificing the energetic being that helps make the rake a "hero." The failure of *The Way of the World* to achieve a perfect concord stems from Congreve's refusal to pretend that there can be a final resolution to the inevitable tensions between men and women, love and conquest, the rake's pleasure and aggression.

CHAPTER 4

The Female Libertine
on the Restoration Stage

I

In moving from the male to the female rake we must recognize that the connection between witchcraft and sexuality implicated women in the demonic realm to a much greater extent than it did men. Penitent Brothel's cry of rage in *A Mad World, My Masters*—"To dote on weakness, slime, corruption, woman!"—testifies to the dramatic equivalence between women and sin that remains a constant in English, indeed in Western, civilization to the present day. The whole question of witchcraft, in fact, can hardly be separated from the question of women's place in Tudor and Stuart England. A. D. J. Macfarlane found that out of 270 suspected witches brought before the Essex assizes during the years 1560–1680, all but 23 were women; Christina Larner estimates that approximately 80 percent of all witchcraft prosecutions in Scotland involved charges against women.[1] The legal aspects of sixteenth- and seventeenth-century witch-hunts were so overwhelmingly directed against women, in fact, that we must be careful not to reduce the witch trials simply to an expression of Tudor and Stuart misogyny. As Christina Larner reminds us, the evil that witches represented "was not actually sex-specific. Indeed the Devil himself was male. Witch-hunting was directed for ideological reasons against the enemies of God, and the fact that eighty percent or more of these were women was, though not accidental, one degree removed from an attack on women as such."[2]

Yet there can be little doubt that sixteenth- and seventeenth-century understandings of female eroticism in partic-

130

ular turned on the intimate association of women with the demonic: "From Christian Europe to West Africa women are witches because they are more wanton, more weak, and more wicked than men."[3] As Wycherley's Pinchwife laments when faced with the wiles of his supposedly "silly and innocent" wife Margery, "Why should Women have more invention in love than men? It can only be, because they have more desires, more solliciting passions, more lust, and more of the Devil" (IV.ii.59–61). At the root of all such complaints lies the account in Genesis of Satan's seduction of Eve, the moment, according to the anonymous poet of "A General Satyr on Woman" (1679), when the "Author's Image" was by woman "betray'd":

> Woman! Thou damn'd hyperbole in Sin,
> Malign *Atropos*, Hell and Woes origin.
>   .   .   .   .
> The Devil and She, alas! too well did know
> The surest way, to work *Man's* overthrow;
> Such subtle arts and means they did contrive,
> That *Man* could not avoid, pass by, and live.
> Could neither Grace nor Law thy Lust dispell,
> *Woman!* thou damn'd Confederate with Hell?[4]

After the Restoration, men did not suddenly cease to regard women as Satan's confederates; indeed, such fears remain, in twentieth-century films like *The Exorcist* or the Dietrich/von Sternberg *The Devil is a Woman*, staples of popular culture. What changes are not the fears and doubts that female sexuality provokes in men, but the ways in which those doubts are expressed and understood. The divine hierarchy that governs Elizabethan and Jacobean explorations of human sexuality becomes less important after the Restoration, when women as well as men find release from the demonic imagery that defines earlier attempts to understand obsessive sexuality. The significant decrease in witchcraft prosecutions after 1650 points to transformations in witch-beliefs; the drama reflects these changing beliefs in a diminution of the demonic rhetoric that conditioned earlier representations of human, particularly female, sexuality. Yet such transformations might themselves be linked to changes in the economic, political, and social status of women. I quote at length here from Lawrence Stone, because the admittedly tentative questions he raises concerning the relations between witchcraft, women, and society will form the background of my examination of representations of female sexuality on the Jacobean and Restoration stages:

> Is it possible that the practice of witchcraft was one of the very few ways in which a woman could impress herself on a male chauvinist world, at a time when economic opportunities were limited, the structure of the family was changing only very slowly, and when female eroticism was strongly condemned? Is it possible that the decline of witchcraft was brought about to some extent by a partial adaptation of the family in order to give women a greater share of respect, authority, and sexual satisfaction? Is it more than coincidence that witches vanish just at the time when Fanny Hill appears? If so then the rise and fall of witchcraft in the West has to be associated with different stages of a revolution of rising female expectations, generated in turn by the growth of literacy and rise of individualism that were accidental by-products of the Reformation. All this is very fanciful, but the sexual element in witchcraft in the West is too obvious to be ignored.[5]

II

Literature before the Restoration presents us with a number of women celebrated for their frank and powerful sexuality. The sexual vitality and attractiveness of Chaucer's Wife of Bath allows her to transcend the conventional satiric attack against women that goes back to Juvenal's sixth satire. In the drama, Shakespeare creates in Cleopatra a woman who forces us to admire the unabashed expression of her sexual potential. Cleopatra's sexuality defines the essence of her character, generating a language that invariably impresses upon an audience the potency of her powers as a human being. Even her simple command to a messenger for information—''Ram thou thy fruitful tidings in mine ears, / That long time have been barren'' (II.v.24–25)—reveals the sexual desires of a woman who sees even her suicide as a sexual act: ''The stroke of death is as a lover's pinch, / Which hurts, and is desir'd'' (V.ii.294–95). To argue the rarity of such figures (whose very memorableness may stem from our understanding of their uniqueness) does not imply that women on the Elizabethan and Jacobean stage are therefore normally sexless or frigid. Shakespeare's Rosalind and Viola, Fletcher's Oriana, Shirley's Mistress Carol, Marston's Crispinella—all display a profound sensuality. Rosalind and Celia in *As You Like It* can jest about putting a man in their bellies, and Crispinella, as we have seen, can even bluntly exclaim that "I dare as boldly speak venery as think venery" (III.i.25–27), revealing the sexual desires that animate her courtship of Tysefew.

Yet for the most part, speaking and thinking venery define the limits of a woman's sexual prerogatives: to indulge those thoughts, to turn speech into action, confronts female characters on the Elizabethan and Jacobean stage with the vast gulf between the maid or wife and the whore. In sexual terms the pre-Restoration drama provides women with a very restricted stock of roles. Beyond the experience of sex within the sanctified context of marriage there is nothing for women except the roles of whore, bawd, or courtesan. By donning the apparel of a man, Moll, the title character of Dekker and Middleton's *The Roaring Girl* (1607–11), may question the double standard that defines relations between men and women, but her effectiveness in doing so depends on her refusal to indulge her sexual appetites. Middleton's prose introduction to the play reassures us that her "doublet and breeches" are "a braue disguise and a safe one, if the Statute vnty not her cod-peice point," while Moll herself demands that we value her "wit, and spirit" that "scorne to llue beholding to her body for meate."[6]

Moll's refusal to accept the proper role assigned to women leads everyone in the play to assume that she will therefore play the whore. The complacent assurance of men like Sir Alexander Wengraue, Laxton, and Trapdoore, that her deviation from the norm points to her sexual availability, demonstrates the inability of male society to imagine any alternatives to the strict dichotomy between maid and whore. As Moll in anger exclaims, "Th'art one of those / That thinkes each woman thy fond flexable whore, / If she but cast a liberall eye vpon thee" (III.i.68–70).

Such a world leads inevitably to the sexual demonic, for the Elizabethan and Jacobean stage invariably links the whore with the devil, the sexual freedom of women with their participation in the demonic. For a woman to forfeit chastity she must abandon God, and the late-sixteenth- and early-seventeenth-century stage rings with denunciations of women who regard their bodies as "meate." The elaborate trappings and spectacle of the trial Monticelso prepares for Vittoria in *The White Devil* provides a perfect setting for the judicial consideration of female sexuality. Monticelso begins by condemning her as a whore; to her ingenuous question "Ha? whore—what's that?" he answers in a twenty-three line tirade that expresses an almost hysterical reaction to her sexual fall:

> Shall I expound whore to you? sure I shall;
> I'll give their perfect character. They are first,
> Sweet-meats which rot the eater: in man's nostril
> Poison'd perfumes. They are coz'ning alchemy,
> Shipwrecks in calmest weather. What are whores?
> Cold Russian winters, that appear so barren,
> As if that nature had forgot the spring.
> They are the true material fire of hell.
>
> (III.ii.78–85)

Monticelso ends his tirade by linking the figure of the whore to the devil, adultery, and murder: "You know what whore is —next the devil, Adult'ry, / Enters the devil, Murder" (108–9).

The ferocity of Monticelso's remarks—even his pawn, the English Ambassador, admits that "the cardinal's too bitter" (107)—indicates that his response to Vittoria's sexuality goes far beyond the attempt to frustrate his political rival Bracciano. For Monticelso, Vittoria represents no longer an individual woman but, as Stephan Greenblatt suggests, the hated Other without which the Self cannot generate its own identity: "Self-fashioning is achieved in relation to something perceived as alien, strange, or hostile. This threatening Other—heretic, savage, witch, adulteress, traitor, Antichrist—must be discovered or invented in order to be attacked and destroyed."[7] Located at the center of the play, the trial of Vittoria exemplifies Monticelso's increasing inability to govern his world; indeed, Vittoria has even undermined his control of the trial, the judicial ritual that should affirm his power. Her sexuality has thus become a symbol of Monticelso's impotence, of his failure to fashion the external world in the image of the masculine Self. In the trial scene he must aggrandize her sexual evil in order to wrest from her the power he covets. Linda Bamber, in describing Shakespearean tragedy, accurately portrays the entangled motivations that impel Monticelso's behavior during Webster's trial scene: "In Shakespeare's tragedy there is a firm connection between self-hatred, reversal of fortune, and misogyny. The hero's view of women reaches bottom at the moment when he is out of control of himself and his world; women are whores to men when it is no longer possible for men to reconcile themselves to what they are."[8]

In the comic realm, perhaps Thomas Dekker's two-part *The Honest Whore* (Part I, written in collaboration with Thomas Middleton, 1604; Part II, 1605-7) best testifies to the complexities of Jacobean attitudes towards the figure of the whore, the mingled fascination, contempt, and fear that female sexuality inspired in pre-Restoration audiences. Both Parts I and II turn on the paradox implied by the title: the apparent impossibility of a whore's proving honest. At the center of both parts stands Bellafront, the honest whore of the title. She begins the first part a notorious whore, a woman with whom men "spend spare howers." Early in the play, however, she meets Hipolito and falls in love. Her promise to "proue an honest whore, / In being true to one, and no more" is met with disbelief by Hipolito: "I know you feine / All that you speake, I: for a mingled harlot, / Is true in nothing but in being false" (II.1.310-15). Hipolito goes on for almost a hundred lines to anatomize her character, damning her not only as a sexual being who exposes her own corruption, but also as a vessel who contains the sinfulness of all the men she has betrayed:

> You haue no soule,
> That makes you wey so light: heauens treasure bought it,
> And halfe a crowne hath sold it: for your body,
> Its like the common shoare, that still receiues
> All the townes filth. The sin of many men
> Is within you, and thus much I suppose,
> That if all your committers stood in ranke,
> Theide make a lane, (in which your shame might dwell)
> And with their spaces reach from hence to hell.
> (322-30)

As Hipolito's condemnation reaches a climax, he describes a
woman divided from god, the property of the devil:

> your eye-lids hang so heauily,
> They haue no power to looke so high as heauen,
> Youde sit and muse on nothing but despayre,
> Curse that deuil *Lust*, that so burnes vp your blood.
>
> (406-9)

His final portrait of the whore's state anticipates Swift's "A
Beautiful Young Nymph Going to Bed" with its vision of
a sleep filled with nightmare, guilt, and fear:

> Yet your nights pay for all: I know you dreame
> Of warrants, whips, and Beadles, and then start
> At a dores windy creake: thinke euery Weezle
> To be a Constable: and euery Rat
> A long tayled Officer: Are you now not slaues?
> Oh you haue damnation without pleasure for it!
>
> (414-19)

The power of Hipolito's tirade profoundly moves Bellafront, who curses the irrevocable moment of weakness that
caused her to fall: "Curst be that minute (for it was no more,
/ So soone a mayd is chang'd into a Whore)" (427-28). The
finality of the transformation from maid to whore, and the gulf
between these roles, has altered her completely, compromis-
ing all her virtues and undermining her former identity:

> I am not pleasing, beautifull nor young.
> *Hipolito* hath spyed some vgly blemish,
> Eclipsing all my beauties: I am foule:
> Harlot! I, that's the spot that taynts my soule.
>
> (440-43)

Determining to change her ways—"Would all Whores were as
honest now, as I" (456)—Bellafront moves through the rest of
both plays condemning herself for adopting a role that damns
her and the men who solicit her:

> Ile say Ime worse, I pray forsake me then,
> I doe desire you to leaue me, Gentlemen,

> And leaue your selues: O be not what you are,
> (Spendthrifts of soule and body)
> Let me perswade you to forsake all Harlots,
> Worse then the deadliest poysons, they are worse:
> For o're their soules hangs an eternall curse.
>
> (I, III.iii.45–51)

The divine hierarchy that rebukes her sexual sins—the references to "spendthrifte of soule" and "eternall curse" reveals the self-loathing with which she regards her life as a whore.

Bellafront's attempts at virtue first meet universal disbelief; as one character notes, "There's more deceit in women, then in hel" (III.iii.86). Matheo, the man for whose love Bellafront first fell, begins the play convinced that "women when they are aliue are but dead commodities, for you shall haue one woman lie vpon many mens hands" (I.i.88–90); later, he best expresses the male conviction of the futility of Bellafront's attempts at reformation: "Ist possible, to be impossible, an honest whore! I haue heard many honest wenches turne strumpets with a wet finger; but for a Harlot to turne honest, is one of *Hercules* labours: It was more easie for him in one night to make fifty queanes, then to make one of them honest agen in fifty yeeres: come, I hope thou doost but iest" (III.iii. 100–105). The odd construction, "Ist possible, to be impossible," which at once denies what it first presents, points to the logical impossibility of her transformation, rejecting not only its probability, but the comic freedom of possibility. And as Matheo's final comment attests, men not only refuse to believe in her ability to change, but actively discourage it. Her reform frustrates both their lust and their easy assumptions of male superiority and female weakness. Male definitions of a woman's nature simply do not allow for the possibility of reform.

Part II reveals that behind these male attitudes lies a view of women that assumes their irrevocably fallen nature. Even after the play rewards Bellafront's virtue by marrying her to Matheo at the end of Part I, the resistance to her transformation remains unchanged. During the first scene in Part II, the courtier Lodovico voices the common male response to her change when he calls her "the Blackamore that by washing was turned white" (I.i.89), the metaphor suggesting his refusal to admit that she has done more than disguise her true self. In Part II, in fact, the two characters who most attempt to frustrate her reformation are the two agents of her conversion: Matheo, her seducer and husband, and Hipolito. Matheo's incredulous initial response to her suggestion that he marry her—" How, marry with a Punck, a Cockatrice, a Harlot? mary foh, Ile be burnt thorow the nose first" (I, III.iii. 116–17)—registers his moral and sexual disgust even as Bellafront insists on the justice of her proposal: "You loue to make vs lewd, but never chaste" (120). When the Duke finally forces Matheo to do Bellafront justice by marrying her, Matheo cannot see beyond the injustice he suffers: "Cony-catcht, guld, must I saile in your flie-boate, / Becaue I helpt to reare your maine-mast first?" (I, V.ii.440–41).

In Part II, Matheo emphasizes his refusal to acknowledge her transformation or its possibility by persistently urging his wife to return to her old profession in order to support his drinking and gambling. Near the beginning of the second part Matheo registers his refusal to believe in her virtue, arguing that "there is a whore still in thine eye" (II.i.185); throughout the play he returns obsessively to his knowledge of his wife's former state. In Act III he visits Bellafront after having lost all his money, exposing his desire that she adopt her old identity to keep his pockets full: "Will you goe set your limetwigs, and get me some birds, some money?" (III.ii.28–29). Bellafront protests, "Build not thy mind on me to coyne thee more, / To get it wouldst thou haue me play the whore?" but Matheo's only response is " 'Twas your profession before I married you" (70–72). When Bellafront asks how they will pay the rent now that he has wasted their substance, he responds that they will "doe as all of your occupation doe against Quarter daies; breake vp house, remoue, shift your lodgings, pox a your Quarters" (77–79). And when he finally leaves her, he again reveals his obsession with her whoredom: "It's base to steale, it's base to be a whore: / Thou't be more base, Ile make thee keepe a doore" (146–47). The scene dramatically represents his efforts to "undo" her by having him strip off her gown in order to pawn it. Like Hipolito, who earlier charged that Bellafront's lack of a soul made her "wey so light," Matheo expresses his contempt for women by insisting that they are "light," lacking in spiritual substance and identity: "Oh, it's Summer, it's Summer: your onely fashion for a woman now, is to be light, to be light" (44-45). Matheo simply refuses to see or accept her change; for Matheo Bellafront's original identity, which he created, remains her only identity.

Even more indicative of the male failure to perceive Bellafront's new self are Hipolito's attempts in Part II to subvert the change in Bellafront that he originally wrought. Having initiated her fall, Matheo refuses ever to see beyond it; Hipolito, on the other hand, having instigated her reform, tries constantly to undo it. Part II finds him bored with his wife, Infelice, and involved in persistent attempts to make Bellafront his mistress. In a long scene in Act IV the two engage in a mock debate in which he tries to "beate downe this Chastity" (IV.i.247) while she argues that a whore's bed is "like a Cabin hung in Hell, / The Bawde Hells Porter" (356-57). The scene clearly parodies the earlier scene in Part I in which Hipolito maintained the sinfulness of a whore against her entreaties that he become her lover. Here his attempts to argue the nobility of the whore's profession are doomed to failure, for Bellafront's arguments, which both parts of the play have supported at every turn, clearly carry the day. Hipolito can only conclude by maintaining that "Ile pursue thee, / (Tho loaden with sinnes) euen to Hells brazen doores. / Thus wisest men turne fooles, doting on whores" (399-401).

Hipolito's transformation from moral paragon in Part I to whoremonger in Part II stems from his need to use women as vehicles to transcend mundane experience. When, in Part I, he thought his beloved Infelice dead, she became an idealized memory through which he could hope to reform his own life. In honor of her death he determines to spend every Monday "lockt vp / In my close chamber, . . . [where] Ile meditate / On nothing but my *Infelices* end, / Or on a dead mans scull drawe out mine owne" (I, I.i.124-27). In Act IV, scene i, of Part I we see him practice this rite, attempting to sustain an ideal world in the darkness of his shuttered room. Isolated from the common world, Hipolito uses Infelice's portrait to purify his existence; her memory provides him access to an unspotted realm of meditation, melancholy, and transcendence:

> looke! a painted board,
> Circumscribes all: Earth can no blisse affoord.
> Nothing of her, but this? this cannot speake,
> It has no lap for me to rest vpon,
> No lip worth tasting: here the wormes will feed,
> As in her coffin: hence, thou idle Art,
> True loue's best picturde in a true-loues heart.
> Here art thou drawne sweet maid, till this be dead,
> So that thou liu'st twice, twice art buried.
>
> (IV.i.46–54)

In Part I Hipolito moves between his sublime appreciation of Infelice, whose death raises him to a transcendent spiritual realm, and his terrible contempt for Bellafront, who represents to him an irrevocably fallen world of sin, blood, and flesh.

His transformation in Part II reveals that his idealization of the one woman cannot be separated from his debasement of the other. Infelice alive is merely an ordinary woman who cannot sustain the reach of his exalted visions: the first scene in Part II exposes his boredom with the flesh-and-blood Infelice he could worship only when he thought her dead. His debate in Part II with Bellafront on the moral value of the whore thus represents not simply a selfish and expedient reversal of his earlier argument in which he damned whores, but a companion to the earlier scene in which he idealized Infelice. Both scenes occupy the same position in their respective plays—Act IV, scene i—and both emphasize his need to escape mere earthly existence. In Part II he would idealize his life, not with the portrait of a dead mistress, but with the body of a living one:

> Who liues in bondage, liues lac'd, the chiefe blisse
> This world below can yeeld is liberty:
> And who (than whores) with looser wings dare flie?
> As *Iunoes* proud bird spreads the fairest taile,
> So does a Strumpet hoist the loftiest saile.
>
> (IV.i.273–77)

Hipolito's transformation from Part I to Part II thus defines a man who can understand women only as repositories of his most exalted dreams or most terrible fears. Hipolito can respond to women only as angels or whores, spiritual saviors or demonic betrayers. He represents the man who cannot generate an exalted Self without a female Other to worship or destroy. This truth remains hidden from the other characters in the play, for whom Hipolito's transformation is inexplicable. The Duke, his father-in-law, attempts to explain the change by blaming Bellafront for having used her devilish wiles to "bewitch" him: "The Harlot does vndoe him, / She has bewitched him, robd him of his shape, / Turnd him into a beast" (IV.ii.75–77). Here the vocabulary of demonic sexuality allows the Duke to link Bellafront with traditional accounts of Circe, thus vindicating his conventional assumptions of female evil. For Elizabethan and Jacobean audiences, as Hipolito himself argues, Bellafront's guilt lies in the sexual temptation with which fallen womankind inevitably corrupts man:

> oh women
> You were created Angels, pure and faire;
> But since the first fell, tempting Devils you are,
> You should be mens blisse, but you proue their rods:
> Were there no Women, men might liue like gods.
> (III.i.161–65)

The demonic imagery associated with women throughout both parts of *The Honest Whore* would seem to reinforce Hipolito's despairing condemnation of women, except that in this case Hipolito's remarks are part of his mistaken assumption of his wife's infidelity. Infelice, however, vindicates her own conduct and, in possession of the letters that her husband has sent to Bellafront, proves that not she but he would stain their marriage bed. She neatly turns the tables on him and, simply by rearranging the terms of his outrage, demonstrates that "Were there no Men, Women might liue like gods" (190). In this particular scene Infelice's sentiments triumph; yet considering the play as a whole, Hipolito's remarks carry the most weight.

The ambiguity of the play's attitude here is reflected in its final celebration of Bellafront. Throughout both parts of the play Bellafront succeeds in maintaining her virtue in spite of male disbelief and ridicule, in spite of her own sense of sinfulness and self-loathing, in spite of the play's clear convic-

tion, here expressed by the chief judicial figure, the Duke, that
"to turne a Harlot / Honest, it must be by strong Antidots, /
'Tis rare, as to see Panthers change their spots" (IV.ii.45–47).
Bellafront does change her spots, however, and her father's
final "euerlasting blessing" seals her pardon, if, as he still feels
obligated to add even after all the trials through which she has
passed, she "play . . . the Whore no more" (V.ii.477–78).
The play vindicates Bellafront, however, in a scene that
exemplifies the uniqueness of her nature and demonstrates the
play's inability to separate its ethos from a pervasive mistrust
of and contempt for women. The long final scene of the play
takes place in Bridewell, home of "the Bawd, the Rogue, and
Whore" (V.ii.44). Here the Duke dispenses punishments and
rewards, ordering a society that has fallen into chaos. Though
Bellafront establishes her innocence in the face of her
husband's lies, her virtue stands against a background that
assumes the inherent and uncontrollable sexual corruption of
women. Even this late in Part II, her protestations of innocence
still call forth disbelief because, as her father claims, "Say
thou art not a Whore, and that's more than fifteene women
(amongst fiue hundred) dare sweare without lying" (179–80);
even women, he tells us, who appear virtuous to the world
"sure will sinne behind a Skreene" (75). Matheo, for instance,
attempts to implicate the innocent Bellafront in the robberies
he has committed in order to feed his debased appetites. When
the Duke asks "What fury prompts thee on to kill thy wife?"
(143), Matheo reiterates his conviction that Bellafront remains
a whore: "It's my humor, Sir, 'tis a foolish Bag-pipe that I
make my selfe merry with: why should I eate hempe-seed at
the Hangmans thirteene-pence halfe-penny Ordinary, and
haue this whore laugh at me as I swing, as I totter?" (144–47).
For Matheo, only the destruction of the female Other will satisfy the disintegrating male Self.
    The Duke concludes the play by having three convicted
whores brought before the assembled members of the court in
order to impress upon them the worst of evils: "Now pray, set
open Hell, and let vs see / The Shee-Deuils that are here"
(252–53). In contrast to Bellafront's hard-won innocence, all
three—Dorathea Target, Penelope Whore-hound, and Cathyryna Bountinall—refuse to abandon their corrupt profession.
Dorathea, who has been forced to spin as a sign of her

repentance, laughs at their justice and explains that "I had rather get halfe a Crowne abroad, then ten Crownes here" (293–94). The second, Penelope, has been in Bridewell "Fiue times at least," while the third, Cathyryna and her bawd Mistres Horsleach, talk of being "burnt at fourteene, seuen times whipt, sixe times carted, nine times duck'd, search'd by some hundred and fifty Constables" (374–76).

In emphasizing Bellafront's honesty even while he drama tizes the horror of women through this judicial parade of sexual sin, Dekker makes of our honest whore an exception that can scarce balance the evil we see. Cathyryna, the final whore, asks, "Is this World, a World to keepe Bawds and Whores honest?" (377). The play's odd concluding scene emphatically answers "No." Bellafront emerges from the play as Juvenal's *rara avis*, that virtuous woman as rare as the black swan. In stressing her uniqueness Dekker suggests the obsessive mistrust of women's sexual nature that conditions almost all portraits of female sexuality on the Elizabethan and Jacobean stage. Bellafront proves that an "honest whore" can exist, but the play clearly reveals how exceptional is such a combination of attributes in a woman.

III

Care must be taken in attempting to describe transformations in the economic, social, and political status of women that may be related to the decline in witchcraft prosecutions and witch-beliefs. In regard to the status of women, the years up to 1714 have been called an "Age of Transition,"[9] for no definitive changes in the position of women in society can be defined for the seventeenth century. In the eighteenth century, the 1792 publication of Mary Wollstonecraft's *A Vindication of the Rights of Woman* crystallizes our sense of the powerful but normally unseen forces that must have been involved in questioning the subordination of women to men; in the nineteenth and twentieth centuries the great feminist legislative triumphs perform the same function. The seventeenth century contains no such moments, and it becomes correspondingly harder to develop broad generalizations about the changing condition of women.

Attempts to deal with this issue in seventeenth-century

England are further complicated by the fragmentary nature of institutional documents dealing with women. As Hilda L. Smith observes in her recent book on seventeenth-century English feminists, "Seventeenth-century women can still be seen only obliquely through fragments of information. . . . We are only beginning to create a portrait of their lives through isolated remarks in contemporary letters and diaries, or the eulogistic information in funeral sermons on women, and to gain some sense of the more general characteristics of women's life cycle and life expectancy from demographic materials."[10] Though feminist criticism has begun to rewrite male histories of the period, Mary Astell's caution about the difficulty of using historical sources to question the subjugation of women remains true to a certain extent even today: "To say the truth Madam, I can't tell how to prove all this from Ancient Records; for if any Histories were anciently written by Women, Time, and the Malice of Men have effectually conspir'd to suppress 'em; and it is not reasonable to think that Men shou'd transmit, or suffer to be transmitted to Posterity, any thing that might shew the weakness and illegality of their Title to a Power they still exercise so arbitrarily."[11]

Yet in spite of these difficulties, our picture of women's lives during the seventeenth century has undergone a substantial change. In the late 1970s few would have challenged Christopher Hill's generalization that "no one . . . in the late seventeenth century claimed that women were wholly equal to men."[12] Today, however, Hill's conclusion would spark considerable debate, particularly from those, like Hilda Smith, who have seen in late-seventeenth-century feminists—Mary Astell, Elizabeth Elstob, Sarah Fige—the beginnings of a sociological approach to the status of women that guides modern feminist research: "Those seventeenth-century feminists, . . . by linking their personal experiences to those of women generally and by speaking of women's past and present relationships with men in terms of one sex's treatment of the other, established that feminist construct which became the model for later feminist theorists."[13]

Though the importance of late-seventeenth-century feminism should not be undervalued, there are indications that the status of women, particularly their economic status, may have declined during the seventeenth century. A number of historians argue that during the sixteenth and seventeenth centuries production gradually shifted from the household unit to larger capitalistic enterprises. As part of a "household firm," or domestic industry, women shared in the economic responsibilities of production; when this form of financial activity grew less important, women may have lost a measure of economic dignity and equality.[14] According to Rosemary Masek, research into such matters remains as yet inconclusive, though evidence exists to suggest that women played a more active economic role prior to the Restoration:

> In the Elizabethan and early Stuart eras, women were active as speculators in salt, estate managers, buyers of wardships, money lenders, shipping agents, ship owners, and contractors to the army and navy. After the Restoration, fewer women seem to be involved in such capitalist enterprises. Nor were women in the professions of teaching and nursing any better off by the end of the seventeenth century. Indeed, only midwifery had reached a professional status, but as women were excluded from advanced instruction, they were gradually displaced by men practitioners.[15]

Yet caution must be exercised in evaluating such evidence, particularly when Restoration drama is the object of study. In many Restoration comedies young women possess far greater economic security than the rakes who woo them. Many witty virgins owe their popularity not simply to their intellectual and physical charms, but to their attractive fortunes. While rakes never lose sight of the sexual pleasures they would enjoy, Dorimant reminds us that they are not indifferent to more practical matters: "*The wise will find a difference in our Fate, / You wed a Woman, I a good Estate*" (IV.ii.192–93). In the plays considered so far, when money is a consideration of the love game, usually a woman has it. This is particularly true in the plays of Congreve: Cynthia represents the key to the Touchwood estate, Angelica's fortune is her own, and both Millamant and Mrs. Fainall possess wealth in their own right. Though we cannot presume a direct correspondence between the Restoration play-world and its society, Rochester's notorious kidnapping of Elizabeth Mallet, the "Heiress of the West," testifies to the economic power of women, particularly after the civil war and confiscation of many Royalist estates.

Yet "economic power" may not be the best way to describe
the role that women played in the marriage market. Single
women did not possess the same legal rights as single men,
while the social penalties for remaining single and in control of
their fortunes seemed prohibitive to almost all women. Most
women were psychologically and intellectually unprepared to
exercise meaningful control over the money they theoretically
possessed, and all such control ended upon marriage, when
women lost both their legal and their economic independence.
Though Mary Astell addresses a very different "Undertaking,"
her anger at the lack of educational opportunities for women
suggests the inability of women to command whatever economic independence they may have enjoyed: "Through the
Usurpation of Men, and the Tyranny of Custom (here in
England especially) there are at most but few, who are by
Education and acquir'd Wit, or Letters sufficiently quallified
for such an Undertaking."[16]

The problem of the economic status of women becomes
even more complex when we recognize, as Sheila Rowbotham
has argued, that the values associated with the early capitalism
that may have undermined women's economic power also
complemented those ideas involved in the questioning of
women's inferiority:

> The questioning of authority, the idea of individual responsibility
> and conscience as a guide for political action, the elevation of activ-
> ity, the notion of control and change of the outside world . . . were
> as relevant for women as they were for men. The difference was in
> the material situation of men and women in relation to production.
> . . . The separation of family from work had occurred before
> capitalism, but as industry grew in scale it appeared in its most
> distinct and clear form.[17]

A similar contradiction, in fact, exists in the libertine attitudes, developed primarily by French philosophers during the
middle of the seventeenth century, that played so notorious a
role at the court of Charles II after the Restoration. Such attitudes, with their emphasis on the arbitrary nature of social
restrictions and the naturalness of the passions that people
shared with beasts, might seem as applicable to women
as men. Yet the men who fashioned such doctrines reveal a
hostility and ambivalence towards women that appears little

different from the misogyny of society at large. La Rochefoucauld merely participates in clichés about women's natural lust when he notes that "we may find Women who have never been in Love, but 'tis rare to find those who have never had but one Lover." And he remains entirely conventional when explaining that "the Wit of the greatest part of Women, serves more to fortifie and demonstrate their Folly, than their Reason."[18] Likewise, La Bruyère, in his influential *The Characters; or, The Manners of the Age,* can celebrate the woman who possess male virtues: "A Beautiful Woman that has the qualities of a Man of Honour, is of all the Conversation in the World the most delicious." In the next moment, however, the thought of such a hybrid fills him with disgust: "'Tis strange to see Passions in some Women, stronger and more violent than that of their love to Men: I mean Ambition and Play. Such Women make the Men chaste, and leave nothing of their own Sex but the Cloaths they wear."[19]

Even at the licentious court of Charles II, where both men and women indulged in the generous sexual freedoms initiated by that "merry monarch" who "loves fucking much," the double standard of sexual morality put women at a distinct disadvantage. Though the king's mistresses might enjoy a certain protection from public censure, those women at court who failed to keep a modicum of public modesty could pay dearly for their sexual indiscretions. The *Memoirs of the Comte de Gramont* testify to the sexual indulgence of Charles's court, where "the atmosphere . . . was redolent of gaming, pleasure, and all the refinements of splendour and urbanity which could be suggested by the influence of a Monarch who was naturally tender and amorous. Its beauties were bent on charming; the gentlemen had no other end but to please."[20] Another foreign visitor to the court, Lorenzo Magalotti of Florence, judiciously indicates just how freely these court "beauties" participated in this world of pleasure: "Now that I come to speak of the intrigues at the English court I have to establish a rule, for the truth or falsehood of which I cannot answer at this time. True or false, it was certainly put to me as indubitable. The rule is that in all the Court of England there was not at that time any honest women except the Queen, but she was universally reputed to be weak and not very clever."[21]

Yet in the midst of this amoral society of intense sexual

play and easy freedoms, a modern reader may be struck by the severe morality directed against women when what all knew to go on in private suddenly became public. Gramont tells the story of Miss Warmestry, one of the Queen's Maids, whose affair with Lord Taaffe unfortunately comes to public attention: "Warmestry, surprised apparently by some error in her calculations, took the liberty of being brought to bed in the sight of the whole Court. A mishap so public, as one may imagine, made a considerable stir. All the prudery of the Court was let loose; ladies, whose age and face were not of a kind to allow themselves to cause scandal, being particularly vociforous in demanding justice."[22] When Taaffe refuses to recognize her as his wife, the "unhappy Warmestry" is forced to leave the court. Even though libertine attitudes depended on assumptions that would seem to promise acceptance of female sexuality, women remained unable to enjoy the sexual liberties taken for granted by men. Women after the Restoration, even among the most debauched section of the population, occupy a world of strict sexual limitations.

Yet there can be little doubt that the English Revolution was a seminal event in the questioning of this related matrix of economic, sexual, and political limitations. As historians have long recognized, the profound dislocation caused by the civil war and the execution of the king allowed a host of radical ideas to surface in England during the 1640s and 1650s. Though the most radical of these ideas were effectively thwarted by the conservative character of the Cromwellian settlement, the intellectual intensity of this "world turned upside down" was not without important implications for English society. While, as Hilda Smith notes, "general essays calling for social or political reforms almost never addressed the status of women, . . . they obviously helped establish an intellectual milieu which encouraged the questioning of the fundamental principles which bind a society together."[23]

The Puritan character of the Revolution, of course, would inevitably have involved women in the rising tide of expectations with which so many greeted the collapse of Charles's government. Women were active in the advance of radical Protestant sects even during the sixteenth century, for, according to Rowbotham, "Puritanism effected a species of moral improvement in the position of women. Within a very confined sense it allowed women a certain restricted dignity. It provided an impetus for a more humane concept of relationships between the sexes, protesting against wife-beating and opposing rituals like churching which had emphasized the uncleanness and animal baseness of women."[24] Radical sects not only promoted an ideology that provided an intellectual rationale for the improvement of women, but allowed women to achieve prominence in religious and political activities. During the 1640s and 1650s women were able to take part in the church government of radical sects as preachers, prophets, and authors.[25] Indeed, women took part in the Revolution as soldiers, siege workers, couriers, spies, and nurses.[26]

The clearest expression of this increased prominence and activity of women can be seen in the series of petitions that women presented to Parliament during these two decades. Certainly these petitions reveal that women continued to accept their inferiority to men: the petitions of 1642, 1643, and 1649 refer repeatedly to their "frail Condition," their status as the "weaker sex," the "weak hand of Women."[27] Yet the petitions also suggest that though women could not challenge the overt superiority of men, they nonetheless possessed a significant interest in the Commonwealth and its legal rights and privileges. As their 1649 petition, *To the Supreme Authority . . . Petition of divers well-affected Women*, argues, "Have we not an equal interest with the men of this Nation, in those liberties and securities contained in the Petition of Right, and other good Laws of the Land? Are any of our lives, limbs, liberties or goods to be taken from us more than from Men?"[28]

Yet even here, where the documents provide the clearest examples of women's expressions of increasing social and political expectations, the evidence suggests that no simple progression of women's rights or equality can be charted. Patricia Higgins, who has studied the women petitioners of the 1640s and 1650s, argues that the petitions expose an intellectual tension between the assertions of women's rights and admissions of their weakness: "There appears to be a contradiction between the female petitioners' admissions of the inferiority of their sex and the intellectual case they made out for the equality of the sexes. It would be fair to say that this contradiction was more than apparent, it was real."[29] Neither the Revolution nor Puritanism could satisfactorily resolve this contradiction, for the rhetoric and ideology of both rested on conservative principles that assumed the inferiority of women. Though Puritanism introduced the possiblity of religious equality for both sexes, it did so within the framework of the patriarchal family structure that emphasized the subjugation of women to men. And while the Revolution challenged many of the basic political assumptions of seventeenth-century England, most revolutionary leaders not only showed little interest in the rights of women, but cast their revolution in a rhetoric that assumed, in its emphasis on traditional notions of property and family, conventional conceptions of female weakness.

Attempts to come to terms with the changing status of women during the seventeenth century again and again involve the historian in a web of contradictions: contradictions within an economic change that seems to have undermined the economic importance of women at the same time that it provided an intellectual basis for questioning their inferiority; within a libertine attitude towards human nature whose creators reveal a conventional condescension towards women at the same time that they generated ideas that could be used to argue the equality of men and women; within a political activism that moves between expressions of women's inferiority and assumptions of equal rights with men in the Commonwealth; within, as Mary Poovey notes, a Puritanism that "simultaneously reinforced the injunctions against the free expression of female desires *and* provided women a role that seemed constructive rather than destructive."[30] In short, any theory of a linear progression involving the increased status or equality of women simplifies the historical evidence. If, as Christopher Hill has suggested, the seventeenth century describes a "Century of Revolution," there is no easy way to decide precisely how that revolution affected women. Old attitudes remain even while new values question the intellectual and moral assumptions that gave such attitudes their power.

This same sense of contradiction characterizes not only the treatment of women in plays written after the Restoration, but the theatrical world of Restoration London itself. The emergence of actresses and female playwrights after the reopening of the theatres in 1660 provides two clear examples of the greater freedom enjoyed by women after the Restoration. Prior to the reopening of the theatres there is no evidence that women attempted to write for the public stage. After the Restoration, however, women played an active part in the theatrical world: Arthur H. Scouten has determined that during the years 1660–1720 seventy-two plays written by fourteen women were produced in London theatres.[31] The career of Aphra Behn, for example, reveals a woman's ability to enter, and succeed in, a sphere that had previously been considered solely masculine. Behn's output was large, and at least for a few years, her activities as a professional playwright allowed her a measure of financial support. Yet the public ridicule she suffered reveals the very high price she had to pay for her success. Angeline Goreau, in her recent biography, chronicles the difficulties of Behn's unique position as the first woman professional playwright. In attempting to move outside of the restricted roles ordinarily occupied by women, Behn became a convenient target for those who refused to accept the participation of women in the larger social world: "'To publish one's work, then, was to make oneself 'public': to expose oneself to 'the world.' Women who did so violated their feminine modesty both by egressing from the private sphere which was their proper domain and by permitting foreign eyes access to what ought to remain hidden and anonymous.''[32] Behn refused to remain anonymous: in doing so, in opening herself up to public scrutiny, she placed herself in a position where both her morality and her femininity could be questioned. The attacks on Behn's licentiousness that Goreau documents reveal male contempt for a woman who chose to assume a public, and therefore masculine role.

The emergence of female players provides possibly the best example of how sexual change could both elevate and degrade women at the same time. On the one hand, the ability of women to join men on the stage points to the increased freedom available to women after the Restoration. The opportunity to play themselves, to project in public their own personalities, reflects an important gain in social freedom. We have become so accustomed to thinking of Shakespeare's theatre as one of the glories of English civilization that we forget just how the refusal to allow women on the stage demeans the sex. The Elizabethan and Jacobean theatre assumes that women are not fit to play themselves, and Shakespeare's Cleopatra recognizes just how much the substitution of boys for women undermines the dignity of her sex:

> The quick comedians
> Extemporally will stage us, and present
> Our Alexandrian revels: Antony
> Shall be brought drunken forth, and I shall see
> Some squeaking Cleopatra boy my greatness
> I'the posture of a whore.
> (V.ii.215-20)

On the other hand, in practical terms, the freedom women gained to play themselves on stage was to a large extent the freedom to play the whore under a different, more polite, guise. Acting was not a particularly remunerative profession, and the sexual availability of actresses was taken for granted. Actresses were convenient sexual prey for Charles's courtiers, while the king himself seems to have frequented the theatre as much for sexual as for aesthetic satisfaction. Anne Goreau relates the not uncommon career of Elizabeth Farley, who began acting with the King's Company during the season of 1660-61. After a short interlude as Charles's lover, she became the kept mistress of a lawyer at Gray's Inn. An unfortunate pregnancy and desertion by her keeper left her bereft of both reputation and financial support. She continued to act until the theatres closed during the Great Plague of 1665. After that she became a common though rather notorious prostitute.[33] Not all actresses, of course, were prostitutes, but Anne Bracegirdle's notorious chastity suggests how unusual it was for an actress to maintain her reputation.

IV

In turning to the Restoration plays that deal most fully with female sexuality I intend to concentrate on two character-types. The Restoration treatment of the first, the courtesan, will stand in sharp contrast to what we have seen in *The Dutch*

Courtesan and *The Honest Whore*, where the pervasive context of demonic sexuality made it difficult to see women who exchanged sexual favors for money as anything but monstrous expressions of our fallen state. The second figure, the female libertine, represents a character rare enough on the Restoration stage, but almost impossible to imagine in the earlier theatre because of the strict dichotomy between maid and whore. The female libertine imitates her male counterpart on the Restoration stage through her desire to participate in the sexual freedoms usually denied by a social world intent on subordinating the individual to the larger dictates of society. In such a context the female libertine's refusal to accept the limitations placed on her becomes an act of rebellion by an individual against the arbitrary restrictions of a corrupt and unnatural society. Like the male rake, the female rake commands both respect and scorn, admiration and fear; unlike the male rake, however, the female rake proves difficult to domesticate. As a projection of male fantasies about, and fears of, female sexuality, the female rake generates ambivalences even greater than those aroused by the male rake. Though she is never simply dismissed as an expression of human degeneracy and postlapsarian evil, her sexual vitality and defiance of male authority create fears that remain unresolved by the conventional resolution of Restoration comedy.

Thomas Killigrew's *Thomaso; or, The Wanderer* predates the Restoration by six years. Written in 1654, and published in a handsome edition of Killigrew's plays in 1664, *Thomaso* may never have been produced on the Restoration stage. Killigrew prepared the play for production, deleting large sections of Part II and making smaller excisions in Part I; he even drew up a partial cast list for the first part. Nevertheless, the play has no stage history, and though William Van Lennep suggests that it may have been performed at the Theatre Royal early in 1665, no firm evidence to prove this assertion has come to light.[34] Performed or not, the play certainly intrigued Aphra Behn, whose adaptation, *The Rover* (1677), was quite successful, holding the stage until the middle of the eighteenth century. While Behn's version remains a much more successful dramatic vehicle than Killigrew's, it is also far more conventional and predictable; unwieldy and ponderous, Killigrew's

original—thought by contemporaries to be semi-autobiograph-
ical—nonetheless explores more fully the sexual and moral
potential of its characters.
Killigrew's Spain is inhabited by men and women con-
sumed by insatiable sexual appetites. None, however, can
match the sexual exuberance or experience of the two chief
libertines of the play, Thomaso and the courtesan Angellica
Bianca. Thomaso resembles Jordan's extravagant rake: called
by one of his companions the "Wanton Wanderer," Thomaso
has drunk, fought, and whored his way across Europe as part of
the English navy. Convinced that "beauty cannot be divided
from variety, no face is too new, or wine too old, nor a friend
too true,"[35] Thomaso's lust expresses itself as a wild and
gallant affirmation of the life of passion. There is a splendid
vitality to his outlandish appetites and exaggerated lust, his
contempt for "Secrecie" and desire to celebrate his lovers
before the eyes of all observers:

> Secrecie a virtue; a damn'd ingrateful vice, only known where small
> beer is currant, despis'd where *Apollo* or the Vine bless the Country;
> and though *Joves* Wife was a shrew, yet we find none of his Mis-
> tresses hid in Roots or Plants, but fix'd stars in heaven, for all to
> gaze and wonder at, though few have wit to admire, or power to imi-
> tate; and though I am not *Jove*, to place my Angellica, or my Paulina
> there; yet my kind heart shall proclaim how fit for such places such
> starry beauties are.
>
> (P. 371)

Angellica's celebration of her own sexuality lags not far
behind Thomaso's. When she first appears on stage, she sings a
song that identifies her sexuality with the plenitude and
regenerative powers of Nature; like Aphrodite, or Shakespeare's Cleopatra, she is animated by a sexuality that renews
itself constantly, transcending the decay of the mundane physical world:

> Come hither, you that Love, and hear me sing
>   of joys still growing;
> Green, Fresh, and Lusty, as the pride of Spring,
>   and ever blowing.
>   .   .   .   .

> Come hither you that hope, and you that cry,
> > leave off complayning
> Youth, Strength and Beauty, that shall never die,
> > are here remaining.
>
> .   .   .   .
> And in an hour, with my enchanting Song,
> You shall be ever Pleas'd, and ever Young.
>
> > (Pp. 334–35)

Having lost her last keeper in the wars, Angellica has had her picture mounted in the town square with a caption promising a month of delights to any man willing to pay a thousand Crowns for her favors.

Thomaso has but to see her picture to respond to her promises. Though too poor to pay her price—always in trouble, he is ever out of money—he claims her picture as his right and outfights a Spanish rival, Don Pedro, and the two bravos hired to guard it in order to retain her visage. Angellica observes his gallantry, invites him to her rooms, and after a few minutes of conversation, decides that their relationship should continue in the bedroom.

The understanding they reach is best described by Thomaso:

> All the hony of Marriage, but none of the sting, *Ned*; I have a Woman without that boundless Folly, of better or worse; there's a kind of Non-sense in that Vow Fools onely swallow; I can now bid my Friends well-come without Jealousie; Our vows are built upon kindness only, they stand and fall together; We neither load, nor enslave the mind with Matrimony; No laws, nor tyes, but what good Nature makes, binds us; we are sure to meet without false well-comes, or dissembling smiles, to hide the Sallary of a sin, or blinde the fornication of a *Platonique* Friendship; Our knots hold no longer then we love; No sooner wish a liberty but we take it.
>
> > (P. 346)

The two libertine-rakes, quick to recognize their similarities in character and temperament, attempt to create a "natural marriage." In doing away with "Matrimony"—that "Vow Fools onely swallow"—and the social laws and ties which it represents, they try to build a relationship upon a mutual kindness and generosity that stem from their recognition that each is much the mirror of the other. The contrast in Thomaso's speech between "good Nature" and "false well-comes, or dissembling smiles" indicates their contempt for arbitrary social formulations that distort people's instinctive behavior. Their vows, which unite them without at the same time taking away their liberty, allow them to realize all the pleasures that a conventional marriage provides—love, sexual fulfillment, emotional intimacy—without sacrificing the freedom that remains central to their libertine beliefs.

Killigrew, however, has little sympathy with such an ideal; no sooner is it formulated than undercut. Without social laws to bind its participants, the natural marriage exists only as long as the initial inclination. Angellica makes this clear early in the play when she explains why she has led the life of a courtesan: "How should I become a Lover that have not so much leasure as to wish or long for any man; All I see are offered before I ask'd; I have refus'd many, and enjoy'd more, but never yet desired one since I parted with my first Friend" (pp. 332–33). In Thomaso she does find a man she desires, but falling in love proves her undoing. Killigrew uses her love as a way to punish her for her immoral life, because she understands from the beginning that Thomaso will never marry a whore. When she learns that he may very well marry the Platonic Serulina, Angellica's bitterness leads her to join an intrigue against him.

Her decision to plot against her lover marks a crucial moment in the play, not only because it reveals the moral corruption that Killigrew insists we see in her libertine beliefs and sexual freedoms, but also because it becomes the chief incident in preparing Thomaso's transformation from rake to husband. When Thomaso discovers her plot he is forced to reflect on his own life:

> It vexes me she should be guilty of so mean an action, because I thought her of a gallant temper, but she's a common Whore; and this life of mine, that which some men may pass some moneths in for humour, but no trade for men of honour; Wisdom and Conscience bids us seek a Nest ere Age and Diseases find us; . . . A gray Wanderer is but a bad Tragedy to himself, though an old Beggar may be a Comedy to others: These thoughts, and the noble nature of this

vertuous Maid [Serulina], have made me resolve to abjure this humour; and having bid farewell to all the follies of my youth vow my whole thoughts to the friendship of the fair *Serulina.*

(P. 438)

Thomaso's rejection of his youthful follies is, of course, characteristic of the extravagant rake. Yet Killigrew's ability to make this transformation psychologically compelling is something few Restoration dramatists could imitate. As the ironic conclusion of Lee's *Princess of Cleve* suggests, too often the rake's repentance is nothing more than a necessary dramatic convention, occasioned not by the psychological needs of the character but by the proximity of the fifth-act curtain. Behn's adaptation of Killigrew's play provides a perfect example, for Behn's hero, Willmore, changes from committed rake to devoted husband in mid-speech. But in presenting Angellica as a libertine mirror of Thomaso, Killigrew makes plausible the latter's reformation because it stems from Thomaso's recognition of what he might become if he refuses to give up his youthful humor.

In Thomaso's transformation and Angellica's punishment Killigrew demonstrates his condemnation of the libertine and the sexual attitudes that their relationship epitomizes. Yet the play departs significantly from Jacobean dramatic language in its refusal to dismiss Angellica as a demonic presence, her ideals and desires as the product of a satanic mind. Thomaso's utter contempt for a "common Whore" accentuates the play's ambivalence towards female sexuality—its desire to punish in the female what can be forgiven in the male rake—but his immediate movement to "this life of mine" demonstrates that the female no longer represents simply a despised and alien Other. Thomaso certainly distances himself from Angellica, who finally does not share his "gallant temper," but he does perceive her as a distorted image of himself; her extravagant sexuality matches his own, while her refusal to restrict her freedom by marrying shows him his own future should he not "seek a Nest ere Age and Diseases find us." Thomaso's speech implicitly recognizes that Angellica's life and sexuality represent, not the Other, but a version of the male Self; as the male libertine Philidor in James Howard's *All Mistaken; or, The*

Mad Couple (1665) remarks when he first sees the female rake Mirida, "A brave wench by this light, sure 'tis I / In Petty coates."[36] The conclusion of Killigrew's play even saves Angellica for virtue by making it clear that she was unaware of the full implications of the plot she joined. Forgiven by Thomaso, and accompanied by Thomaso's friends on an extended trip to Italy, Angellica, it is hinted, may even become Don Pedro's lover. Equally important, however, is Killigrew's decision to allow Angellica to plead the cause of sexual equality. In both parts of the play she engages in an extended debate over the morality of the sexual double standard; though she hardly emerges victorious, her arguments compel attention—unlike those in *The Honest Whore*, which only satirize expressions of female sexual equality.

In the first part of the play she challenges Thomaso, who has just admitted that the passion he feels for her is not love but "Lust his bastard-brother":

> After all this severe truth, what are we [women] guilty of that you have not confess'd? What crime staines us that you would not now act? You men are strangely partial to your selves, you would not despise us else; Is the fault single in us? If not, why should we lose our Honours in the Act, when you think it an Honour to be the Actors? Who made the Law against Love? Or where will you find it obligeth women onely? If the Law be general, must not the crime be so too?
>
> (P. 339)

In focusing on the twin conceptions of Honour and Law, Angellica questions the legitimacy of social categories that arbitrarily assign a moral distinction to the expressions of male and female sexuality. In a simple lyric entitled "Woman's Honor," Rochester would later attempt to take advantage of the different meanings of the term "honor" by using the distinction between male honor ("noble confidence") and female honor ("mean mistrustful shame") to compose a poem of seduction.[37] Here, however, Angellica wants to ask how it can be honorable for a man to fulfill his sexual needs, but dishonorable for a woman. Though she does not explicitly refer to

Nature, it is evident that behind the artibrary measures of society lies a natural standard that belies the unjust creations of man. In his answer Thomaso admits the justice of her natural standard while explaining the reason why she cannot justly claim it:

> Love 'tis equal, but not in you, because you will be paid; you sell your blood which is your guilt: 'Tis Mercenarines in you that make the sin, Nature else would plead for you too; When I hang out my picture, and at a rate expose my self to all comers, then I will not wonder if you despise me.
>
> (P. 339)

Thomaso's point is well-taken, but Angellica responds in a language that anticipates Mary Astell's later charge in *An Essay in Defence of the Female Sex* (1696) that "Women, like our Negroes in our Western Plantations, are born slaves, and live Prisoners all their Lives":[38]

> And I could urge, when you'll take a House and furnish it, deliver up your Youth and Liberty a slave to our Sex, and wait like a spider in your Web, for all flies that pass; When *Angellica* knocks at your door, and leads you to your bed, I will not wonder if you ask a price before I enjoy you; Nor ought you to wonder when we desire some satisfaction for the slavery we suffer.
>
> (P. 339)

By insisting that women must demand money because of the social inequality that otherwise makes them slaves to men, Angellica indicts male society for a crime that men complacently regard as a matter of female weakness and degeneracy. As Angellica observes, "Onely (once a whore and ever) is the world adage" (p. 339).

Angellica's argument with Don Pedro, in Part II, follows a similar course, with Angellica wondering why chaste women are considered virtuous when "chaste men [are] ridiculous, neither believ'd, esteem'd or trusted by either sex" (p. 396); and with Don Pedro imitating Thomaso's argument that "our guilt is not so general, we like and enjoy some one; you like nor refuse none that will buy" (p. 397). Angellica's reply again insists on the injustice of arbitrary social standards, and like a true rake she ends by asserting the essential nobility and exuberance of sexual passion:

> What partial folly then is that governs the minds of men; and what fools are women to submit to their Lunacy? I prize my self as high for having enjoy'd a gallant man, as you would do for having won his sword, or a gallant womans heart; despis'd because enjoy'd by others! tell me, to morrow, if you find any paths or steps upon my body where former Lovers trod, or any print of pass'd kisses cleaving to their lips; if you can miss those Graces, those Roses they gather'd, and not find as fresh and full handfulls for you to reap, as if he or they had not found their harvest.
>
> (P.397)

By dwelling on the vitality of men and women's sexual natures, and questioning the contradictions that lay behind the assertions of socially approved morality, Angellica continues to identify her charms with the regenerative powers of Nature. Promising those who would share her delights a perpetual spring of youth, vitality, and sensuality, Angellica remains, in spite of Killigrew's condemnation and the triumph of Serulina, the play's most powerful female presence. While her arguments hardly carry the day, they are not implicitly degraded by the demonic context that shapes our responses to the sexuality of a Franceschina or Bellafront. In this play the sexuality of both Thomaso and Angellica links them to a natural world that elevates rather than diminishes their natures. Thomaso, of course, by marrying Serulina, can more easily atone for his past and play a more central role in the comic resolution, but even Angellica partakes in the celebration that ends the comedy. Both must learn to control their extravagant sexuality, to subordinate it to the dictates of society, but neither is portrayed as the alien, the Other, whose sexuality overwhelms their individuality or humanity.

V

Men have rarely accepted with equanimity women's attempts to participate in the freedoms and pleasures of the male world. The prospect of women's usurping the roles of men has usually produced the most emphatic accents of male rage. Juvenal has few kind words for women at any point in his sixth satire, but some of his severest censure falls on those women who as athletes, intellectuals, or politicians attempt to deny their sexual sterotypes and adopt ''masculine'' poses and activities. Yet men have been excited by that which ostensibly repels them: for instance, the legends of the Amazons, those female warriors who must remove one breast in order to employ their bows with all the accuracy of a man, have never ceased to fascinate the male imagination.

During the seventeenth century men found particularly unnatural the possibility that women might assume male roles, because, as the anonymous author of *Marriage Asserted* (1674) argues, while men represent "*the glory of God,*" women "answer the end of their Creation" when they reflect "*the glory of man.*" Each sex thus possesses its own particular virtues and vices: "What [St. Paul] therefore condemns as a fault in [the female] Sex, is so far from being one, and gives them so good a lustre, that I question (though a vice in a man) whether it is not a perfection in them."[39] This strict dichotomy between the sexes can enforce a view of women as different almost in kind from their male superiors. According to Marin La Chambre, whose *L'art de Connoistre les Hommes* (1659) was translated into English in 1665 as *The Art of How to Know Men*, "Woman is *cold* and *moist*" and thus it follows that she "should be *Weak,* and consequently *Fearfull, Pusillanimous, Jealous, Distrustfull, Crafty,* apt to *Dissemble, Flatter, Lie,* easily *Offended, Revengefull, Cruel* in her revenge, *Unjust, Covetous, Ungratefull, Superstitious.* And from her being *moist,* it follows that she should be *Unconstant, Light, Unfaithfull, Impatient,* easily *Perswaded, Compassionate, Talkative.*" Though these qualities appear to be vices, La Chambre continues, yet they "are not, to speak exactly, so many defects, but rather, on the contrary, so many natural perfections, as being correspondent and conformable to the feminine Sex." Indeed, were a woman to possess the same virtues as a man, these virtues should become vices in her: "It must be acknowledg'd, but what is a perfection in one subject, may be a defect in another: as for instance, courage in a Lion, is a vertue, in a Hare, a vice; and so what is a perfection in the man, is a default, and imperfection in the Woman, because it makes her recede from the natural perfection of her Sex."[40]

The figure of the courtesan does not entirely address this question of women's engrossing male roles because the economic terms of her sexual transactions—as the debates between Thomaso, Don Pedro, and Angellica reveal—isolate her from conventional expressions of sexual desire. Though the courtesan enjoys the sexual variety usually reserved for men, by making explicit the translation of the sexual self into an economic commodity she removes herself from polite society. It is the female libertine on the Restoration stage who best confronts the tension between male and female roles because the libertine has always been regarded as a primarily male identity. The *Oxford English Dictionary* properly warns us that the term "libertine" was "rarely applied to a woman," though as Lady Mary Wortley Montagu rather cynically noted in 1723, wives were committing adultery so freely that "the Apellation of Rake is as genteel in a Woman as a Man of Quality."[41]

In *Sir Anthony Love; or, The Rambling Lady* and *The Wives Excuse; or, Cuckolds Make Themselves*, produced almost within a year of one another, in 1690 and 1691, Thomas Southerne explores the dramatic possibilities of the female libertine-rake, dramatizing her diverse psychological and moral potential in the figures of Sir Anthony and Mrs. Wittwoud. Southerne's radically different responses to these two characters, who share a common identity, point to the curious mixture of excitement and fear that the female libertine inspires, for while Sir Anthony's extravagant sexuality clearly fascinates the author, Mrs. Wittwoud's sexual liberties disgust and repel. Yet in spite of the substantial differences in their personalities, neither Sir Anthony nor Mrs. Wittwoud can be assimilated into a conventional comic structure. Southerne's treatment of these figures reveals not only how Restoration dramatists struggled to create a comic form capable of both expressing and controlling the rake's desires, but how the female rake in particular created problems for a comic drama based on conventional notions of male aggression and female passivity.

Sir Anthony Love was probably first produced in November 1690, performed by the United Company with Mrs. Mountfort in the title role.[42] At that time Susannah Mountfort dominated the comic stage as the reigning queen of the gay couple, and in the dedication to the first printed edition of the play in 1691, Southerne pays generous tribute to her powers as an actress: "I am pleased, by way of Thanks, to do her that publick Justice in Print, which some of the best Judges of these Performances, have, in her Praise, already done her, in publick places; that they never saw any part more masterly play'd: and as I made every Line for her, she has mended every Word for me; and by a Gaity and Air, particular to her Action, turn'd every thing into the Genius of the Character."[43] Yet Mrs. Mountfort's importance to the play went beyond the excellence of her performance. As Peter Holland has noted, in Restoration London the smallness of the theatrical world emphasized the peculiar intimacy that normally arises between performers and their audience.[44] Audiences, for instance, quickly recognize the type of character a particular performer chooses to play, and that knowledge creates certain expectations about a new performance. Today we certainly would not expect Katharine Hepburn to portray a sentimental old spinster, or Robert Redford a nasty two-bit gunslinger. Such expectations have a private as well as public dimension: Taylor and Burton's *Cleopatra* possessed a certain piquancy because of our knowledge that the screen romance merely echoed the even more passionate backstage romance.

The casting of *Sir Anthony Love* encouraged both public and private expectations. While Mrs. Mountfort had followed Nell Gwyn as the female half of the gay couple, William Mountfort, who during the 1680s had most impressed audiences as the witty rake, had become the new Charles Hart. As the leading gay couple of the day, Susannah and William Mountfort had achieved "the predictive inevitability of union" for which Hart and Gwyn were the originals on the Restoration stage. And in the case of the Mountforts, their status as man and wife emphatically reinforced the expectations created by their stage identities: "By 1691, the theatre audience would expect that any time both Mountforts appeared in the same cast, they would woo each other and end the play together."[45]

Southerne's play begins by encouraging such expectations, for its opening scene makes very clear that Sir Anthony (Mrs. Mountfort) has assumed male garb only so that she can better pursue the object of her passion, Valentine (Mr. Mountfort).

We first meet Sir Anthony while she is alone with her male servant, Waitwell, the only one as yet aware that Sir Anthony is "young and handsome in Petticoats." Why, he asks, does she "part with the pleasures of your own Sex, to Ramble into the Troubles of ours?" Why, indeed, except to secure a lover: "I do it to be better employ'd; to recommend me to *Valentine*, for whose dear sake I first engag'd in the Adventure; robb'd my Keeper, that nauseous fool *Golding*, of Five hundred Pounds and under thy discretion came a Collonelling after him here into *France*" (p. 2).

If Southerne's play begins by creating certain expectations through its casting, these expectations can only be reinforced by the conventions of the breeches role. The breeches role, of course, is one of the most conventional dramatic devices in English comedy. Found originally in medieval French romances and the plays of Italy, the female page became a popular figure on the Elizabethan stage and remained a favorite of audiences and playwrights throughout the Restoration.[46] Elizabethan and Restoration playwrights present many reasons for a woman's assumption of male disguise. One of Shakespeare's most famous heroines, Rosalind, does so in order to protect herself from a dangerous male world in which "beauty provoketh thieves sooner than gold." Margery Pinchwife is dressed as a boy by her husband in order to protect *his* forehead, while Wycherley's most romantic heroine, Fidelia, dons a male disguise in order to pursue the man she loves. Yet self-protection and love do not exhaust the range of possible motivations. In Ravenscroft's *The Careless Lovers*, the heroine Hillaria dresses as a man—"Cock, and Strut, and so Hector the young Cits"—so that she can torment and dominate her suitor, Careless. In Stapylton's *The Slighted Maid*, a male disguise advances a revenge plot against a jilting lover.

What remains constant about the breeches role is not its motivation but its conclusion, not the impetus it gives to dramatic action, but the way in which it brings such action to a close. Typically the female page ends the charade by revealing her true identity, reaffirming her true sexual nature by giving herself in marriage. Though the heroine may enjoy the male disguise and revel in the freedom it provides, by the end of the play she happily trades her male attire for a wedding dress and the love of her man.[47] Duke Orsino's first command

of Viola after he has discovered her true identity at the conclusion of *Twelfth Night* is that she "Give me thy hand, / And
let me see thee in thy woman's weeds" (V.i.270–71). The
breeches role on the Elizabethan and Restoration stage both
advances and delays the climactic "boy wins girl" pattern of
romantic comedy; it promises an eventual union of hero and
heroine once their sexes are properly sorted out, but it titillates
audiences with bisexual fantasies while withholding that
union.[48]

The opening scene of the play, then, promises the eventual
union of Sir Anthony and Valentine both in the dramatic
significance of the casting and the sexual implications of the
breeches role. Indeed, Sir Anthony is already well known to
Valentine as a friend and fellow rake, and Waitwell's questions
concerning the intentions of Sir Anthony stem only from his
surprise that she has not already unmasked. Sir Anthony, however, knows better: "Thou wou'dst have had me, with the true
Conduct of an *English* Mistress, upon the first inclination,
cloy'd him with my Person; without any assurance of his
relishing me; enough, to raise his appetite to a second taste:
No, now I am sure he likes me; and likes me so well in a Man,
he'll love me in a Woman; and let him make the Discovery if
he dares" (p. 2). The amusing movement from being "liked as
a man to loved as a woman" reveals Sir Anthony's recognition
that the male's desires can be raised only upon the firm foun-
dation of the female's ostensible indifference, that delay alone
can prove his passion true. Delay, though, has apparently run
its proper course, for the scene between Waitwell and Sir Anthony ends with the servant commanded to direct Valentine to
Sir Anthony's private lodgings and to prepare Sir Anthony's
female wardrobe.

Accident, however, governs the realm of comedy, and the
very next scene suggests the obstacles that will prevent Sir Anthony's unmasking. Valentine and his friend Ilford enter Sir
Anthony's apartment, and during the conversation of the three
friends we learn that Valentine has fallen in love with
Floriante, the beautiful and rich daughter of Count Canaile.
The count opposes their marriage, of course, for he wishes his
eldest daughter to wed the Count Verole, though Valentine re-
tains an important ally in the Abbè, brother of Count Canaile
and a staunch admirer of his new English friends.

Yet Valentine possesses a second, far more powerful ally, and Southerne's play turns on the revelation that far from attempting to foil Valentine's marriage to Floirante, Sir Anthony has determined to advance it. The obstacle to Sir Anthony's unmasking lies not in Floirante and her rival love for Valentine, but in Sir Anthony herself, for she so enjoys the freedom which her male attire provides that her disguise has come to dominate her personality.

Even during the play's opening scene, when so much serves to confirm our conventional expectations of the play's action, minor details hint that Sir Anthony is not a traditional romantic heroine, that she too thoroughly enjoys her life as a male rake. Waitwell opens the play by assuring us that she "so perfectly act[s] the Cavalier, that cou'd you put on our Sex with your Breeches, o' my Conscience you wou'd carry all the Women before you" (p. 1). Sir Anthony cannot, of course, transform her anatomy, though she does more than parade about in male disguise. She has, for instance, taken fencing lessons that have allowed her just that morning to skewer a stranger who refused to celebrate Valentine's virtues: "My Constant Exercise with my Fencing Master, And Conversation among men, who make little of the matter, have at last not only made me *adroit*, but despise the Danger of a quarrel too" (p. 1). Sir Anthony's fascination with swordplay reveals that she has learned not just the outward forms, but the psychology that defines male freedom. In *Twelfth Night*, Viola fails to outface the cowardly Sir Andrew not simply because she has never learned to make a pass with a sword, but also because she remains always a woman in spite of her disguise. Her fear proves her femininity, and in Shakespeare's play the audience welcomes such proofs because they point to the happy ending that depends on her assumption of her proper female shape. That the female page should apologize for her male dress, that she should earnestly affirm her essential femininity, are traditional aspects of the breeches role.[49] Sir Anthony will suffer no such apologies to be made; her unhesitating acceptance of her new role indicates an attitude at odds with a willing return to her old identity. In learning to "despise the Danger of a quarrel," Sir Anthony has come to despise an essential feature of her female role.

As the play develops, we become more aware of how completely Sir Anthony's male disguise takes over her personality. Though surrounded by a number of genuine male rakes, the high-spirited Valentine among them, Sir Anthony is truly, as the witty Abbè remarks, "all in all; the whole Company thy self, / Thou art every thing with every body" (p. 17). She enjoys the freedom that her male attire provides, finding the sexual aggressiveness that her role demands much to her taste. She celebrates the perpetual holiday in which she can now participate—"We make a Carnival; all the year a Carnival" (p. 28) —and comes to understand, too, the kinds of pleasure that arise from conquering women. When Ilford asks her not to ruin the woman he loves, the Abbè's daughter Volante, Sir Anthony reveals how entirely she thrives on the privileges that her role provides:

> *Ilf.* Do me a favour, and don't undoe her Fame.
> *Sir A.* But there's the pleasure on't—
> *Ilf.* To ruine the Woman that loves you, —
> *Sir A.* Not so much out of ill Nature to her, as good Nature
> to myself: Reputation must be had: And we young Men
> generally raise ours out of the Ruine of the Womens.
> (P. 57).

Though we perceive the irony of her remarks, we see too how much she has come to enjoy the vitality of a role that depends more on the aggression she can enjoy than the sexuality she cannot. Though her remarks here are little more than cliché, their very conventionality reveals how she has learned to appreciate the dimensions of the male role she has adopted. Like her earlier use of the metaphors of appetite to talk about sexuality, Sir Anthony here employs a language most often spoken on the Restoration stage by men. She quickly recognizes the relationship for men between sexual and verbal aggression:

> *Ilf.* Whoever has the Woman; you have your Wit, Sir
> *Antony—*
> *Sir A.* They go together, Sir, — You'll find it so.
> (P. 5)

The freedoms Sir Anthony enjoys seem particularly vital and attractive when measured against the helplessness of the other female characters. Though Floriante desperately wishes not to marry the Count Verole, and though her sister Charlott would avoid the convent with which she has been threatened, both remain unable on their own to evade the demands of masculine authority. This authority is first represented by the father, Count Canaile, who maintains a firm sense of the duty owed him by his daughters: Floriante, he says, "too well knows what's owing to a Father and her self, / To my Authority and her own Birth, now to dispute / What I design for her" (p. 23). Only marriage can free women from such rule, but as Floriante bitterly recognizes, that institution merely allows women to exchange one master for another:

> So you promise all before you have enclos'd us,
> But possess'd our Fortunes, and our Persons are your Slaves,
> Us'd like your Slaves, and often both abus'd.
>
> (P. 24)

Such sentiments, of course, are the clichés of Restoration comedy, expressed by a host of women who prove eager to assume the chains of matrimony by the play's end. Southerne's play accentuates such feelings through the presence of a woman whose participation in male freedoms reveals the passivity that most women in this society must accept. Like her male counterparts, the female rake reminds us of just how much the individual must sacrifice to the demands of society.

Sir Anthony refuses to capitulate to those social demands, however much the play has excited our expectations of her eventual union with Valentine. If dramatic conventions reflect social conventions, then Sir Anthony's refusal to participate in the former reveals her rakish disdain for the latter. When Sir Anthony finally reveals her true identity to Valentine, we discover her unwillingness to discard her male disguise. The moment we have awaited as a romantic climax to the play's complex fabric of intrigue and deception now marks only another stage in Sir Anthony's rakish plots. Though she clearly desires the sexual satisfactions that only a man can provide, she refuses to abandon the aggressive pleasures that animate her behavior as a male:

Sir A. Not to marry me, I hope, *Valentine!* But, if you
cou'd be in that mind (which I neither desire nor deserve)
I know you too well, to think of securing you that way.
Val. But I wou'd not have engag'd my self, any where
else—
Sir A. I know your engagements, to *Floriante;* and you shall
marry her. That will disengage you, I warrent you.
Val. You continue your Opinion of Marriage.
Sir A. Floriante, I grant you, wou'd be a dangerous Rival
in a Mistress—
Val. Nothing can Rival thee.
Sir A. And you might linger out, a long liking of her, To
my uneasiness, and your own, but Matrimony, that's her
security is mine: I can't apprehend her in a Wife.
(Pp. 49–50)

This unmasking marks the first time in the play that Sir
Anthony appears dressed as a woman, though the scene's distance from a conventional scene of revelaton lies precisely in
the disjunction between her female dress and male sentiments:
the assumption of her proper female identity only serves to
emphasize the impropriety of her masculine understanding. In
the above exchange it is Valentine who timidly seems to suggest marriage, Sir Anthony who treats such alternatives with
disdain; Valentine who speaks the language of romantic cliché
("Nothing can Rival thee") and Sir Anthony who disregards
such silly talk, Valentine who deludes himself as to their true
libertine desires and natures, Sir Anthony who knows "too
well" their inability to accommodate themselves to marriage.
Sir Anthony's indifference to marriage stems from her
understanding of what the security of marriage will demand
from both her and Valentine. Having played the rake for much
of the play, she realizes that marriage can only cloy both of
them, that marriage means an end to holiday, a diminution of
vitality and sexual fervor. Far better to remain lovers than
become husband and wife, for as lovers they can maintain the
generous playfulness and rakish extravagance that has characterized their relationship as friends.

The play demonstrates just how strong is their friendship
when near the end Sir Anthony asks Valentine to stand up for
her at an assignation with a lady. Sir Anthony, of course, cannot sample the sexual joys that her liaison promises, but by

using Valentine as her agent she intends that both shall receive
as much pleasure as possible:

> *Val.* 'Tis a whimsical Undertaking methinks,
>   To support another Woman's Intrigue, at your Expence—
> *Sir A.* There's no buying such a Frolick to [*sic*] dear.
> *Val.* And part with your Lover to oblige her!
> *Sir A.* So long, I can't part with you; to provide for your
>   pleasure as well as my own:
>   Besides, 'tis a diverting piece of Roguery:
>   And will be a Jest as long as we know one another.
>
> (P. 64)

Of "Roguery" and "Jest," as Sir Anthony suggests, will their
relationship consist, and the play becomes an amusing series
of sophisticated tricks played by the libertine couple. In the
course of the play Sir Anthony succeeds in exposing the
hypocrisy that lies behind the mask of an ostensibly devout
pilgrim, duping twice more her original keeper, Sir Gentle
Golding, who has the misfortune of happening on her again,
"marrying" Volante, Ilford's love, and then sending Ilford to
consummate the marriage; she also reveals the homosexual
passion that animates the Abbè, and, most important, helps
Valentine in his plot to marry Floriante.

The success of this final plot signals the play's close,
though the manner in which it does so suggests Southerne's
difficulty in accommodating the unrepentant Sir Anthony.
Valentine and Sir Anthony in breeches go out one night to
rescue Floriante and Charlott from the convent that protects
their virtue by enforcing their father's will. While spiriting the
women away, their party is set upon by Count Verole and his
hired bravos. In order to frustrate the count, Sir Anthony and
Floriante exchange clothes. When the confusion abates, when
plot and counterplot fulfill themselves, the company gathers
on stage with marriage, parental blessings, and substantial fortunes promised Volante and Ilford, Charlott and Count Verole,
and Floriante (dressed as Sir Anthony) and Valentine. The
general merriment increases when Sir Golding and Sir Anthony (dressed as Floriante) enter, the former trumpeting his
success in having revenged himself on all by marrying Floriante. Confronted with the sad truth, that he has really married
his female nemesis, Sir Golding quickly agrees to provide Sir

Anthony a separate maintenance that will allow her to "begin to rove" again. Four marriages and a final dance should provide a conventional comic resolution, but Sir Anthony remains a troubling presence in the play. Though dressed now as a woman, the clothes she wears are not her own: her female identity has still not been restored. Moreover, in using their disguises to suggest that Floriante is Sir Anthony and vice versa, Southerne only makes us more aware of Sir Anthony's earlier boast that she "can't apprehend . . . [Floriante] in a Wife." Four marriages celebrate the play's resolution, but from this celebration Sir Anthony stands well apart, the unrepentant libertine who earlier remarked that "I make love sometimes, but do not often Marry" (p. 36).

Southerne's decision to leave Sir Anthony unattached at the play's conclusion gives the play a somewhat disquieting air; like Horner in Wycherley's *The Country-Wife*, Sir Anthony refuses to sacrifice her private world of pleasure for the dubious rewards promised by society. For Margaret McDonald, "Sir Anthony is the most blatantly immoral of all Restoration heroines. In her striving for mastery she goes beyond the threats of other coquettes . . . to become the most militant of all these feminists. Sir Anthony is almost unreal: a dream-like projection of the power fantasies of Isabelle, Lady Betty and a gaggle of other coquettes."[50] Though McDonald certainly overstates the case, there remains something menacing about Sir Anthony's unwillingness to betray her conviction that "In all plays, one side must be the looser; / But Marriage is the only Game, where no body can be the winner" (p. 59). Sir Anthony exemplifies more than the frustrated desires of other less successful women; she reveals the aggression which, as we have seen, lies at the heart of all rakes, male as well as female. While Sir Anthony and Valentine charm us with their frank passion and sophisticated playfulness, they also provide a glimpse of the pleasure they take in aggression and destruction. In doing so they reveal the complex libertine beliefs that lead to the rake's determination to remain an outsider.

If *Sir Anthony Love* only alludes to the dark side of the female rake's personality, *The Wives Excuse* makes explicit the destructive nature of the Hobbesian female libertine. Set in an imprecisely realized France, the earlier play allowed its English audience to distance itself from the rake's antics. *The*

Wives Excuse, however, insists on its English setting; its opening scene, where servants gossip about their masters and mistresses outside of a Musick-Meeting, emphatically places the play in the contemporary London social world. Here, so close to home, playfulness and wit emerge as no more than masks that disguise the rake's aggression and self-interest, while the exciting and attractive freedoms of Sir Anthony become perverted by a female rake who exemplifies not male fantasies about female eroticism, but male fears of a destructive female sexuality that challenges assumptions of masculine superiority.

The rake's antisocial power reveals itself first in the gallery of male libertines who dominate the play's action. Friendall, acted by Mr. Mountfort in the play's December 1691 première, represents, like Goodvile, the rake married, a man tired of his wife almost before he has time to enjoy her. As he cheerfully admits, in fact, he married without any intention of enjoying her: "To tell you the Truth, the chief End of my marrying her, (next to having the Estate setled upon me) was to carry on my Entrigues more swimmingly with the Ladies."[51] A second figure, Wilding, plays the rake who, like Etherege's Dorimant, takes as much pleasure in triumphing over a woman as in receiving her embraces; ruining those women he has enjoyed defines Wilding's particular taste for pleasure. As one of his friends notes, "*Wilding*, you know, never Debauches a Woman, only for himself; where he visits, in a little time, every Man may be received in his turn" (p. 32).

Unlike Friendall and Wilding, who early in the play reveal their less attractive sides, Lovemore, the last of the male rakes, engages our sympathy for much of the play. A "friend" to Friendall, Lovemore recognizes the charms of Mrs. Friendall and attempts throughout the play to solace her for her husband's neglect. Lovemore possesses a charm, wit, and self-knowledge that Friendall does not, and for much of the play an audience may even encourage his attentions towards Mrs. Friendall; she deserves to be valued, and Lovemore's assiduous wooing suggests a desire that may involve genuine feelings. In the fifth act, however, Lovemore exposes his true nature when Mrs. Friendall firmly articulates her desire for him yet refuses to betray her virtue by cuckolding her husband. Lovemore's contempt for her dilemma and integrity exposes his inability to appreciate anything beyond his own desires:

> *Mrs. Fr.* But I am marry'd, only pitty me— [*Goes from him*
> *Love.* Pity her! She does not deserve it, that won't better
> her condition, when she may: But she's marry'd she
> says; why, that was the best of my reasons of following
> her at first; and I like her so well, as she's another Man's
> wifc, I shou'd hardly mend the matter by making her my
> own.
>
> (P. 50)

His admission that he pursued her only because she was already married makes clear his inability to respond emotionally to any woman; this rake exists simply as a sexual predator.

These portraits of the male rake are conventional enough, unusual only in the grimness of Southcrne's treatment and his bitter satiric tone. The most unusual character in the play, however, and the one who most fully reveals the degraded nature of the rake-hero, is Mrs. Wittwoud. Hardly a year after playing Sir Anthony, Susannah Mountfort again found herself cast as the female rake, uttering as Wittwoud lines that might have been spoken by her earlier heroine:

> *Witt.* I would have a man know just enough
>   Of me, to make him a Lover; and then, in a little time,
>   I should know enough of him, to make him an Ass.
> *Sight.* This will come home to you one day.
> *Witt.* In any shape but a Husband, Cozen.
>
> (P. 7)

> *Witt.* . . . if any Man pretended to follow and like me, I
>   shou'd never believe what he said; if he did not do some-
>   thing to convince me, I should think he affronted me
>   extreamly; if upon the first handsome occasion, he did
>   not offer me every thing in his power.
>
> (P. 31)

> *Witt.* Indeed the Woman shou'd cheat the Man, as much as
>   she can,
>   Before Marriage, because after it,
>   He has a Title of cheating her, as long as he lives.
>
> (P. 22)

The two women share an impatience with the promises of marriage, as well as a sure recognition of their needs and desires. Yet in the earlier play Mrs. Mountfort's role contains a playfulness and good cheer that Mrs. Wittwoud doesn't possess. Wittwoud quickly emerges as a nightmare version of Sir Anthony, a coarse woman cheapened and corrupted by her freedoms. Here Wilding's admission that "I see, Madam, we differ only in our Sexes" (p. 23)[52] unites her in a rakish partnership that displays none of the attractiveness so evident in the behavior of Sir Anthony and Valentine, or even Angellica and Thomaso. When Wittwoud attempts to lead Wilding to an assignation with a lady—a business that reminds us of Southerne's earlier play—it reveals none of the "Roguery" and "Jest" celebrated in the earlier couple. Here when the female libertine's plotting comes to light, Mr. Wellvile characterizes Wittwoud in the most humiliating terms: she is "every thing that's mischievous; abandon'd and undone; undone her self, she wou'd undo the Sex: she is to bawd for *Wilding:* I know her bad enough for any trade. But Bawds have some good Nature, and procure pleasure for pay: *Wittwoud* has baser ends, A general Ruine upon all her friends" (p. 32).

In *Sir Anthony Love* the female rake enjoyed freedoms that unmasked the hypocrisy of others; Sir Anthony's "liberation" stood in marked contrast to the limitations and dishonesty of conventional society. In *The Wives Excuse*, however, the female libertine represents a distillation of what is worst in the contemporary social world. Wittwoud's plots reveal nothing positive in her character, for her energies fulfill themselves only in the destruction of others; "general Ruine" defines Wittwoud's taste for pleasure. At the play's opening we learn that Wittwoud's vicious example has led to the corruption of her cousin Fanny, a simple girl whom Wilding debauches early in the action. In return for Wilding's promise not to expose Fanny to the town, Wittwoud agrees to help him seduce her virtuous friend Mrs. Sightly. Even for herself, Wittwoud can procure only the most degraded of liberties. She has been, Mrs. Sightly charges, "notoriously abandon'd to the Beastly Love of a Fellow, that no Body else can look upon" (p. 44). This lover, whom we never see, is referred to throughout the play as an ugly rogue, a philandering husband who shames her—a "Curse," as she puts it, rather than a pleasure.

If Southerne assails all of the libertine characters, the play's conclusion emphasizes the particular horror that the female libertine inspires. *Sir Anthony Love*, as we have seen, turns on the audience's expectation of the union of Susannah and William Mountfort. *The Wives Excuse* raises no such expectations, for William Mountfort's role as husband to Mrs. Friend all (acted by Mrs. Barry) seems to preclude the possibility of any relationship between the real husband and wife. The climax of *The Wives Excuse*, however, comes when the entire company discover Wittwoud and Mr. Friendall embracing during the masquerade at Friendall's house; Wittwoud has deliberately disguised herself as Mrs. Sightly in order to ruin her friend's reputation by sleeping with Friendall. The discovery of Wittwoud and Friendall—with its clever allusion to their off-stage relationship—uncovers Wittwoud's designs, leaving her open to the contempt of all. Southerne uses the movable scenery of the Restoration stage to great effect here, for he quite literally exposes the guilty pair to both company and audience: "*Scene draws, shows* Friendall *and* Wittwoud *upon a Couch*" (p. 53).

In spite of their villainy, the play's male rakes remain within the acceptable limits of their social worlds: Lovemore and Wilding will simply move on to other conquests, and even the contemptible Friendall still possesses a secure social position. Wittwoud, however, represents the outsider who cannot be forgiven by or integrated into her society. Here the female libertine becomes the blocking character who must exile herself from civil society:

> *Sight.* You have paid dear enough for that Scarf; you may
>   keep it for a pattern for your friends, as 'twas borrow'd
>   for: I won't insult over you, and am only pleas'd, that I
>   have scap'd your snares.
> *Witt.* That disappointment is my greatest Curse; and
>   Disappointments light upon you all.   [*Goes out.*
>   (P. 54)

Wittwoud's departure, like Malvolio's in Shakespeare's romantic comedy, or Fainall's in Congreve's comedy of man-

ners, represents the only way to deal with a character who
cannot be accommodated by the comic resolution. Her final
curse reveals the depths of her depravity, both her antisocial
nature and the self-destructive consequences of her vicious
conception of freedom.

Wittwoud suffers the heaviest punishment for the libertine's disregard of conventional morality, for in this play the
female rake cannot be forgiven those sins that define the rake's
nature. While Southerne allows his male rakes to participate in
the play's comic resolution, Wittwoud must bear the weight of
the audience's moral opprobrium, fulfilling Sarah Fige's observation that "Woman now is made the Scape-goat, and / 'Tis
she must bear the sins of all the land."[53] Only once in Southerne's play does Wittwoud court the sympathy of her audience,
and that comes when she herself recognizes the unfulfilling
nature of the life she has chosen:

> Now from one of my Character,
> Who have impertinently prated away so much of my time,
> (In setting up for a Wit, to the ruine of other Peoples pleasure,
> And loss of my own) what encouragement,
> Or probability can there be, but that, as I have liv'd a fool,
> I ought to dye repenting, unpity'd, and a Maid:
> If I had dy'd a Maid, 'tis but what I deserv'd,
> For laughing so many honest Gentlemen
> Off their charitable design of making me otherwise.
>
> (P. 24)

This speech, delivered just prior to her partnership with Wilding, emphasizes not simply her selfish desires, her need to
"ruine . . . other Peoples pleasure," but the unsatisfactory
nature of the character she has adopted. Wittwoud here
laments her loneliness, the isolation that a woman suffers
when she rejects the conventional course of marriage. In a
society in which marriage was the only career open to women,
Wittwoud has made her position in society untenable. This
society can offer no other channel for her energies; in refusing
to accept the fate of Mrs. Friendall, Wittwoud dooms herself to
live "unpity'd, and a Maid." Her vitality corrupted, she can
fulfill herself only, as Mrs. Sightly charges, by working to

make others "as despicable as your self." Such a passion, Sightly continues, is ultimately satanic: "There must be the Devil in the bottom on't, and I'le fly from him in you" (p. 44). *The Wives Excuse* has little regard for the freedoms embraced by the female libertine. While the play savages conventional society and the corrupted institution of marriage that props up this sterile order, it has only contempt for libertine attempts to subvert the manners that define a civilized society. Southerne concentrates his disapproval on the female libertine, though only a hint of the demonic rhetoric that characterized Jacobean drama remains to remind us of the immoral creed such a figure once represented.

The relative critical neglect suffered by Southerne's two plays may stem from our inability to place these plays comfortably within the conventional patterns of Restoration comedy. While both plays possess many features typical of the Restoration theatre, the presence of a female libertine changes their shape in subtle but unmistakable ways. Quite prepared to deal with a male who boasts that "Conquest is our destiny: we must follow it," critics remain uncertain just how to treat a woman who claims as her motto "Conquer or perish."[54] The female libertine generates unusual relationships with her male counterparts: if Sir Anthony and Valentine, Wittwoud and Wilding, suggest any other couple, it is not the conventional gay couple, but Laclos's Merteuil and Valmont, those evil geniuses who dominate *Les Liaisons dangereuses.* In a society governed by a strict dichotomy between male and female roles, the female libertine must, as Merteuil explains to Valmont, take particular care if she wishes to enjoy those freedoms available to the male:

> And where, after all, is the achievement of yours that I have not a thousand times surpassed? You have seduced, even ruined a great many women: but what difficulty did you have in doing so? What obstacles stood in your way? Where is the merit you can truly claim as your own? . . . Believe me, Vicomte, unnecessary virtues are rarely acquired. Since you risk nothing in your battles, you take no precautions. For you men, defeat means only one victory the less. In this unequal contest we are lucky not to lose, you unlucky when you do not win.[55]

The harsh punishment suffered by the marquise at the conclusion of Laclos's novel supports her understanding of the disadvantages under which women labor in the battle of the
sexes: while Valmont dies nobly in a duel, Merteuil suffers the
ignominy of a disfiguring disease that "has turned her inside
out, . . . [making her soul] now visible on her face."[56]
Southerne's fascination with the female libertine expresses
itself in the fantasy world of *Sir Anthony Love*, where libertine
impulses and the female rake who most fully displays them
have free play. His later play, however, reveals his distaste for
these same impulses and his determination, in a more realistic
setting, to exact retribution from the woman who dares to
enjoy privileges not hers by custom.

CHAPTER 5

Sexual Discourse
in the Eighteenth Century

I

The Restoration rake, I have argued in my first four chapters,
reflects a remarkable transformation in conceptions of sexuality, inaugurating the culture's attempt to transfer the control of sexuality from the divine to the secular world. This
transformation, seen through its literary models, creates a
unique type of drama and new types of sexual discourse. In
considering, in this final chapter, the development of these
discourses in the eighteenth century, I will not maintain that
the seventeenth-century rhetoric of demonic sexuality is
abandoned and replaced. What distinguishes the eighteenth
century is the diversity of languages within which sexuality
could be understood. Demonic sexuality is not replaced by a
single language or discourse, but itself becomes one of a
multitude of sexual languages. Demonic sexuality, for example, is central to Richardson's portrayal of Lovelace in *Clarissa*
and, later in the century, to the dark sexual overtones of the
gothic novel. But various secular languages become just as important, if not more so, and we may derive an understanding of
the number of sexual languages available to the eighteenth
century by considering one of Chesterfield's letters to his il-
legitimate son:

> I come now to another and very material point; I mean women; and
> I will not address myself to you upon this subject either in a
> religious, a moral, or a parental style. I will even lay aside my
> age, remember yours, and speak to you as one man of pleasure,
> if he had parts too, would speak to another. . . . By what goes
> before, you will easily perceive that I mean to allow you what-

ever is necessary, not only for the figure, but for the pleasures of a gentleman, and not to supply the profusion of a rake. . . . Having mentioned the word Rake, I must say a word or two more on that subject, because young people too frequently, and always fatally, are apt to mistake that character for that of a man of pleasure; whereas, there are not in the world two characters more different. A rake is a composition of all the lowest, most ignoble, degrading, and shameful vices; they all conspire to disgrace his character, and to ruin his fortune; while wine and the p——x contend which shall soonest and most effectually destroy his constitution. . . . A man of pleasure, though not always so scrupulous as he should be, and as one day he will wish he had been, refines at least his pleasures by taste, accompanies them with decency, and enjoys them with dignity. Few men can be men of pleasure, every man may be a rake.[1]

Chesterfield begins by choosing between the different personae available to him, each of which assumes a different "style," a different mode of discourse. The one he chooses, that of the "man of pleasure," defines itself in opposition to the Hobbesian rake whom we have considered in Wycherley and Etherege, Otway, and Lee. We might recall Etherege's boast—that "[I] have followed what was likelier to ruin a fortune already made than make one: play and women. Of the two the Sex is my strongest passion"—in order to mark the vast gulf between Chesterfield's understanding of pleasures refined "by taste" and accompanied "with decency," and the Hobbesian libertine's obsessive and anarchic pursuit of pleasure that invariably leads, both Etherege and Chesterfield agree, to "ruin." Chesterfield's man of pleasure has much more in common with the philosophical libertine and that figure's "science of voluptuousness," though even here we can detect a new accent characteristic of the eighteenth-century concern for sex with sensibility, erotic fire tempered and civilized by a capacity for refined feeling.[2] Though commentators typically, and justifiably, stress the cynical and worldly nature of Chesterfield's advice to his son, in sexual matters he maintains a decorum that consistently elevates and purifies the grosser sexual passions of the Restoration rake: "Remember that when I speak of pleasures, I always mean the elegant pleasures of a rational being, and not the brutal ones of a swine. I mean *la bonne chère*, short of gluttony; wine, infinitely short of drunkenness; play, without the least gaming; and gallantry, without debauchery."[3] Chesterfield's use of the term "gallantry" reveals what Peter Wagner has referred to as the eighteenth-century desire to use "words of love" that are purged of their moral connotations:

> Given the frequency of extra-marital relations, a word like *adultery* almost lost its former connotation with sin. The new usage of words of love was partly influenced by French romances of seventeenth- and early eighteenth-century origin: formerly negative words were upgraded. Thus, adultery became *gallantry*, a love affair was an *amour*, and an attempt at seducing someone was labelled *intrigue*. The titles of the published divorce trials bear witness to this gradual change of usage and, in particular, to the euphemistic application of the term *gallantry* to what in essence was nothing else but adultery.[4]

Such euphemisms legitimize sexuality by removing it from the moral realm, making decorous what a previous century defined as sinful. The connection between sex and sensibility that developed during the eighteenth century is most important, because, Roy Porter argues, it "seemed to solve that constant problem of the English Enlightenment: how individuals could indulge their own selfish passions without danger to the social order."[5]

Both Porter and Wagner suggest that the eighteenth-century language of erotic sensibility testifies to that century's attempt to come to terms with the basic conflict between social order and sexual license that the Restoration struggled with in the figure of the libertine-rake. Yet this language of sensibility is not the only discourse developed during the eighteenth century that confronts the problem of sexual excess. Tony Tanner, for instance, in explaining the importance of adultery in the bourgeois novel of the eighteenth and nineteenth centuries, defines a legal terminology of "contract and transgression" that characterizes "the possible breakdown of all the mediations on which society itself depends":

> It may be objected here that the theme of cuckoldry is as old as literature and that cuckoldry in no way threatened the actual in-

stitution of marriage. It may also be objected that society learned to contain the ruptures implicit in adultery by the negative ritual of divorce. But in the first case, cuckoldry—or, for that matter, inter-marital games in Restoration comedy—is conceived of as separate from the formal institution of marriage itself, which is unthreatened by wayward sexual behavior on the part of those thus contractually joined. There were so many other religious and social normative and constitutive patterns binding people together. It is only when marriage is seen to be the invention of man, and is felt to be the central contract on which all others in some way depend, that adultery becomes, not an incidental deviance from the social structure, but a frontal assault on it.[6]

Though I hardly wish to argue that *The Way of the World* "anticipates" this novelistic concern, many critics have noted the play's reliance on legal machinery, on contracts that bind and unbind obligations and dependencies: Mirabell insists on Waitwell's marriage to Foible so that his servant cannot "stand upon Terms" and ruin the "Contract" by which Lady Wishfort "is [to be] caught"; the proviso itself, of course, is constructed in terms of a legal contract, while the final scene revolves around the rival contracts and documents of Fainall and Mirabell. When marriage has lost its sacramental character, the legal formulations of society become the chief determinants of the relations between men and women. To a significant extent, *The Way of the World* defines "contract" as the central constituent of a complex society and marriage—in the elaborate proviso scene between Millamant and Mirabell —as an "invention of man." Though the implications of this transformation are not fully worked out in Congreve's play, its dependence on legal discourse suggests a similar concern for the "contract and transgression" that Tanner finds so important in the novel.

Scientific discourse provided another model with which to deal with erotic experience. Though primitive by our own standards, the pseudoscientific and scientific languages of the eighteenth century tried to explain the mysteries of sexuality by providing mechanistic explanations for sexual desires and obsessions; understood as an essential part of nature, sexuality becomes a legitimate object of study for the natural sciences. Robert Wallace (1697–1771), Scottish minister and

mathematician, begins his unpublished essay "Of Venery, or
of the commerce of the two sexes" by assuming that "as
[venery] is necessary for propagating the species of mankind,
nature hath not only indued both sexes, with a strong inclination to Venery, but hath rendered the Venereal Act highly
Delightfull when it is performed in obedience to nature."[7]
G. S. Rousseau has demonstrated that the eighteenth century
attempted to generate a "materialistic science of eros" that
could explain the body's desires in scientific terms. While old
sexual beliefs and myths lived on in anonymous tracts such as
Aristotle's Masterpiece and *Aristotle's Book of Problems*, a
new science of the erotic defined sexuality in terms far removed from the demonic sexuality of the seventeenth century:
"Before the eighteenth century there was no science of the
erotic; . . . As late as the seventeenth-century *fin de siècle*, a
sexually hysterical woman is still labelled 'possessed demon-
ically,' not called nymphomaniacal or discussed in physiolog-
ical, neurological or other medical terms."[8]

The profusion of erotic languages generated by the eighteenth century is matched by a corresponding increase in the
number and types of rakes who figure prominently in literature of the eighteenth century. The rake continues, of
course, his career in the comedy of manners. Recent critical
attention to the types of plays performed as well as written
during the eighteenth century has shown that the rake did not
"desert" the theatre after the Restoration; "sentimentalism"
did not sweep the stage clear of rakes, and comedies of manners continued to be written throughout the century.[9] Many
Restoration comedies continued to be popular well into the
century; Wycherley and Congreve, in fact, enjoyed their greatest popularity on the eighteenth-century stage during the thir-
ties and early forties.[10]

Yet to follow the rake's career in the eighteenth century is
inevitably to move from the well-defined and relatively narrow limits of a single genre—the comedy of manners—to a
consideration of how a variety of other literary forms adopted
and transformed the rake's character. The rake's growth in the
comedy of manners does not extend much beyond the early
part of the eighteenth century, and we will discover the most

compelling examples of his sexual extravagance in other dramatic forms and, particularly, in the emerging novel.[11] Observed through and developed by other literary genres and conventions, the rake undergoes manifold transformations during the eighteenth century; by the nineteenth century important aspects of the rake characterize figures as diverse as Byron's early Romantic heroes, the frightening villains of gothic fiction, and the Wickhams and Crawfords of Jane Austen's prose comedies of manners.

In this final chapter I will attempt neither to trace the genealogy of all the rake's many descendents, nor to survey the many sexual languages generated by other literary forms: both are subjects for another work entirely. I will end, as I began, by focusing on the rake's sexuality, considering two of the erotic discourses that indicate some of the ways in which eighteenth-century England imagined and accommodated the sexual rebellion with which the Restoration rake originally confronted society. The economic terms of the sexual language employed by Millwood, in Lillo's bourgeois tragedy *The London Merchant* (1731), and by Moll Flanders, in Defoe's novel (1722), reveal the struggle of the female rake to express and realize her sexual nature in a society governed and dominated by men. In Millwood we discover the most malignant of all female rakes, a "devil" whose sexuality, like Maskwell's or Fainall's, exists only as a part of an aggressive urge to destroy. Millwood's economic understanding of sexuality acts as a justification for her destructive will: perceiving herself as an economic slave to men, Millwood uses her sexuality to destroy the sex that would dominate her. Moll's sexuality, on the other hand, serves not a love of destruction, but as a means of survival in a hostile male society; like Angellica Bianca, Moll depends on an "economics of desire" that allows her to make her way as a vulnerable woman in a masculine world. In spite of the profound differences between Millwood and Moll, both employ an economic vocabulary of sexuality as a weapon against a society that refuses to legitimize or accept their sexuality.

Standing in opposition to the economic vocabulary of these two women is the pastoral language used by Macheath, in

Gay's comic *The Beggar's Opera* (1728), and by Fanny Hill, the heroine of Cleland's pornographic masterpiece *Memoirs of a Woman of Pleasure* (1748–49). Their discourse expresses the rakish desire to participate in a generous, natural world of erotic ecstasy. While much of my study of the Restoration rake has emphasized the rake's subordination of physical pleasure to the pleasures of aggression—the movement from Horner to Fainall illustrating the diminution of the rake's desire for sexual fulfillment—in Macheath and Fanny Hill we find the most compelling portraits of the rake as sensualist. Like Horner, both characters enjoy Banquets of Sense that reveal their desire to create sensual idylls removed from the mundane world. Both attempt to generate visions of unrestricted sexual delight, while in the novel's luxurious male fantasy, freed from the vocabulary of Renaissance sexuality, Cleland fashions an English language of pornography that even today governs male articulations of erotic pleasure.

II

Lillo's Millwood certainly represents the most emphatic portrait in eighteenth-century drama of the female as the hated, feared, and yet desired Other. We probably have to return to Webster's Vittoria Corombona to find a woman at once so evil and destructive, and yet so dramatically vibrant. Both Vittoria and Millwood dominate the men who oppose their desires, Vittoria's triumph over Monticelso in his judicial ritual paralleled by Millwood's defence of herself to Thorowgood that leads him to admit, "Truth is truth, though from an enemy and spoke in malice. You bloody, blind, and superstitious bigots, how will you answer this?"[12] Both women possess a dramatic power that allows them a measure of triumph even in defeat; the male world succeeds in destroying these women, but not before Vittoria and Millwood suggest the fragility and insignificance of the assumptions and sureties that buttress the masculine order. Lawrence Price may get carried away when he speaks of Millwood's "grandiose possibilities" as reflective of "a passive grandeur that vies with the Greek tragedies,"[13] but, particularly for modern audiences,

Millwood's power is certainly increased when contrasted to the verbose and unrelenting goodness of the play's other characters.

The tragic villainesses of Dryden's heroic drama anticipate the passions that motivate Millwood. Lyndaraxa in *The Conquest of Granada* and Nourmahal in *Aureng-Zebe* both possess an attraction to power that their status as women frustrates. Lyndaraxa's desire "to live without control" and Nourmahal's assertion that "my thoughts no other joys but pow'r pursue" define women who cannot be accommodated by a masculine world in which women must be content to express themselves only through the power of love. Lyndaraxa's and Nourmahal's love of power constitutes a male prerogative, and their horrible deaths punish them for desires that lead them to deny their proper sexual roles. Though Millwood speaks ironically, her outburst to Barnwell—"What have I lost by being formed a woman! I hate my sex, myself!" (I.v.46–47)—reveals the frustrations of those women whose sex denies them the ability to impose their forceful personalities on the world.

Lillo emphasizes Millwood's refusal to accept her inferiority by adding Thorowgood's daughter Maria—not present in the original "Ballad of George Barnwell"—to the cast of characters. In Act I, scene ii, Maria discusses with her father her feelings about marriage, emphasizing her willingness to abide by the terms of his authority: "Had you asserted your authority and insisted on a parent's right to be obeyed, I had submitted and to my duty sacrificed my peace" (51–54). Her inclinations, she explains, "shall ever be submitted to your wisdom and authority" (67–68), completing the picture of a woman perfectly submissive to the male structures of domination that characterize society.

Maria leaves the stage requesting Thorowgood's "permission to retire" (71), and immediately Millwood makes her first appearance, her maid Lucy in attendance. In the movement from Act I, scene ii, to Act I, scene iii, Lillo juxtaposes Maria's willing acceptance of male authority to Millwood's explicit condemnation of the power that men exercise over women: "Men, however generous or sincere to one another, are all selfish hypocrites in their affairs with us. We are no [*sic*] otherwise esteemed or regarded by them but as we contribute to their satisfaction'' (I.iii.10-14). In this scene Lucy acts as Millwood's foil, for the maid cannot see beyond the polite social conventions that govern relations between the sexes:

> *Lucy.* You are certainly, madam, on the wrong side in this argument. Is not the expense all theirs? And I am sure it is our own fault if we haven't our share of the pleasure.
> *Millwood.* We are but slaves to men.
> *Lucy.* Nay, us they that are slaves most certainly, for we lay them under contribution.
> *Millwood.* Slaves have no property—no, not even in themselves. All is the victor's
>
> (15 22)

Lucy, according to Millwood, responds simply to the manners of society, to a love game that pretends to elevate women by making them the object of male advances. Millwood, however, insists that placing women on a pedestal succeeds only in degrading them, that women's apparent superiority only disguises their actual powerlessness. Millwood, like Bellafront in *The Honest Whore* and Angellica Bianca in *Thomaso*, recognizes that men exploit female weakness by forcing women to fulfill men's darkest fears of what women can be: "It's a general maxim among the knowing part of mankind that a woman without virtue, like a man without honor or honesty, is capable of any action, though never so vile. And yet, what pains will they not take, what arts not use, to seduce us from our innocence and make us contemptible and wicked, even in their own opinions? Then, is it not just the villains, to their cost, should find us so?" (31-37). Having idealized women, men take a perverse pleasure in degrading them, demonstrating both that women do not deserve the elevation they supposedly enjoy and that the power of establishing meaning in this culture remains tightly in the male grasp.

Millwood's acute sense of the disadvantages under which women suffer links her to the earlier versions of the female rake we examined in the last chapter. Yet the terms in which she expresses her knowledge show the radical changes in the social context within which the love game takes place. Millwood and Lucy understand their relations to men primarily within an economic vision of the world. Lucy thinks women privileged because men must bear all "the expense," must be laid "under contribution." Millwood, on the other hand, sees women as "slaves" who possess "no property—no, not even in themselves." In the battle between the sexes men are like "Spaniards in the New World, who first plundered the natives of all the wealth they had and then condemned the wretches to the mines for life to work for more" (25–27). Millwood, as Richard E. Brown remarks, "is not merely a 'risible amoral vamp'; she is a sexual vendor, and when she seduces George, she is turning her only asset to profit."[14]

Restoration comedy, of course, does not assume a world removed from economic pressures; Restoration rakes do not inhabit a "Utopia of gallantry" indifferent to the significance of money. Dorimant, as we have seen, responds to financial pleasures, while Congreve's last three comedies depend on the intimate connection between sexual pleasure and economic security. But in *The London Merchant* and *Moll Flanders* economic metaphors dominate the action, characterizing a world in which the power of money is fundamental to all social relations. In Restoration comedy rakes take their definition primarily from their elevation of pleasure over business; in the eighteenth century, however, particularly for the isolated female rake, such a commitment to pleasure represents a luxury the libertine can no longer afford. In *The London Merchant* pleasure must be subordinated to business; as Trueman reminds his now fallen friend Barnwell ("fallen" both sexually and economically), "Business requires our attendance—business, the youth's best preservative from ill, as idleness his worst of snares" (II.ii.92–94).

Even the term "business" itself has taken on a more narrowly economic meaning. When Sir Jasper Fidget talks of his "pleasure, business," he refers to a realm of responsibilities that include, but are not strictly defined by, money. In *The London Merchant*, however, "business" becomes an activity characterized primarily by the "accounts" that Trueman and Barnwell constantly keep. Published in 1733, only two years after the first production of Lillo's play, Pope's "Epistle to Bathurst," the third of his *Epistles to Several Persons*, reveals an analogous world in which the power of money reigns supreme; "fates and fortunes" are as nothing before the "paper-credit" that has made universal the power of gold:

> Blest paper-credit! last and best supply!
> That lends Corruption lighter wings to fly!
> Gold imp'd by thee, can compass hardest things,
> Can pocket States, can fetch or carry Kings;
> A single leaf shall waft an Army o'er,
> Or ship off Senates to a distant Shore,
> A leaf, like Sibyl's, scatter to and fro
> Our fates and fortunes, as the winds shall blow:
> Pregnant with thousands flits the Scrap unseen,
> And silent sells a King, or buys a Queen.[15]

This is a world that Millwood understands well, for she, too, appreciates the economic basis of her society:

> well may I curse your barbarous sex who robbed me of 'em [her uncommon perfections of mind and body], ere I knew their worth, then left me, too late, to count their value by their loss. Another and another spoiler came, and all my gain was poverty and reproach. My soul disdained, and yet disdains, dependence and contempt. Riches, no matter by what means obtained, I saw secured the worst of men from both. I found it, therefore, necessary to be rich and to that end I summoned all my arts.
>
> (IV.xviii.11–18)

Millwood's speech assumes the sovereignty of money. That riches are the object of all her arts is suggested by the economic metaphors that permeate her language: she apprehends her "uncommon perfections of mind and body" only in terms of "worth," "value," and "loss," "gain," "poverty," and "spoil." Millwood recognizes that her sexual arts possess meaning only within a larger economic context that strictly regulates relations between men and women. For Millwood to succeed in such a world she must subordinate her sexual nature to monetary necessity, transforming the erotic into the economic, passion into spoils, sexual adventure into financial manipulation.

For eighteenth-century audiences one of the images that perhaps most powerfully captures Millwood's economic understanding of society is her reference to "the unhospitable natives of Cornwall . . . [who live] by shipwrecks" (IV.xviii. 27–28). In an island nation totally dependent on its ability to dominate the seas, the Cornish practice of luring vessels to their destruction by setting false beacons, and then plundering the ships and even murdering the survivors, represented one of the most heinous of crimes. Legal statutes against "wrecking" were promulgated as early as the reign of Edward I; in 1713 an act was passed specifically designed to reinforce existing legislation against this crime.[16] Millwood's use of these notorious criminals as a model for her own behavior perfectly captures the way in which the elevation of the economic leads to a society in which individuals exist solely as destructive predators; her economic determinism places her outside all social bonds, an isolated individual striving to protect herself in a chaotic state of nature: "I have done nothing that I am sorry for. I followed my inclinations, and that the best of you does every day. All actions are alike natural and indifferent to man and beast who devour or are devoured as they meet with others weaker or stronger than themselves" (IV.xviii.41–45).

Not surprisingly, Millwood's bent for destruction comes to remind us of Maskwell, the first rake we considered whose sexual powers serve only his passion for destruction. Like Maskwell, Millwood revels in her ability to lead the unsuspecting to "swallow the bait" (I.iv.63), to manipulate the passions of others by disguising her true nature: "If I have any skill in physiognomy, he is amorous and, with a little assistance, will soon get the better of his modesty. I'll trust to nature, who does wonders in these matters. If to seem what one is not in order to be the better liked for what one really is, if to speak one thing and mean the direct contrary, be art in a woman, I know nothing of nature" (I.iv.7–13). Like Maskwell, she prefers a feigned to a genuine sexual passion; as her servant Blunt remarks, "I own it is surprising. I don't know which to admire most—her feigned, or [Barnwell's] real passion" (III.iv. 2–3). Like Maskwell, she transforms the vocabulary of sexual pleasure into a language of destructive lust; when Lucy confesses that Barnwell's "youth and innocence . . . moves me mightily" (I.vii.17–18), Blunt recognizes that Millwood as the predatory hawk responds to Barnwell's charms only to destroy them: "Yes, so does the smoothness and plumpness of a partridge move a mighty desire in the hawk to be the destruction of it" (19–20). Even Lucy, as she watches Millwood seduce Barnwell, uses language that suggests the sexual nature of Millwood's desire to destroy: "So! She has wheedled him out of his virtue of obedience already and will strip him of all the rest, one after another, till she has left him as few as her ladyship or myself" (I.vi.84–86). Millwood's sexual attractions lead not to marriage and fertility, but only to ruination. As Lucy suggests when her mistress first appears and asks, "How do I look today, Lucy?" (I.iii.1), Millwood looks "killingly" (2).

The final, and most important, parallel between Maskwell and Millwood involves their depiction as agents of the devil, though Lillo insists on the sexual nature of that demonism to a much greater extent than Congreve. Barnwell immediately identifies his fall with Satan's, seeing himself in "the condition of the grand apostate when first he lost his purity. Like me, disconsolate he wandered, and, while yet in Heaven, bore all his future Hell about him" (II.i.11–13). By the end of Act II Barnwell has come to identify himself, again like Satan, with "Hell, the seat of darkness and of pain" (II.xiv.13). As the play progresses, however, and Lillo prepares us for Barnwell's eventual apotheosis, such imagery comes more and more to characterize Millwood rather than her poor victim. Millwood, Barnwell recognizes, is his "fate, my Heaven or my Hell" (II.xiii.18), and by the time he readies himself to kill his uncle he understands that Millwood has "firm possession of my heart" (III.v.22). Roberta Borkat has argued that this imagery of possession should be taken seriously, "that Barnwell is under a spell, that Millwood and not he controls his actions, that he cannot help what he does"; Borkat even insists that "the actor playing Barnwell should portray the youth as carrying out the murder in a trance-like state."[17]

While one might wonder just how Barnwell's long soliloquy in Act III, scene v, could be delivered effectively in a "trance-like state," the pervasive demonic imagery of the final two acts supports this interpretation of Millwood's "possession" of Barnwell. Acts IV and V raise a veritable chorus of charges testifying to Millwood's demonic nature. Barnwell himself calls her a "devil," one of the "fiends . . . cursed with immortality to be the executioners of Heaven" (IV.xiii.8–9). Her own servant, Blunt, eventually labels her a "devil" (IV.xiv.2), while Thorowgood sees her as a "sorceress" (IV.xvi.22) and Trueman calls her a "devil" (IV.xviii.4).

Just as the juxtaposition of Millwood and Maria emphasizes Millwood's refusal to accept male authority, so too does Maria's constant association with the divine accentuate Millwood's sexual powers as an agent of hell. When, in Act III, Maria joins with Trueman in an attempt to hide from Thorowgood Barnwell's initial crimes, Trueman explicitly links her charity to heaven: "Will you save a helpless wretch from ruin? Oh, 'twere an act worthy such exalted virtue as Maria's! Sure, Heaven in mercy to my friend inspired the generous thought" (III.iii.50–53). Maria appeals to heaven to judge the righteousness of her actions, and Trueman again asserts that "Heaven, I doubt not, will reward it" (63–64). At the play's close Barnwell himself comes to see Maria's "exalted goodness" as an earthly link to the divine salvation he hopes to enjoy: "Would you, bright excellence, permit me the honor of a chaste embrace, the last happiness this world could give were mine. *(She inclines toward him; they embrace.)* Exalted goodness! Oh turn your eyes from earth and me to Heaven, where virtue like yours is ever heard. Pray for the peace of my departing soul!" (V.x.6–11).

The distinction between Maria's "chaste embrace," her "passion so just and so disinterested," and the sexual thralldom of Millwood places us again in a world in which sexual passion bears the taint of the demonic. Like Freevill, who must choose between Beatrice and Franceschina in Marston's *The Dutch Courtesan*, Barnwell confronts two women who represent the powers of darkness and light: Millwood emerges from the play a Lilith figure whose sexual attractions lead to damnation and the disintegration of the individual personality, while Maria offers heaven's salvation, an intensity of sentiment that liberates the individual from the senses. Like the light- and dark-haired women of the nineteenth-century novel, or the Odette/Odile figures in *Swan Lake*, Maria and Millwood represent woman as a divine, finer image of the male Self, and woman as a demonic Other.

We can mark the distinction between Marston's play and Lillo's, however, in the rake's refusal to grant the terms of the divine hierarchy that generates such a scheme. Franceschina, as we have seen, glories in her identification with the demonic powers: "The world sall know the worst of evils: / Woman corrupted is the worst of devils." But Millwood, like Nemours, ridicules society's efforts to dismiss and control the rake's passions. Millwood sees the belief in demonic sexuality as another indication of society's tyranny over the female and attempts to reverse the moral terms of their hierarchy: when Trueman calls her a "devil" she exclaims, "That imaginary being is an emblem of thy cursed sex collected, a mirror wherein each particular man may see his own likeness and that of all mankind!" (IV.xviii.5-7). Millwood does not deny the existence of God; when Thorowgood regrets that she "should be a stranger to religion's sweet but powerful charms" (47-48), she indicates that "I am not fool enough to be an atheist" (49). What she rejects, however, is a divine hierarchy that excuses male attempts to "punish in others what you act yourselves or would have acted" (62-63). For Millwood, demonic sexuality and the "imaginary beings" who embody it represent merely another patriarchal attempt to subjugate women, to create in "women . . . your universal prey" (66-67). In its place she imagines instead an infinity of Millwoods whose generation threatens the dominance that men now enjoy:

> Oh, may, from hence, each violated maid,
> By flatt'ring, faithless, barb'rous man betray'd,
> When robb'd of innocence and virgin fame,
> From your destruction raise a nobler name:
> To right their sex's wrongs devote their mind,
> And future Millwoods prove, to plague mankind!
> (73-78)

III

Though Moll Flanders, who appears nine years before Lillo's play, can hardly be considered a "future Millwood," she nonetheless represents a woman who would have earned the approval of Lillo's doomed heroine. Moll's passage from "innocence and virgin fame" to experience and a hard-won if dubious honesty and repentance provides much opportunity for her to "right their sex's wrongs" and "plague mankind." Moll early recognizes the social inferiority of women, and the deceit that defines her life, as well as the many strategies she employs for survival, demonstrates her knowledge of the ways in which a supposedly powerless woman can make her way in a male world. In spite of a society that ruthlessly enforces male superiority, Moll insists "that a Woman can never want an Opportunity to be Reveng'd of a Man that has us'd her ill, and that there were ways enough to humble such a Fellow as that, or else certainly Women were the most unhappy Creatures in the World."[18] Marlene LeGates, writing of three very different characters (Pamela, Clarissa, and Rousseau's Julie), correctly describes both Moll's plight and her power when she notes that "the defenselessness of these innocent heroines has been sometimes exaggerated. What is truly remarkable about these victims is their strength and resourcefulness in situations where their weakness is sexually determined."[19] Moll's career is a tribute to her ability to survive and even thrive in a social world that would doom her to servitude or extinction; in spite of the social injustice under which women live, only a passive acceptance of their inferiority can make them "the most unhappy Creatures in the World." Moll's extraordinary vitality stems precisely from her refusal to accept this unhappy fate, for she generates her character out of the ingenious responses that convert inferiority into superiority, weakness into strength, powerlessness into power.

Yet Defoe's novel also reveals the price that Moll must pay for her success; though she avoids becoming one of the most unhappy creatures in the world, she emerges from her adventures a curiously limited figure despite her power. Moll is diminished as well as elevated by her struggles, and if we examine her in the context of other rakes, we can understand more precisely just what she must abandon in order to triumph over her social inferiority.

Unlike Maskwell, Fainall, or Millwood, Moll does not become a destructive monster, a rake whose lust for ruin and destruction consumes her erotic passions. The possibility of such a response certainly exists; one of the most quoted of her adventures—the robbery of the "pretty little Child" with the necklace of gold beads—demonstrates how close to the surface are Moll's desires to glory in a senseless destruction of the external world that so restricts her: "Here, I say, the Devil put me upon killing the Child in the dark Alley, that it might not Cry; but the very thought frighted me so that I was ready to drop down" (194). Moll's response to her own demonic impulses indicates their immense power and attraction as well as her own strength in resisting them. Though gratuitous violence often threatens to enter her narrative, she manages always to keep it at bay: "I had a great many tender Thoughts about me yet, and did nothing but what, as I may say, meer Necessity drove me to" (195). Moll remains always aware of her own power, of how easily she can manipulate and even destroy the unsuspecting Other. When, during her years as a thief, she allows herself to be picked up by the drunken gentleman at Batholomew Fair, she characterizes him through Proverbs 7:22–23: "*They go like an Ox to the slaughter, till a Dart strikes through their Liver.*" Drunk and asleep, this gentleman, like the little girl, lies totally in Moll's power. Her "Business," however, "was his Money, and what I could make of him, and after that if I could have found out any way to have done it, I would have sent him safe home to his House, and to his Family" (227). Although tempted, Moll never glories in destruction for its own sake. Like the father of her first lover and first husband, Moll remains always "thoughtful of the main Chance" (54), concerned primarily with money and survival, not with the ruin of others that may attend her desperate efforts.

The rake, therefore, who best illuminates Moll's character is Congreve's Vainlove, for both figures share an obsessive concern for the social manipulations that set the chase in motion, and an ultimate indifference to the sexual pleasures that crown the pursuit. Vainlove and Moll clearly resemble their more destructive counterparts like Maskwell and Millwood, for a glorification of destruction lies at but one remove from Vainlove's and Moll's pleasure in manipulation and power; it does not take much to make Vainlove into a Maskwell, or, as we have seen, to transform Moll into an avenging Millwood. Yet the distinction between these two pairs is important, for

while Maskwell and Millwood seem primarily tragic figures—
the one excluded from the comic resolution of Congreve's
play, the other doomed to a despairing death—Vainlove and
Moll are essentially comic, their unfixed sexual identities
possessing a great vitality that does not ultimately threaten
social conventions. Vainlove's masculine impotence corresponds to Moll's sexual plight, revealing not her "frigidity"—
for Moll never strikes a reader as a frigid character—but her
necessary efforts, in Lady Macbeth's phrase, to "unsex"
herself.

Next to the controversy over Defoe's technical mastery—
the problem of his ironic intentions—the question of Moll's
sexual identity has proven most vexatious for modern critics.
Indeed, Dickens long ago questioned how readers apprehend
Defoe's heroines when he remarked that "De Foe's women . . .
are terribly dull commonplace fellows without breeches."[20] At
least one influential modern critic has agreed with Dickens'
sentiments, for Ian Watt has consistently maintained that
though "the facts show that she is a woman and a criminal . . .
neither of these roles determine her personality. . . . the
essence of her character and actions is . . . essentially masculine."[21] While Watt does not deny that Moll possesses many
female traits, he claims that Moll's ostensible womanhood
"merely seems to endow her with a marketable physiolog-
ical asset."[22] Not all critics, of course, agree with Watt's
response to Moll: Dorothy Van Ghent, for one, insists that
Moll possesses "the immense and seminal reality of an Earth
Mother."[23] Even when critics do not respond directly to the
question of Moll's sexuality, however, they employ a sex-
related terminology that continues to reflect a curious duality
in our reactions to Moll. John Richetti, for instance, refers to
Moll as "essentially an *active intelligence* which transforms
itself to meet the needs of experience, but . . . also . . . a *passive
entity* to whom things happen" (my italics).[24] G. A. Starr, too,
notes a disjunction in the novel between "act and agent," between Moll's quite active and aggressive life and her desire to
"portray herself as a passive instrument."[25]

The key to the critical confusion over Moll's sexual definition lies in her ability to "unsex" herself so completely that as
readers we simply cannot penetrate beyond the emotional and

sexual repression that comes to define her personality. Patricia Meyer Spacks recognizes half of the problem when she explains in her aptly titled essay " 'Ev'ry Woman is at Heart a Rake,' " that "the feeling heart guarantees misery; only by emotional repression can a woman survive successfully in a world which penalizes female expressiveness."[26] Moll goes even further than Spacks suggests, for she extinguishes not just her emotional nature, but her sexual identity as well. She does not become a Lady Macbeth or Millwood, for she makes no attempt to transform her female identity into a male one; Moll does not, like Millwood, wish to be a man, nor, like Lady Macbeth, does she desire to replace her female "weakness" with male "strength":

> Come, you Spirits
> That tend on mortal thoughts, unsex me here,
> And fill me, from the crown to the toe, top-full
> Of direst cruelty!
> . . . .
> Come to my woman's breasts,
> And take my milk for gall, you murth'ring ministers.
> (I.v.40–48)

Lady Macbeth eventually replaces gall with destruction when she imagines her capacity to pluck her "'nipple from [her babe's] boneless gums, / And dash the brains out" (I.vii.57–58) Moll puzzles us precisely because she is neither woman nor man, neither nurturer nor destroyer. When she can, she does worry about the fate of her children: "But it touch'd my Heart so forcibly to think of Parting entirely with the Child, and for ought I knew, of having it murther'd, or starv'd by Neglect and Ill-usage" (173); and when she cannot afford to worry she becomes simply indifferent: "My two Children were indeed taken happily off of my Hands, by my Husband's Father and Mother, and that by the way was all they got by Mrs. *Betty*" (59).

Though unsexed, Moll undeniably possesses a powerful sensuality; her ability to impress herself on her world, to force external reality to bear the stamp of her personality, indicates the considerable erotic energies at her disposal. Particularly at the beginning of her career, before she fully understands the necessity of repressing her sexual instincts, we can glimpse the erotic passions that animate her behavior. The elder brother with whom she first becomes involved—himself "a gay Gentleman that knew the Town" (19)—doesn't even realize how ripe she is for sexual pleasure: "In short, he began to be in Earnest with me indeed; perhaps he found me a little too easie, for God knows I made no Resistance to him while he only held me in his Arms and Kiss'd me, indeed I was too well pleas'd with it, to resist him much" (23). Even her affair with the "*Gentleman-Tradesman*" reveals her sexual desires overcoming her better judgment. "Catch'd in the very Snare, which *as I might say*, I laid for my self" (60), Moll foregoes the safer proposals of "the Dullest and most disagreeable Part of the World" (60) for the dubious but sexually potent charms of her "Rake, Gentleman, Shop keeper, and Beggar all together" (61). John Richetti's analysis of this second marriage emphasizes the sexual potency that for Moll underlies her husband's social versatility.[27]

Yet even these early ventures into the "market," as critics have recognized, reveal Moll's confusion between sexual and economic pleasure. Moll "was more confounded with the Money than . . . [she] was before with the Love" (23), and her greatest pleasure with the eldest brother arises not from their erotic play, but from her solitary enjoyment of the gold with which he rewards her favors: "As for the Gold I spent whole Hours in looking upon it; I told the Guineas over and over a thousand times a Day" (26). Her second marriage displays an identical concern with objects of value: the only story she tells of her married life involves the trip to Oxford in a coach and six with "a rich Coach, very good Horses, a Coachman, Postilion, and two Footmen in very good Liveries; a Gentleman on Horseback, and a Page with a Feather in his Hat upon another Horse" (61). All the sensual details of their jaunt culminate in the final reckoning that eventually defines the trip: "*93 1. Expence*" for "about twelve Days ramble" (62).

Moll responds not to the conventional love game, to the erotic implications of the battle between the sexes, but to the economic resonances of what she calls over and over again "the Market." This becomes apparent when she pursues her third husband, the man who turns out to be her own brother.

The climax of their courtship, the famous scene in which they write on the glass of her sash, demonstrates how far we have come from the world of the Restoration rake. Michael Shinagel perceptively notes that the scene represents "Defoe's self-conscious attempt at witty repartee between lovers in the style of the genteel romances or Restoration comedy."[28] This repartee, however, possesses not the slightest sexual reverberation. Focused strictly on money, his "Gold" and her "Poverty," their negotiations, carried on by means of a diamond ring, reveal an almost complete absence of the sexual tension that characterizes the love game during the Restoration. That love game, of course, depended on the sexual extravagance of Restoration rakes, their understanding that identity depended primarily on an individual's sexuality. By the time Moll has set her sights on a third husband, however, she has learned that economics, not sexuality, defines identity. Earlier she notes that "a Woman should never be kept for a Mistress, that had Money to keep her self" (61), and just before the scene at the window she explains that "it soon began to be found that the Widow had no Fortune, and to say this, was to say all that was Ill of me; for I began to be dropt in all the Discourses of Matrimony: Being well Bred, Handsome, Witty, Modest and agreeable; all which I had allowed to my Character, whether justly, or no, is not to the Purpose; I say, all these would not do without the Dross, which was now become more valuable than Virtue Itself. In short, *the Widow*, they said, *had no Money*" (76). The three states of female identity that Moll recognizes—mistress, wife, and widow—all of which depend on a woman's relationship to a man—make sense to her only in financial terms. No wonder, then, that the "witty repartee" between lovers contains not a hint of sexual desire: as Juliet McMaster recognizes, "money has become not so much the proof of love as the thing itself."[29] Erotic potential has been converted into financial necessity, sexuality into cash, the individual woman into, as one of Moll's most famous similes states, "a Bag of Money, or a Jewel dropt on the Highway" (128). Horner's generous desires to "spend" and exhaust his supplies of china have been converted into Moll's relentless desire to horde her substance, to protect her tenuous identity by never revealing, even to Jamie, either her name or an exact accounting of her fortune.

The wish to accumulate substance, to pile up the wealth that defines one's personality, need not necessarily lead to sexual repression. Jonson's *Volpone*, for instance, depends on the erotic relationship between Volpone and his gold. His first act adoration of his "saint" is rich in sensual detail:

> O thou son of Sol,
> But brighter than thy father, let me kiss,
> With adoration, thee, and every relic
> Of sacred treasure in this blessed room.
>   (I.i.10–13)

The erotic potential of Volpone's "dumb god" powerfully manifests itself in his later seduction of Celia, when he imagines their sexual play amidst a landscape of luxurious sensuality:

> Thy baths shall be the juice of July-flowers,
> Spirit of roses, and of violets,
> The milk of unicorns, and panthers' breath
> Gathered in bags and mixed with Cretan wines.
>   (III.vii.213–16)

In Moll, however, the completeness of her sexual repression allows us to catch only glimpses of this economic eroticism, most notably in her relationship with the married gentleman she meets at Bath and in her brief encounter with gambling during her years as a thief. The former, Juliet McMaster says, perfectly demonstrates "an ingenious translation into financial terms of a sexual encounter."[30] The fortune he produces from his "Walnuttree box" quite overwhelms the little horde that Moll takes from her "little private Drawer" and strews across her bed. Her "lover" has to force her to accept his largesse: "He held my Hand hard in his Hand, and put it into the Drawer" (112). The scene ends with a lavish erotic display as he mingles their money in her lap, "and pour'd out all my own Money among his" (112). This economic eroticism explains why they can live for so long without the sexual consummation that their behavior, particularly the sharing of a bed, seems to demand.

The scene in the gaming house near Covent Garden depends on similar gestures that reveal the erotic power of money. Again Moll finds herself with a considerable sum of someone else's gold in her lap, "out of which I every now and then convey'd some into my Pocket; but in such a manner . . . as I was sure he cou'd not see it" (261). And again her male partner must force her to "put my Hand into it [the pile of coins], and take some for myself, and bid me please myself" (262). This very public scene possesses not quite the same erotic power of the earlier one, though we can again see how exciting Moll finds all this economic/erotic play. On the ad-vice of her old governess she avoids returning to the gaming house, "for I knew as well as she, if the Itch of Play came in, I might soon lose that, and all the rest of what I had got" (262). The scene's emphasis on Moll's desire to "please myself," her attraction to the "Itch of Play," points at once to the sexual fears and desires that animate her behavior and relations to money. Contrasted to the Restoration rake's fondness for gam-bling metaphors as an expression of sexual excitement, Moll's ultimate denial of gambling reveals the extent of her sexual re-pression.

The conversion of erotic potential into economic power de-termines the shape of Moll's career, for seen in these terms her life as a thief satisfies the same basic impulses as her life in the sexual marketplace. Robert Erickson has noted that "Defoe's language for describing Moll's commencement, apprentice-ship, and career as a professional thief bears remarkable resem-blance to the rhetoric and lore of the noble 'Art of Midwifery,' a resemblance which makes her transition from the life of sex-ual intrigue to the life of a thief seem the most natural thing in the world."[31] Though Moll herself never seems conscious of the connection between the two halves of her career, her language consistently points to the identity between her desires for sexual pleasure and her attraction to a life of thievery. Moll understands both pleasures, for example, in terms of the distinction between necessity and inclination:

I had resisted some Casual offers of Gallantry, and had manag'd that way well enough; I was not wicked enough to come into the Crime for the meer Vice of it, and I had no extraordinary Offers made me that tempted me with the main thing which I wanted. (107)

I was now very far from being poor, that the Temptation of Neces-sity, which is generally the Introduction of all such Wickedness was now remov'd. . . . but *I say*, I had not so much as the least inclina-

tion to leave off; . . . From hence 'tis Evident to me, that when once
we are harden'd in Crime, no Fear can affect us. (221)

In the first passage Moll refers to her introduction to Bath and
her attempts to secure a lover or a husband, whereas in the
second she considers her initial successes as a thief. Taken out
of context, however, the passages might confuse us as to which
"Crime" she contemplates: the vocabulary of "Crime" and
"Temptation," "Wickedness" and "Necessity," remains the
same for both. When she finally allows her "wicked" nature to
bring her to the bed of the gentleman from Bath, the resemblance between her "crimes" becomes even more prominent:
"These mutal assurances harden'd us in the thing; and after
this we repeated the Crime as often as we pleas'd" (117). In
both cases the initial "bars of Virtue and Conscience" break
down, leading to a "harden[ing] in Crime" that makes her
unable to control herself. Perhaps the most emphatic linking
of the sexual and economic is found not in Moll herself, but in
the woman she describes who steals from her lover even as
they make love: "I Knew a Woman that was so dexterous with
a Fellow, who indeed deserv'd no better usage, that while he
was busie with her another way, convey'd his Purse with
twenty Guineas in it out of his Fob Pocket, where he had put it
for fear of her, and put another Purse with guilded Counters in
it into the room of it" (228). Here indeed do we discover a
perfect correspondence between sex and theft, for sexual
pleasure itself becomes an act of theft, the male's sexual
spending translated by his female partner into economic gain.

Yet Moll's own narrative reveals a crucial distinction between her sexual and economic crimes that depends on the
demonic rhetoric we have traced from Jacobean drama through
the seventeenth century. As a penitent, of course, Moll consistently criticizes and degrades the sexual desires that she
indulged during her long and active life. Whenever she ac-
knowledges such impulses, she characterizes them as wicked
or felonious. She explains, for instance, the transformation of
her relationship with the gentleman from Bath as a result of
her own wicked nature. While he may have enjoyed their non-
sexual intimacy, "I do not say that I was so wholly pleas'd
with it as he thought I was: For I own I was much wickeder

than he" (116). The "first Breach," she explains, "was not on his part" (116), and she attributes this to her own "Weakness," her desire to indulge in "loose and lewd Freedoms" (119). However wicked Moll may have been during the first part of her life, only after she becomes a thief does she begin to understand herself as a prey to genuinely demonic impulses and consistently turn to the devil to characterize her evil:

> I neither knew or considered where to go, or on what Business; but as the Devil carried me out and laid his Bait for me, so he brought me to be sure to the place, for I knew not whither I was going or what I did. . . . This was the Bait; and the Devil who I said laid the Snare, as readily prompted me, as if he had spoke, for I remember, and shall never forget it, 'twas like a Voice spoken to me over my Shoulder, take the Bundle; be quick; do it this Moment; it was no sooner said but I step'd into the Shop. (191–92)

Moll as a penitent recognizes the evil of her sexual passions, even explaining, in regard to her affair with the elder brother, that "the Devil is an unwearied Tempter" (26). But only the wickedness of her economic crimes calls forth an emphasis on her "evil Counsellor within" (193), her assurance that "the Devil put things into my Head" (195), her sense that it was "as if he had spoke." For Moll the Devil manifests himself in the mundane world not primarily through sexual indulgence, but through economic misdeeds. The sexual demons of Renaissance England have become economic demons for eighteenth-century England, their presence conjured not by sexual but by economic anxieties. In charting the rake's career we attend to the transformation of the language of the sexually demonic into a language of economic demonism.

IV

In both *The London Merchant* and *Moll Flanders*, the heirs of the Restoration rake confront societies in which money determines not simply all social relations, but the mysteries of personal identity as well. Both Millwood and Moll must subordinate their sexual energies to their economic selves, subsuming sexual pleasure in their relentless struggle for the wealth that alone guarantees personal autonomy and social identity. In such worlds erotic pleasure becomes not simply a self-indulgent luxury but a positive danger, for it seduces the rake from the pursuit of the financial identity that would secure her place in society. The criminality of Millwood and Moll is defined by their economic weakness rather than by their extravagant sexuality; both exist as outsiders because of their vulnerable femininity for which society has provided no legitimate economic role.

The opening scene of Gay's *The Beggar's Opera* provides perhaps the most powerful image of such a world, for the tableau of Peachum at his accounts represents a world in which the individual life has nothing more than a simple, and easily definable, economic value. Tom Gagg, "a lazy dog" who refuses to "mend his hand," must die because then he will be worth "forty pounds"; Betty Sly, on the other hand, can be saved from transportation because Peachum "can get more by her staying in England."[32] As Peachum does his accounts, considering the men and women who work for him and listing the articles of luxury that define their worth—"Sixteen snuff-boxes, five of them of true gold. Six dozen of hankerchiefs, four silver-hilted swords, half a dozen of shirts, three tie-periwigs, and a piece of broadcloth" (I.iii.8–11)—we confront a society in which human life has lost all significance apart from a strict economic valuation. In Webster's *The White Devil*, Monticelso's "black book" defines individuals solely in terms of their demonic natures. Here Peachum's account book reduces individuals simply to their economic worth; all other meaning or significance has been taken from them.

The rest of Act I makes clear just how far Peachum's economic determinism dominates his life. He understands even his own family solely in terms of his account book, assured that human relationships can be transfomed into economic transactions: "Married! If the wench does not know her own profit, sure she knows her own pleasure better than to make herself a property" (I.iv.85–87). Polly's marriage to Macheath horrifies Peachum only because she refuses to turn her husband into an economic entity, an entry in Peachum's account book; her refusal means that Peachum will lose both Polly and Macheath as properties without securing their true economic worth. Peachum is at an utter loss to understand how his own daughter could forget that all things exist only insofar as they possess financial significance: "I dare say, the Captain himself would like that we should get the reward for his death sooner than a stranger. Why, Polly, the Captain knows that as 'tis his employment to rob, so 'tis ours to take robbers. Every man in his business. So that there is no malice in the case" (I.x. 34–39). Here is Sir Jaspar Fidget's "business" with a vengeance. In the world of Peachum there is no longer any tension between pleasure and business, for pleasure exists only in business, in the ability to translate all emotion, all relations, all life, into financial terms.

The opening of Act II presents the attempt of Macheath's gang to generate an alternative world. Contrasted to Peachum's account book is their tavern world *"with wine, brandy, and tobacco,"* the intoxicants that define the degraded "green world" that would oppose the inhuman social vision of Peachum. They challenge Peachum's desire to hoard and engross value with a generous desire to spend their substance; the song sung by Matt of the Mint reminds us of Rochester's "Upon His Drinking a Bowl," for both song and poem elevate drinking and sex to the chief "employ" of life:

> Fill ev'ry glass, for wine inspires us,
>   And fires us
> With courage, love, and joy.
> Women and wine should life employ.
> Is there aught else on earth desirous?
>   (Air XIX, II.i.30–34)

"Women and wine," "Cupid and Bacchus," stand in the place of Peachum's money and interest.

This attempt to present a healthy alternative to Peachum fails, of course, for the gang, no less than Peachum and Lockit, remains fatally compromised by the power of money. Jemmy Twitcher, one of the most forward in proclaiming that "the present time is ours" (II.i.8), eventually betrays Macheath, leading to the tragic recognition that "'Tis a plain proof that the world is all alike" (III.xiv.4–5). Few satiric revelations possess quite the force of Macheath's simple remark, for few satires would level all the world so completely, would make of everyone a Peachum or Lockit. The ultimate bankruptcy of

Macheath's green world leads us to a society in which, as Lockit boasts, "you should never do anything but upon the foot of interest" (III.i.36–37), a veritable state of nature in which humanity's place is even more degraded than that of the beasts: "Lions, wolves, and vultures don't live together in herds, droves, or flocks. Of all animals of prey, man is the only sociable one. Every one of us preys upon his neighbor, and yet we herd together" (III.ii.4–7). Even Pope's *Dunciad*, with its terrible evocation of a "Universal Darkness [that] buries All," does not possess the blackness of Gay's "light" satire, for the power of art to order and contain chaos that so many readers respond to at the close of Pope's poem is missing from Gay's play, where the corrupt "taste of the town" degrades even the artist and his art.

Yet the green world in this "Newgate Pastoral," however corrupt and illusory, does provide a space within which the rake Macheath can indulge his passions with a freedom and energy allowed few other rakes. However much Macheath is hedged around with voracious enemies and lovers, however much the politics of Walpole's England press upon his identity, he emerges as one of the most erotically powerful of literary creations. Even the substantial changes wrought in Gay's play by the Brecht/Weill *Three Penny Opera* leave undiminished the powerful sexual energy of their more deadly Mac. Macheath, of course, is not an easy figure to come to terms with. His association with Walpole as "the great man" makes him suspect from the very start, while his callous treatment of Polly and Lucy can hardly recommend him to an audience enthralled by the illusions of romantic love. Like Nemours, Macheath revels in his mastery of romantic cliché; to secure Polly's favors he uses the most commonplace pastoral imagery to claim that his wandering heart has been tamed: "I sipped each flower, / I changed ev'ry hour, / But here ev'ry flower is united" (Air XV, I.xiii.21–23). Macheath's dubious sexual ethic has led Robert Hume to dismiss him, for "however dashingly he is often played in the theatre, [Macheath] is a lying scoundrel."[33]

Yet Macheath is surely more than simply a "lying scoundrel." While Macheath's moral stature lies open to question, he nonetheless represents the only saving grace in a society utterly corrupt and degraded. We discern this corruption not simply in Peachum and Lockit, but even in their daughters Polly and Lucy, endearing romantic heroines who nonetheless emerge from the play as distorted reflections of their parents. Polly's conception of love depends on "cursed playbooks" and the cheap "romances" Macheath lends her, fictions that have taught her only that "none of the great heroes were ever false in love" (I.xiii.16–17); Lucy, meanwhile, as she recognizes herself, possesses an "education" that has ruined her: "When young at the bar you first taught me to score, / And bid me be free of my lips, and no more" (Air XLI, III.i.24–25). Pursued by both the fathers and the daughters, betrayed by his women and his gang, Macheath is systematically isolated in the course of the play. For everyone from Peachum to Lucy, from Jemmy Twitcher to Jenny Diver, Macheath exists only as an object to be translated into a "property." As Lucy's attempt to poison Polly demonstrates, the difference in this play between an economic and a romantic property is not great: Macheath remains always a victim, whether of the economic valuations of the fathers or of the romantic illusions of the daughters.

Caught between the debased definitions of human nature proferred by Peachum and Lockit on the one hand, and by Polly and Lucy on the other, Macheath pursues his own vision of an erotic paradise. In his first soliloquy, in Act II, scene iii, Macheath reveals his understanding of the green world when he flatly states: "I love the sex. And a man who loves money might as well be contented with one guinea as I with one woman" (2–3). Though he begins with an analogy that equates sex and money, he ends his reflections on love by depicting a pastoral world of "pleasure, and soft repose" that triumphs over the economic world that defines the rest of the play:

> Roses and lilies her cheeks disclose,
> But her ripe lips are more sweet than those.
>   Press her,
>   Caress her;
>   With blisses,
>   Her kisses
> Dissolve us in pleasure, and soft repose.

I must have women. There is nothing unbends the mind like them. Money is not so strong a cordial for the time. (12–20)

Macheath's desire for intoxication, his need to "dissolve . . . in pleasure" and "unbend the mind," should remind us of Nemours' powerful evocation of a world of erotic ecstasy. While Peachum translates all the world into his account book, Macheath attempts to transform that world into a pastoral dream of sexual pleasure and satisfaction. "Nor," as Rochester writes of a very different figure in his "Satyr on Charles II," "are his high desires above his strength," for Macheath possesses a sexual potency every bit as extravagant as that of Horner or Nemours. Poor ambitious Filch, desirous of filling Macheath's place as "the favorite child-getter," finds himself reduced to a "shotten herring," convinced that "if a man cannot get an honest livelihood any easier way, I am sure 'tis what I can't undertake for another session" (III.iii.1–9). Like Horner, Macheath emerges as the phallic center of his world, a rake who values above all else the outsized sexual desires that are unregarded or despised by the other characters in the play.

Macheath's most powerful attempt to realize this dream of erotic pleasure and freedom comes in the fourth scene of Act II, when he and his many women enjoy a private party at the tavern near Newgate. Like Horner's more elegant dinner party, this Banquet of Sense depends on the frank acceptance of the sexual desires that bring the company together. The initial dance and song, Air XXII, recognize that "Youth's the season made for joys" (30), placing us firmly in a fleeting pastoral world that must be enjoyed now, for "Time's on the wing; / Life never knows the return of spring" (43–44). The theme of *carpe diem* emphasizes the fragility of their retreat from the world of Peachum and Lockit, mortality and economic necessity. But the mock pastoral accents of the next song, Air XXIII, pay tribute to the power of Macheath's extravagant sexuality and lust for erotic pleasure:

> Before the barndoor crowing,
>   The cock by hens attended,
> His eyes around him throwing,
>   Stands for a while suspended.
> Then one he singles from the crew,
>   And cheers the happy hen,
> With how do you do, and how do you do,
>   And how do you do again.
>   (84–91)

Much of the animal imagery that pervades the play—like the wolves and tigers that emphasize the predatory nature of this society—serves to characterize the degraded condition of humanity. Such imagery perfectly captures a fallen world in which the connection between people and beasts deflates the pretensions of what Rochester calls "that vain animal / Who is so proud of being rational." Gay's play, like Rochester's "A Satyr Against Reason and Mankind," posits a world in which "'Tis evident beasts are, in their degree, / As wise at least, and better far than he."[34]

Yet Macheath, as the ebullient cock-of-the-walk, possesses the wisdom and morality of a creature who has not been corrupted by human vanity. Here the "naturalness" of the mock pastoral world is a virtue, for Macheath enjoys a vitality that contrasts sharply with the relentless desire to hoarde that defines Peachum and Lockit. An audience cannot help but laugh at the marvellous comic implications of these lines and the joyous sexual energy celebrated by the witty repetition of "With how do you do, and how do you do, / And how do you do again." Macheath, like Horner, asks nothing more than to spend his substance. His sexual generosity here corresponds to his later largess in offering assistance to his gang when the road proves "so barren of money" (III.iv.1); and both his sexual and economic freedom are without parallel in the play. Macheath, like Horner, attempts in his Banquet of Sense to extend to others those freedoms he himself enjoys. The extended greetings to his eight women that open the banquet express his wish that all who participate freely reveal their desires. Though Macheath's sensual paradise represents a particularly male fantasy of phallic power and domination, Macheath treats his eight women not as an undifferentiated mass of flesh, but as individuals whose personalities he understands and appreciates: Jenny Diver is—much to his cost—his "dear, artful hypocrite" (16), while Molly Brazen is a "freehearted wench . . . as willing as a turtle" (24–25). Each, his recognition of their individuality implies, should enjoy the pleasures they will, for the banquet depends on the openness of its participants, their ability to recognize their needs that the larger society frustrates: "If any of the ladies choose gin, I hope they will be so free to call for it" (48–49).

Like Horner's banquet, however, Macheath's cannot displace that larger and even more corrupt society that surrounds it. What marks Macheath's distance from Horner is that Macheath takes too seriously the banquet's promises of honesty and plain dealing. While Horner holds part of himself aloof, never revealing the presence of another mistress in the next room, Macheath puts himself entirely in the hands of his women and pays the price. In *The Country-Wife*, Horner himself refuses to extend the confidences of the dinner party to the larger society; in Gay's play, Macheath becomes a victim of his own generosity, sacrificed to the greed and secrets of his own women. As in *The London Merchant* and *Moll Flanders*, eroticism here represents a dangerous self-indulgence, for it renders its victims vulnerable to the exploitation of others: "Was this well done, Jenny? —Women are decoy ducks; who can trust them! Beasts, jades, jilts, harpies, furies, whores!" (II.v.2–4).

Macheath's vulnerability, here and throughout the play, reveals a very different resolution to the basic tension between the rake's often contradictory desires for sexual satisfaction and aggressive dominance. Up to now, the subordination of the former to the latter has marked the careers of the rakes we have examined: Dorimant, Maskwell, and Millwood have all elevated their desires to secure social dominance above their erotic longings. Macheath, however, does not. Even after his betrayal by Jenny and his damning of the female sex, Macheath continues to place his safety in the hands of women, and in Act III, scene vi, his assignation with Mrs. Coaxer allows Mrs. Trapes to trade his life for her "own price upon any of the goods" she wants (66–67). Macheath consistently values his erotic satisfactions above all else. After all the betrayals he has suffered, Macheath remains a figure whose erotic delights define his relationship to the world:

> Thus I stand like the Turk, with his doxies around;
> From all sides their glances his passion confound;
> For black, brown, and fair, his inconstancy burns,
> And the different beauties subdue him by turns.
>   (Air LXIX, III.xvii.12–15)

Surrounded by his host of "wives," "subdued" by their beauty and joined by them in a festive dance, Macheath imagines himself amidst voluptuous Eastern splendors that define the triumph of his erotic nature. In complying with the corrupt "taste of the town," Gay can both implicate his audience in his satiric attack and fashion the most elaborate vision of the male rake's sexual fantasies.

V

Her fantasy world uninhibited by the strictures of mundane reality and conventional society, Fanny realizes, more than any other female rake, the vision of sexual liberty evoked by Hipolito in Part II of Dekker's *The Honest Whore*:

> Who liues in bondage, liues lac'd, the chiefe blisse
> This world below can yeeld is liberty:
> And who (than whores) with looser wings dare flie?
> As *Iunoes* proud bird spreads the fairest taile,
> So does a Strumpet hoist the loftiest saile.
> (IV.i.273–77)

Perhaps no strumpet in English literature hoists as lofty a sail as Fanny, though her fulfillment of Hipolito's erotic fantasy suggests the extent to which Fanny exists as a male projection of female sexuality. There has been, in fact, some critical confusion regarding the significance of Fanny's sexual liberation, of the way in which Cleland's pornographic novel relates to an emerging feminism. Brigid Brophy, for instance, finds in Fanny an indication "that women had emerged into social articulateness. No longer mere objects of men's pleasure, they can themselves be pleased and say so." And Leo Braudy has argued that "Cleland through Fanny is transmuted into the first feminist" because "sexuality . . . makes all men and women equal."[35] Our consideration of the female rake, however, should make us wary of such claims. Like Killigrew's Angellica Bianca and Southerne's Sir Anthony and Mrs. Wittwoud, Fanny fulfills male expectations of female sexuality, providing a specifically erotic portrait of the female Other and her relations to the male Self. As Nancy K. Miller recognizes in her excellent essay " 'I's' in Drag: The Sex of Recollection," "female drag allows the male 'I' not so much to please the Other—by subscribing or capitulating to women's 'taste'—as to become the Other . . . the better to be admired by and for himself."[36] What these contradictory responses to Cleland's masterpiece reveal, Robert Markley suggests, is that the novel "flirts with something approaching an incipient feminism, with the possibility of a non-discriminatory sexuality, but it always returns to its dominant language of rationality, common sense, and phallocentric repression. In this respect, *Fanny Hill* becomes bourgeois mythmaking at its most disarming— and effective: it sustains a masculine mythology of power from within the guise of a feminine confession."[37]

Robert Scholes has isolated a number of the assumptions of male narcissism that underlie Cleland's depiction of erotic pleasure: women can achieve genuine satisfaction only with men; the extent of the satisfaction depends primarily on the size of the male organ; women achieve orgasm only as often as their male partners; "the male genitals are described in considerable detail and are individualized by unique features as often as possible"; and "the female genitals are described in a kind of soft focus, as if airbrushed, so that no details beyond hair color are reported. The clitoris is certainly invisible and for all practical purposes nonexistent."[38] I would like to examine in detail Scholes' final two points, not only because I think some revision necessary to his formulations, but because Cleland's establishment of the English language of pornography depends on his ability to translate the Restoration love game into physical description, to reconceptualize the witty repartee and social conventions of the love game in terms of a pornographic vocabulary of "furious engines" and "pleasure-thirsty channels."

The nature of Cleland's erotic landscape is best revealed during Fanny's initiation into Mrs. Cole's "family of love." Characterized in Eastern terms of luxury similar to those in *The Beggar's Opera*, Mrs. Cole's "little Seraglio" allows Fanny to participate in a world in which pleasure becomes "the universal port of destination, and every wind that blew thither a good one, provided it blew nobody any harm."[39] The freedoms of this society, and the physical descriptions that represent them, are seen in the party that Mrs. Cole arranges to welcome Fanny to the group, a Banquet of Sense that attempts, however ironically, to recapture a prelapsarian Eden: "The authors and supporters of this secret institution, would, in the height of their humour, style themselves the restorers of the liberty of the golden age, and its simplicity of pleasures, before their innocence became so unjustly branded with the names of guilt, and shame" (94). This Banquet, which takes place in a drawing room "with a Turkey-carpet, and all its furniture voluptuously adapted to every demand of the most study'd luxury" (111), fulfills all the erotic promise of the earlier banquets of Horner and Macheath. In addition, it achieves an honesty and intimacy denied those other banquets, for all participate freely and without constraint: "The parties intended at once to humour their taste of variety in pleasures, and by an open publick enjoyment, to see me broke of any taint of reserve or modesty, which they look'd on as the poison of joy. . . . I was perfectly at my liberty to refuse the party, which being in its nature one of pleasure, suppos'd an exclusion of all force, or constraint" (112–13).

The climax of this banquet occurs when Fanny watches the three love bouts that precede her own. Though it means quoting at great length, the descriptions of these amorous encounters provide illuminating examples of the pastoral vocabulary that Cleland uses to define female sexuality:

Her petticoats thrown up with her shift, discover'd to the company the finest turn'd legs and thighs that could be imagin'd, and in a broad display, that gave us a full view of that delicious cleft of flesh, into which the pleasingly hair-grown mount over it parted, and presented a most inviting entrance, between two close ledges, delicately soft and pouting. Her gallant was now ready, having disincumbered himself from his cloathes overloaded with lace, and presently his shirt remov'd, shew'd us his forces in high plight, bandied, and ready for action: but giving us no time to consider dimensions, and proving the stiffness of his weapon, by his impatience of delay, he threw himself instantly over his charming antagonist. (113)

But what infinitely enrich'd and adorn'd [her thighs], was the sweet intersection, form'd where they met, at the bottom of the smoothest, roundest, whitest belly, by that central furrow which nature had sunk there, between the soft relievo of two pouting ridges, and which in this girl was in perfect simmetry of delicacy

and mignature with the rest of her frame: no! nothing in nature
could be of a beautifuller cut: then the dark umbrage of the downy
sprig-moss that over-arch'd it, bestow'd on the luxury of the landscape, a touching warmth, a tender finishing, beyond the expression
of words. . . . Her truly enamour'd gallant . . . addressed himself at
length to the materials of enjoyment, and lifting the linnen veil that
hung between us and his master-member of the revels, exhibited
one whose eminent size proclaim'd the owner a true woman's hero.
(115–16)

Her posteriours, plump, smooth, and prominent, form'd luxuriant
tracts of animated snow, that splendidly fill'd the eye, till it was
commanded down the parting or separation of those exquisitely
white cliffs, by their narrow vale, and was there stopt, and attracted
by the embower'd bottom-cavity, that terminated this delightful
visto, and stood moderately gaping from the influence of her bended
posture. . . . Her gallant . . . encouraging her with kisses and caresses
to stand him through, drew out his affair ready erected, and whose
extreme length, rather disproportion'd to its breadth, was the more
surprising, as that excess is not often the case of those of his corpu-
lent habit. (118–19)

   Most striking about these three descriptions is the cursory
consideration of the male in comparison to the female body.
Though Michael Shinagel notes that Cleland's novel contains
''roughly half as many references to the female sexual organ''
as to the male,[40] here descriptions of the female body are far
more elaborate and luxurious than the corresponding descriptions of the male body. In this scene the inequity is even
greater, for the breasts of two of the women also receive a fair
share of attention. Fanny looks on with the eyes of a heterosex-
ual male observer, interested more in the female than in the
male anatomy. The penis does not always get such short shrift
in the novel—indeed, it often receives a great deal of scrutiny
—but for the most part the female body defines the chief sexual
focus of Cleland's work. This should not, of course, come as a
surprise, for Cleland's primary aim lies in titillating his male
audience. In this scene, in particular, Fanny enjoys the
prerogatives of the male gallants who ''stood absorb'd''—''no
fear of glutting!''—as the women disrobe, but the men do not
themselves participate in this elaborate striptease.

At the same time, however, Cleland's depictions of the female genitals lack genuinely "individualized" features. In each of the three descriptions the predominate metaphor for the female body is a naked landscape. Though Cleland's figurative language differs in each case, all three depend with few exceptions on rather generalized and imprecise depictions of topological features: "mount," "ledges," "furrow," "ridges," "sprig-moss," "landscape," "snow," "cliffs," "vale," "vista." The men, on the other hand, are characterized only by size: Harriet's gallant possesses "a master-member of the revels . . . one whose eminent size proclaim'd the owner a true woman's hero," whereas Emilia's beau boasts an "extreme length, rather disproportion'd to its breadth."

In spite of numerous exceptions, a careful study of Cleland's physical descriptions supports the general impression that Cleland defines female sexuality in terms of pastoral imagery and male sexuality through mechanical images.[41] This imagistic disjunction serves to emphasize, in fact, not just the sexual beauty of women, but their passivity. In the banquet scene the male organ represents the "master-member of the revels," the "mighty machine" upon which female pleasure absolutely depends. If pastoral landscapes depict the female body, then the penis represents the mechanical male force that works, tills, and eventually despoils that landscape. Cleland describes Charles's imminent destruction of Fanny's virginity in precisely such terms: "for still, . . . my virgin-flower was yet uncrop'd" (40); "I was still mistress of that darling treasure, that hidden mine, so eagerly sought after by the men, and which they never dig for but they destroy" (39). Cleland's descriptions of the female body are pastoral not simply because they depend on images of nature, but because the landscape depicted remains easily controlled, rarely threatening, representative of a world in which men labor without effort or pain. The men who support Mrs. Cole's establishment, as we have seen, consider themselves "restorers of the liberty of the golden age, and its simplicity of pleasures": in Cleland's novel the luxurious and inviting female body represents that Golden Age.

Cleland's physical descriptions thus provide a way in which males can control the outrageous desires that characterize his depiction of female sexuality, for women clearly do not emerge from the novel as sexually passive figures. Fanny's seduction of Mr. H——'s servant Will, and Louisa's lustful enjoyment of the idiot, are just the most obvious examples of the unquenchable natural appetites that women supposedly possess. In Dekker's *The Honest Whore* and Webster's *The White Devil* the frightening sexual powers of women are expressed and degraded by the persistent demonic imagery that characterizes obsessive sexuality. In Cleland's novel the physical descriptions perform a similar function, for they allow Cleland to present the extravagant erotic desires of women while at the same time subordinating those desires to male control. Female sexuality is validated in the novel only in linguistic terms that reinforce female passivity and male domination; as Nancy Miller insists, "The natural impulses of women as a sex are negatively coded."[42] It is a rather large jump from eighteenth-century England to twentieth-century Latin America, but the first of Pablo Neruda's *Twenty Love Poems and a Song of Despair* makes clear the implications of this pastoral imagery:

> Body of a woman, white hills, white thighs,
> you look like a world, lying in surrender.
> My rough peasant's body digs in you
> and makes the son leap from the depth of the earth.[43]

The male body is powerful, generative, brutal; the female body, weak, passive, vulnerable.

The use of pastoral imagery to describe the human body is not restricted in the novel solely to women; Cleland often describes men in a similar fashion. Used in terms of men, however, these pastoral images are occasionally satiric, as when Mr. Barvile, whose perverse taste for pleasure involves beatings, displays a penis "scarce showing its tip above the sprout of hairy curls that cloath'd those parts, as you may have seen a wren peep its head out of the grass" (146), or when the idiot for whom Louisa late in the novel hungers "swells, and vegetates" under Fanny's touch, eventually showing an "enormous head . . . in hue and size, not unlike a common sheep's heart" (162).

When not satiric, however, the pastoral depiction of the

male body defines a very different prospect from the female pastoral landscape. After her first night with Charles, Fanny wakens and, while Charles sleeps, surveys his body, "devour[ing] all his naked charms with only two eyes" (44). Her extended description contains many pastoral images, including his "snow-white bosom"—"that . . . presented on the vermillion summet of each pap, the idea of a rose about to blow" (44)—and his genitals: "Then the beautiful growth of the hair, in short and soft curls around its root, its whiteness, branch'd veins, the supple softness of the shaft, as it lay foreshorten'd, roll'd and shrunk up into a squob thickness, languid, and born up from between the thighs, by its globular appendage, that wondrous treasure-bag of nature's sweets" (45). In repose, Charles's vulnerable body suggests the same pastoral delights that the female body offers. Yet once Charles awakes, and Fanny's caresses raise his passion, that easy pastoral world is rent by "such ungovernable fury" that his "storm fall[s]" on her still tender "wound": "the instrument . . . now cased home, so gorged me with pleasure, that it perfectly suffocated me, and took away my breath: then the killing thrusts! the unnumber'd kisses!" (46–47).

Fanny's description, which moves between the extremes of suffocation and pleasure, "killing thrusts" and "unnumber'd kisses," calls attention to the fierce and dominating force of the now animated male landscape. The male body possesses an awful power alien to the more vulnerable female body. When Fanny first sees Will's "may-pole of so enormous a standard" (72), she waxes eloquent on its pastoral beauty, but ends by reminding us that "it stood an object of terror and delight" (73). The male body, and the penis in particular, is seen, Robert Markley notes, "as naturally—and irrevocably—being part of the God-given order of things; it is the pristine origin of power."[44]

Yet Cleland's pornographic language expresses not simply male fears of, and desires to control, female sexuality, but the male fantasy of an inexhaustible sensual paradise. Like Killigrew's Angellica Bianca, Fanny represents a pastoral erotic landscape "Green, Fresh, and Lusty, as the pride of Spring, and ever blowing." Part of an eternal natural world, Fanny emerges from the novel, in spite of her frequent sexual adventures, as a modern Venus who perpetually renews her virginity. After her first sexual encounter with Will's "over-siz'd machine" (73), Fanny wonders "what innovation that tender soft system of mine might have sustain'd from the shock of a machine so siz'd for its destruction" (79). She discovers, of course, that her body remains unchanged, still a symbol of a world in which, again in Angellica Bianca's words, "Youth, Strength, and Beauty, . . . shall never die": "The silky hair that cover'd round the borders, now smooth'd, and re-prun'd, had resum'd its wonted curl and trimness; the fleshly pouting lips, that had stood the brunt of the engagement, were no longer swoln or moisture-drench'd: and neither they, nor the passage into which they open'd, that had suffer'd so great a dilation, betray'd any the least alteration, outward or inwardly" (79). "Re-prun'd," Fanny's erotic landscape again represents what Thomas Stretzer, in his extended geographical description of the female genitals, *A New Description of Merryland* (1740), calls "the lovliest and sweetest Region of the World."[45]

Cleland's erotic celebration of the female body allows him to transform Defoe's harsh and threatening social landscape into a benign pastoral prospect upon which Fanny can indulge the sexual passions that Moll must repress. Both Moll and Fanny recognize that female sexuality in a male world represents a marketable commodity, and that for a woman to succeed she must, as Rosalind advises in *As You Like It*, "sell when you can, [for] you are not for all markets" (III.v.60). This, certainly, is the frank advice of Mrs. Jones, who exploits Fanny's vulnerability after Charles's removal by insisting that "do not you now stand upon your punctilio's, and this and that, but make your market while you may" (58). This advice comes at a moment when Fanny, like Moll, has lost any male protector and is haunted by the threat of the prison that "every drop of my blood chill'd" (57).

In Defoe's novel such moments define the recurring crises of Moll's life: again and again Moll must generate a Self capable of staving off the external world that would destroy her fragile identity. Moll, of course, comes alive precisely at such moments, her narrative concerned not with the domestic stasis that she periodically enjoys—she dismisses most of her marriages in a paragraph or a page—but with the long periods of uncertainty and fear that lie between. In Cleland's fantastic world, on the other hand, Fanny moves gracefully from protector to protector, recognizing the dangers of her moments of vulnerability, but dismissing them as blithely as Moll does her marriages. When Mr. H—— throws Fanny off after discovering her indiscretions with Will, Fanny, like Moll, finds herself "once more a-drift, and left upon my own hands" (86). Barely a page later, however, she finds Mrs. Cole and another safe haven within which to express and enjoy her passions. Moll defines her life and narrative by those periods when she must repress her sexuality in order to survive; Fanny, on the other hand, exists only during those seasons when she can revel in her erotic desires.

Fanny, of course, must learn a certain caution and prudence; like Moll, she must grow from a naive and vulnerable country girl to a knowledgeable woman of the town. Like Moll, Fanny begins her adult life as a woman of naturally warm desires; her first sight of the "old last act," when she observes Mrs. Brown and the young horse-grenadier, reveals the extremity of her untutored passions: "I could scarce hear the sighs, and murmurs, the heaves, and pantings that accompanied the action, from the beginning to the end; the sound and sight of which thrill'd to the very soul of me, and made every vein of my body circulate liquid fires: the emotion grew so violent that it almost intercepted my respiration" (25). Cleland initially defines Fanny solely in terms of her erotic longings, with little education and "neither virtue, or principles" (21).

For Moll the transition from innocence to experience marks a long and painful process, in the course of which she must shed not only her virtue and principles, but even the desires that define her as a woman; Moll succeeds precisely because she learns to evade or ignore her virtues and principles, to repress her natural desires. In Cleland's novel, however, both Fanny and her world are governed by a "natural instinct" in which rampant male members and warm female "centers of sense" possess an ineffable attraction for each other. At the beginning of her career, Fanny "did what I did, because I could not help it" (38); yet even near her story's conclusion, when she should know better, Fanny remains self-indulgent with her

desires. Meeting a young and unknown sailor after a particularly frustrating evening with Mr. Norbert, she gives in to her
"pressing calls" and plays a "common street-plyer": "in
short, it was not my head that I now obey'd" (140). Mrs. Cole
rebukes Fanny for being "so open-legg'd," but Fanny suffers no
penalty for her indiscretion. Fanny's transition from innocence
to experience describes no dangerous passage, for she inhabits
a fantasy world in which her instinct for pleasure rarely finds
itself at odds with the necessity for profit: "You may be sure a
by-job of this sort interfer'd with no other pursuit, or plan of
life, which I led in truth with a modesty and reserve that was
less the work of virtue, than of exhausted novelty, a glut of
pleasure, and easy circumstances, that made me indifferent to
any engagements in which pleasure and profit were not
eminently united" (153).

Fanny's life and adventures are the stuff of purest daydream
precisely because Cleland dissolves the recurrent tension between business and pleasure that has characterized the rake's
desires ever since Sir Jaspar Fidget commanded that Horner
"go to your business, I say, pleasure, whilst I go to my pleasure, business." Fanny's narrative displays not the slightest
disjunction between the two terms, for she lives in a world in
which business is pleasure, and pleasure business. The culmi-
nation of this identity comes in Part II, when Fanny joins Mrs.
Cole and enjoys "a rare alliance of pleasure with interest" (93).
The Banquet of Sense that introduces her into Mrs. Cole's
establishment climaxes not just with her initiation on the
couch, where she receives "a double payment of tribute" from
her gallant, but with the "purse of guineas" (124) that he also
leaves her: "tribute" and "payment" for Fanny inevitably involves, as her language demonstrates, both sexual and economic consummation. And both are realized in the book's climax, when Fanny marries Charles, her sexual license having
in no way compromised her economic value as a wife.

Like the rake's fifth-act conversion in Restoration comedy, Fanny's marriage thus qualifies her libertine sexual freedoms, subordinating her pastoral world of pleasure to the
economic realities of society. As Robert Markley suggests, her
sexual experiences "become a way of temporarily transcending
one's mundane existence, of celebrating a nearly Dionysian

release from the constraints of bourgeois propriety."[46] Cleland translates the Restoration rake's dream of a sensual paradise into a pornographic language which assumes that the erotic is an integral part of human nature; nonetheless, this vision of sexual freedom remains bounded and controlled by the power of conventional society. Even though in Enlightenment England, according to Roy Porter, "public visibility and tolerance of sexuality . . . encompassed a large section of society, certainly much more extensive than the libertine elite of the Restoration court,"[47] the rake's extravagant sexuality had still to be tamed and degraded. At the same time, Porter insists, the greater sexual freedoms of the eighteenth century applied "principally to males. Male Enlightenment attitudes were highly ambiguous with regard to women."[48] This, too, marks Cleland's novel, for its pornographic vocabulary displays the same male ambivalences towards female sexuality that we explored in earlier versions of the whore and female rake. Cleland's secular pornographic vocabulary differs greatly from the seventeenth-century rhetoric of demonic sexuality, but both reveal male fascination with, and fear of, female sexuality, the complex relationship between male desires to enjoy and control the tempting and yet threatening female body.

NOTES

INDEX

NOTES

INTRODUCTION

1. John Wilmot, earl of Rochester, "Upon His Drinking a Bowl," in *The Complete Poems of John Wilmot, Earl of Rochester*, ed. David M. Vieth (New Haven: Yale University Press, 1968), p. 53.

2. William Cavendish, duke of Newcastle, *The Humorous Lovers* (London: Printed by J.M., 1677), p. 2.

3. Sir George Etherege, "So soft and amorously you write," in *The Poems of Sir George Etherege*, ed. James Thorpe (Princeton: Princeton University Press, 1963), p. 43.

4. Rochester, "A Satyr on Charles II," in *The Complete Poems*, pp. 60–61.

5. Thomas H. Fujimura, *The Restoration Comedy of Wit* (Princeton: Princeton University Press, 1952); Dale Underwood, *Etherege and the Seventeenth-Century Comedy of Manners*, Yale Studies in English 135 (New Haven: Yale University Press, 1957); Virginia Ogden Birdsall, *Wild Civility: The English Comic Spirit on the Restoration Stage* (Bloomington: Indiana University Press, 1970); Robert Jordan, "The Extravagant Rake in Restoration Comedy," in *Restoration Literature: Critical Approaches*, ed. Harold Love (London: Methuen, 1972), pp. 69–90.

6. Sigmund Freud, *Civilization and Its Discontents*, tr. and ed. James Strachey (New York: Norton, 1961), p. 42.

7. Ibid., p. 62.

8. Sigmund Freud, " 'Civilized' Sexual Morality and Modern Nervousness," in *Sexuality and the Psychology of Love*, ed. Philip Rieff, The Collected Papers of Sigmund Freud (New York: Collier Books, 1963), p. 25.

9. *Reflexions on Marriage, and The Poetick Discipline: A Letter, by the Author of Remarques on the Town* (London: Printed for Allen Banks, 1673), p. 58.

10. Sir Richard Blackmore, *Prince Arthur* (London, 1695), sigs. A^v–a.

11. John Dryden, "Astraea Redux," in *The Works of John Dryden*, ed. Edward Niles Hooker, H. T. Swedenberg, Jr., and Alan Roper,

19 vols. (Berkeley: University of California Press, 1956–), 1:23, lines 43–48.

12. Ibid., p. 25, lines 105–10.

13. Michel Foucault, *The History of Sexuality*, vol. 1, *Introduction*, tr. Robert Hurley (New York: Pantheon Books, 1978), p. 34.

CHAPTER ONE: THE RAKE AND THE DEVIL

1. For a history of the gay couple prior to the Restoration, see John Harrington Smith, *The Gay Couple in Restoration Comedy* (Cambridge: Harvard University Press, 1948), esp. pp. 3–28. For a discussion of the rake's relation to the Vice see Birdsall, *Wild Civility*, esp. pp. 16–32. William W. E. Slights, "The Trickster-Hero and Middleton's *A Mad World, My Masters*," *Comparative Drama* 3 (1969): 87–98, does not discuss the rake, but his examination of the Jacobean trickster-hero indicates some of the ways in which the two are related.

2. Peter Holland, *The Ornament of Action: Text and Performance in Restoration Comedy* (Cambridge: Cambridge University Press, 1979), p. 82.

3. Ben Jonson, *Volpone; or, The Fox*, ed. Alvin B. Kernan, The Yale Ben Jonson (New Haven: Yale University Press, 1962), III.i.23–29. All references are to this edition.

4. For a discussion of Volpone's speech, and the type of language it uses, see L. A. Beaurline, *Jonson and Elizabethan Comedy: Essays in Dramatic Rhetoric* (San Marino: The Huntington Library, 1978), ch. 5, esp. pp. 177–92.

5. Jean H. Hagstrum, *Sex and Sensibility: Ideal and Erotic Love from Milton to Mozart* (Chicago: University of Chicago Press, 1980), p. 50.

6. John Donne, "Show me deare Christ," in *John Donne: The Divine Poems*, ed. Helen Gardner (Oxford: Clarendon Press, 1952), p. 15.

7. Sir Walter Raleigh, "A Farewell to false Love," in *The Poems of Sir Walter Raleigh*, ed. Agnes M. C. Latham (Cambridge: Harvard University Press, 1951), pp. 7–8.

8. All quotations from Shakespeare's plays are from the Arden Edition.

9. J. M. Armistead, "Occultism in Restoration Drama: Motives for Revaluation," *Modern Language Studies* 9 (1979): 62.

10. Foucault, *History of Sexuality*, p. 156.

11. Ibid., p. 35.

12. Keith Thomas, *Religion and the Decline of Magic: Studies in Popular Beliefs in Sixteenth- and Seventeenth-Century England* (London: Weidenfeld and Nicolson, 1971), pp. 498, 499.

13. Ibid., pp. 475, 472.

14. In writing this section on sixteenth- and early-seventeenth-century witchcraft I have depended heavily on the work of the following four social historians: Norman Cohn, *Europe's Inner Demons: An Enquiry Inspired by the Great Witch-Hunt* (New York: Basic Books, 1975); Christina Larner, *Enemies of God: The Witch-Hunt in Scotland* (Baltimore: Johns Hopkins University Press, 1981); Alan Macfarlane, *Witchcraft in Tudor and Stuart England: A Regional and Comparative Study* (London: Routledge and Kegan Paul, 1970); and Keith Thomas, *Religion and the Decline of Magic.* I have also consulted H. R. Trevor-Roper, "The European Witch-Craze of the Sixteenth and Seventeenth Centuries," in *The Crisis of the Seventeenth Century: Religion, the Reformation, and Social Change* (New York: Harper and Row, 1968), pp. 90–192, and Robert Rentoul Reed, Jr., *The Occult on the Tudor and Stuart Stage* (Boston: Christopher Publishing House, 1965).

15. A. D. J. Macfarlane, "Witchcraft in Tudor and Stuart Essex," in *Crime in England, 1550–1800,* ed. J. S. Cockburn (Princeton: Princeton University Press, 1977), pp. 75, 77; Thomas, *Religion and the Decline of Magic,* p. 449.

16. Peter Laslett, *The World We Have Lost* (London: Methuen, 1965), notes how powerful was this fear of damnation as a mechanism for social control: "Submission to the powers that be went very well with the habit of obedience to the head of the patriarchal family, and it had the extremely effective sanction of the universal fear of damnation to the defiant. 'Short life,' so the doctrine went, 'was the punishment of disobedient children'" (p. 178).

17. Cohn, *Europe's Inner Demons,* p. 261.

18. James I, *Daemonologie, In Forme of a Dialogue, Divided into three Bookes* (1597; rpt. New York: Da Capo Press, 1969), p. 67.

19. For descriptions of the demonic pact see Cohn, *Europe's Inner Demons,* pp. 99–100 and 229–33, and Larner, *Enemies of God,* esp. pp. 145–51.

20. Macfarlane, "Witchcraft in Tudor and Stuart Essex," p. 75.

21. John Webster, *The Displaying of Supposed Witchcraft* (London: Printed by J. M., 1677), sigs. a2v–a3.

22. Larner, *Enemies of God,* p. 200; Trevor-Roper, "The European Witch-Craze," pp. 162–63.; Thomas, *Religion and the Decline of Magic,* pp. 444–46.

23. Thomas, *Religion and the Decline of Magic,* p. 441.

24. Thomas Ady, *A Perfect Discovery of Witches. Shewing The Divine Cause of the Distractions of this Kingdome, and also of the Christian World* (London: Printed for R. I., 1661), pp. 6–7.

25. Thomas, *Religion and the Decline of Magic*, pp. 442–44.

26. Evidence for this is noted by Muriel West, *The Devil and John Webster*, Salzburg Studies in English Literature 11 (Salzburg: Universität Salzburg, 1974), p. 237.

27. Thomas, *Religion and the Decline of Magic*, p. 439.

28. D. P. Walker, *Unclean Spirits: Possession and Exorcism in France and England in the Late Sixteenth and Early Seventeenth Centuries* (Philadelphia: University of Pennsylvania Press, 1981), p. 62; Thomas, *Religion and the Decline of Magic*, pp. 481–82.

29. Richard Sibbes, *The Soules Conflict with it selfe, and Victory over it selfe by Faith. A Treatise of the inward disquietments of distressed spirits, with comfortable remedies to establish them*, 4th ed. (London: Printed for R. D., 1651), p. 184.

30. *A Complete Collection of State-Trials, and Proceedings for High Treason, and Other Crimes and Misdemeanours; From The Reign of King Richard II To The End of the Reign of King George I*, 2d ed., 6 vols. (London, 1730), 1:311.

31. The murder of Sir Thomas Overbury can be followed in ibid., pp. 313–52. The Overbury scandal is discussed by William Lloyd McElwee, *The Murder of Sir Thomas Overbury* (New York: Oxford University Press, 1952), and Beatrice White, *Cast of Ravens: The Strange Case of Sir Thomas Overbury* (New York: G. Braziller, 1965). J. L. Simmons, "Diabolical Realism in Middleton and Rowley's *The Changeling*," *Renaissance Drama* 11 (1980): 135–70, uses the murder of Overbury to discuss, in ways similar to my own, aspects of demonic sexuality in Jacobean society and literature.

32. For a discussion of this incident, see Thomas Longueville, *The Curious Case of Lady Purbeck: A Scandal of the Seventeenth Century* (London: Longmans, Green, 1909), pp. 94–101. See also Roger Lockyer, *Buckingham: The Life and Political Career of George Villiers, First Duke of Buckingham, 1592–1628* (London: Longman, 1981), pp. 285–86.

33. See Barbara Breasted, "*Comus* and the Castlehaven Scandal," in *Milton Studies III*, ed. James D. Simmonds (Pittsburgh: University of Pittsburgh Press, 1971), pp. 201–24.

34. For a brief discussion of the use of "hell" to refer to the female sexual organ, see Stephen Booth, ed., *Shakespeare's Sonnets* (New Haven: Yale University Press, 1977), note to sonnet 144, line 12.

35. John Webster, *The White Devil*, ed. John Russell Brown, The Revels Plays (1960; rpt. Manchester: Manchester University Press, 1977), I.ii.3. All references are to this edition. See M. C. Bradbrook,

John Webster: Citizen and Dramatist (New York: Columbia University Press, 1980), p. 122.

36. For a work which develops the demonic imagery that implicates all of the play's characters, see West, The Devil and John Webster, esp. pp. 295-97.

37. Thomas Otway, Venice Preserv'd, in The Works of Thomas Otway, ed. J. C. Ghosh, 2 vols. (Oxford: Clarendon Press, 1932), vol. 2, II.66-76. All references to the plays of Otway are to this edition.

38. My conception of the play corresponds to the "pessimistic satire" of a "world corrupt beyond redemption" that Judith Milhous and Robert D. Hume posit as one of the "four basic production potentialities" of Venice Preserv'd; see their Producible Interpretation: Eight English Plays, 1675-1707 (Carbondale: Southern Illinois University Press, 1985), pp. 172-200.

39. For an account that explores the play's pervasive eroticism, see William H. McBurney, "Otway's Tragic Muse Debauched: Sensuality in Venice Preserv'd," Journal of English and Germanic Philology 58 (1959): 380-99.

40. For an explanation of Vittoria's dream and its demonic details, see West, The Devil and John Webster, pp. 157-65.

41. In Civilization and Its Discontents, pp. 46-47n, Freud talks of how the failure of dogs to be "ashamed of . . . [their] sexual functions" makes them objects of contempt in human eyes. This helps explain the power of Flamineo's scornful suggestion that "women are like curst dogs."

42. Jordan, "The Extravagant Rake in Restoration Comedy," in Love, Restoration Literature, pp. 87-88.

43. Thomas Middleton, A Mad World, My Masters, ed. Standish Henning, Regents Renaissance Drama Series (Lincoln: University of Nebraska Press, 1965), IV.v.63-64. All references are to this edition.

44. Richard Levin, "The Dampit Scenes in A Trick to Catch the Old One," Modern Language Quarterly 25 (1964): 149-50; Anthony Covatta, Thomas Middleton's City Comedies (Lewisburg: Bucknell University Press, 1973), p. 123. William W. E. Slights feels that "the perplexing element in the farcical plot is not so much the appearance of a dream-figure as it is the moralistic language of Penitent's long soliloquy" ("The Trickster-Hero," p. 95).

45. See Brian Gibbons, Jacobean City Comedy: A Study of Satiric Plays by Jonson, Marston, and Middleton (Cambridge: Harvard University Press, 1968), who recognizes the nature of this resolution when he notes that "Middleton drains away the force of the bad characters, particularly the whore, so that the final scene can be festive in mood and the play satisfactorily symmetrical in design" (p. 114).

46. John Marston, *The Dutch Courtesan*, ed. M. L. Wine, Regents Renaissance Drama Series (Lincoln: University of Nebraska Press, 1965), I.i.14–15. All references are to this edition.

47. Paul M. Zall, "John Marston, Moralist," *ELH* 20 (1953): 193. Samuel Schoenbaum, "The Precarious Balance of John Marston," *PMLA* 67 (1952): 1069–78, describes this as Marston's fundamental problem: "Man has a soul, but he has a body as well. . . . Marston cannot bring himself to accept this duality; it is at the core of his disgust with mankind. And yet, if the body is a source of revulsion, it exerts nevertheless a peculiar fascination" (p. 1074).

48. The moral and sexual extremes of the play are discussed by Robert K. Presson, "Marston's *Dutch Courtezan*: The Study of an Attitude in Adaptation," *Journal of English and Germanic Philology* 55 (1956): 406–13, and Gustav Cross, "Marston, Montaigne, and Morality: *The Dutch Courtezan* Reconsidered," *ELH* 27 (1960): 30–43.

49. Michel Eyquem de Montaigne, "Upon Some Verses of Virgil," in *Essays of Michael Lord of Montaigne*, tr. John Florio, 3 vols. (1603; rpt. Boston: Houghton Mifflin, 1904), 3:95.

50. Anthony Caputi, *John Marston, Satirist* (Ithaca: Cornell University Press, 1961), p. 232.

51. George L. Geckle, *John Marston's Drama: Themes, Images, Sources* (Rutherford, N.J.: Fairleigh Dickinson University Press, 1980), emphasizes this point when he notes that "Crispinella herself receives high praise from most critics and scholars. . . . Considering Marston's other plays, however, Beatrice, and not Crispinella, is the ideal woman" (p. 165).

52. Laslett, *The World We Have Lost*, pp. 131 and 130. Though I accept Laslett's conclusion here, I wonder if his sweeping generalization sufficiently attends to divergences in behavior between different social and economic classes. Conduct at the court of Charles II may well overshadow the statistical consensus that Laslett seeks, particularly if one suspects that ecclesiastical courts are not the forum in which people were likely to speak candidly concerning their sexual habits.

53. Rochester, "The Fall," in *The Complete Poems*, p. 86.

54. Carole Fabricant, "Rochester's World of Imperfect Enjoyment," *Journal of English and Germanic Philology* 73 (1974): 338–50.

55. David Foxon, *Libertine Literature in England, 1660–1745* (New York: University Books, 1965), pp. 45–51.

56. Lawrence Stone, *The Family, Sex, and Marriage in England, 1500–1800* (London: Weidenfeld and Nicolson, 1977), p. 135. As I have indicated, a general consensus among historians concerning Stone's conclusions has yet to be reached. For the grounds of disagree-

ment on this issue, see the debate between Miriam Slater and Sara Mendelson in "The Weightiest Business: Marriage in an Upper-Gentry Family in Seventeenth-Century England," *Past and Present* 85 (1979): 126–40. For a helpful review of the scholarship concerning these issues, see Stone's "Family History in the 1980s: Past Achievements and Future Trends," *Journal of Interdisciplinary History* 12 (1981): 51–87. A recent essay that takes issue with Stone's position regarding the relations between parents and children is Mary Joe Hughes, "Child-Rearing and Social Expectations in Eighteenth Century England: The Case of the Colliers of Hastings," *Studies in Eighteenth-Century Culture* 13 (1984): 79–100. Two essays that approach Stone's conclusions from a more "literary" perspective are David Blewett, "Changing Attitudes toward Marriage in the Time of Defoe: The Case of Moll Flanders," *Huntington Library Quarterly* 44 (1981): 77–88, and Laura A. Curtis, "A Case Study of Defoe's Domestic Conduct Manuals Suggested by *The Family, Sex, and Marriage, 1500–1800*," *Studies in Eighteenth-Century Culture* 10 (1981): 409–25.

CHAPTER TWO: THE HOBBESIAN LIBERTINE-RAKE

1. Rochester to Savile, spring 1676, in *The Letters of John Wilmot, Earl of Rochester*, ed. Jeremy Treglown (Oxford: Basil Blackwell, 1980), p. 119.
2. Charles Sackville, earl of Dorset, "A Letter from the Lord Buckhurst to Mr. George Etherege," in *The Poems of Charles Sackville Sixth Earl of Dorset*, ed. Brice Harris (New York: Garland Publishing, 1979), p. 106, lines 33–42.
3. William Wycherley, *The Country-Wife*, in *The Plays of William Wycherley*, ed. Arthur Friedman (Oxford: Clarendon Press, 1979), II.i.567–68. All references are to this edition.
4. William Congreve, *The Old Batchelour*, in *The Complete Plays of William Congreve*, ed. Herbert Davis (Chicago: University of Chicago Press, 1967), I.i.5–14. All references to the plays of Congreve are to this edition.
5. Rochester, "A Ramble in St. James's Park," in *The Complete Poems*, p. 40.
6. Susan Staves, *Players' Scepters: Fictions of Authority in the Restoration* (Lincoln: University of Nebraska Press, 1979), p. 115.
7. Birdsall, *Wild Civility*, p. 39.
8. Robert D. Hume, "The Myth of the Rake in 'Restoration' Comedy," *Studies in the Literary Imagination* 10 (1977): 45. Max-

imillian E. Novak discusses this question at length in *William Congreve*, Twayne's English Authors Series (New York: Twayne, 1971), esp. pp. 41-51.

9. This tension in an audience's response to the rake is what Judith Milhous and Robert Hume, in *Producible Interpretation*, identify as the central determinant of theatrical production during the Restoration: "Our best guess—and we offer it as no more than that—is that a seventeenth-century director (whether author or actor/manager) would have thought of contrasting production concepts largely in terms of sympathy with and alienation from the characters" (p. 68).

10. Underwood, *Etherege and the Seventeenth-Century Comedy of Manners*, pp. 26 and 28.

11. For an excellent analysis of Horner and his behavior during the china scene, see C. D. Cecil, "Libertine and *Precieux* Elements in Restoration Comedy," *Essays in Criticism* 9 (1959): 239-53.

12. Gerald Weales, ed., *The Complete Plays of William Wycherley*, Stuart Editions (New York: New York University Press, 1967) p. xii; David M. Vieth, "Wycherley's *The Country Wife:* An Anatomy of Masculinity," *Papers on Language and Literature* 2 (1966): 346; William Freedman, "Impotence and Self-Destruction in *The Country Wife*," *English Studies* 53 (1972): 421-31. In his recent book *Language in Wycherley's Plays: Seventeenth-Century Language Theory and Drama* (Alabama: University of Alabama Press, 1984), James Thompson repeats the same charge: "It is a commonplace that Horner first pretends to be impotent but later becomes so, figuratively when he has no more 'china,' and more broadly in the sense that 'the reputation of impotency is as hardly recover'd again in the World, as that of cowardise' (II.i.550-52)" (p. 86). However significant we judge Horner's "figurative" impotence, we should not forget, as Margery assures us during the final scene, that "literally" he is not impotent: " 'Tis false Sir, you shall not disparage poor Mr. Horner, for to my certain knowledge—" (V.iv.369-70).

13. W. R. Chadwick, *The Four Plays of William Wycherley: A Study in the Development of a Dramatist* (The Hague: Mouton, 1975), p. 117.

14. Birdsall, *Wild Civility*, p. 156. As Birdsall's reference to staging makes clear, performances of the play can reveal very different conceptions of the rake-hero's personality. Vieth, for example, views Horner's statement that "I, alas can't be one [a husband]" as "a belated recognition that he was capable of something better" (p. 346). A relatively "straight" delivery of that line is necessary to support Vieth's view of Horner, and though I grant the possibility of such a

reading, my own staging of the play would see in such a remark only another instance of Horner's pervasive irony and insider's fun at the expense of those who have only "an innocent, literal understanding."

15. Although Weales suggests that he does not share this attitude (*Complete Plays of William Wycherley*, p. xii), he does not go on to elaborate his own opinion of the women's relation to Horner.

16. Chadwick, *Four Plays of William Wycherley*, p. 102.; Rose A. Zimbardo, *Wycherley's Drama: A Link in the Development of English Satire*, Yale Studies in English 156 (New Haven: Yale University Press, 1965), pp. 150–52; Jocelyn Powell, *Restoration Theatre Production* (London: Routledge and Kegan Paul, 1984), p. 141.

17. Frank Kermode, *Shakespeare, Spenser, Donne: Renaissance Essays* (New York: Viking Press, 1971), pp. 84–115.

18. Ibid., p. 99.

19. For a study of the relationship between *préciosité* and the Restoration stage, see David S. Berkeley, "*Préciosité* and the Restoration Comedy of Manners," *Huntington Library Quarterly* 18 (1955): 109–28.

20. Rochester, "A Satyr against Reason and Mankind," in *The Complete Poems*, p. 99, lines 150–52.

21. Powell, *Restoration Theatre Production*, p. 135.

22. Alexander Pope, "Epistle to Miss Blount, With the Works of Voiture," in *The Poems of Alexander Pope*, ed. John Butt, Twickenham Edition, 11 vols. (London: Methuen, 1939–69), 6:63, lines 31–32.

23. John Traugott, "The Rake's Progress from Court to Comedy: A Study in Comic Form," *Studies in English Literature* 6 (1966): 381–407.

24. Though James Thompson is not speaking specifically of this exchange, he also feels that Horner's decision to betray Alithea is a "pivotal moment of choice. . . . From an especially bright and witty comedy of intrigue, this play takes a nasty turn, deliberately disturbing the audience. . . . we are not entirely prepared for the change in Horner, whom we have found quite amusing for four acts" (*Language in Wycherley's Plays*, pp. 71–72).

25. Northrop Frye, *Anatomy of Criticism: Four Essays* (Princeton: Princeton University Press, 1957), p. 173.

26. Anthony Kaufman, "Wycherley's *The Country Wife* and the Don Juan Character," *Eighteenth-Century Studies* 9 (1975–76): 216.

27. This raises again the questions asked at the end of my first chapter concerning the possibility of changing conceptions of marriage. While the argument is primarily one involving the discipline of social history, for literary criticism that deals with some of these prob-

lems, see Maximillian E. Novak's "Margery Pinchwife's 'London Disease': Restoration Comedy and the Libertine Offensive of the 1670's," *Studies in the Literary Imagination* 10 (1977): 1–23. Novak amasses considerable evidence to suggest that what he labels a "libertine offensive" of the 1670s actively questioned the morality of regarding marriage as simply a property arrangement. And P. F. Vernon, in "Marriage of Convenience and the Moral Code of Restoration Comedy," *Essays in Criticism* 12 (1962): 370–87, also deals with the complex problem of social realities and dramatic illusions in regard to satiric portrayals of marriage on the Restoration stage.

28. B. Eugene McCarthy, *William Wycherley: A Biography* (Athens: Ohio University Press, 1979), p. 67.

29. Frye, *Anatomy of Criticism*, pp. 177–79.

30. See Hume, "Myth of the Rake in 'Restoration' Comedy," pp. 25–55.

31. Zimbardo, *Wycherley's Drama*, p. 16; Vernon, "Marriage of Convenience," pp. 385 and 386. In the 1970s similarly contradictory positions were defended by B. Eugene McCarthy and W. R. Chadwick; McCarthy argues that "even recognizing Horner's role as satirist of his society . . . we are not confronted with the whole of Horner" (*William Wycherley*, p. 64), whereas Chadwick describes Horner as a *pícaro*, "neither admirable or reprehensible," who focuses the satire more on the corrupt world he moves through than on himself (*Four Plays of William Wycherley*, esp. pp. 116–19). James Thompson has recently repeated Zimbardo's argument, insisting that in the figure of Horner "we witness the satire of satire, the irony of irony, the hypocrisy of hypocrisy" (*Language in Wycherley's Plays*, p. 75).

32. Madame de Lafayette, *The Princesse De Clèves*, tr. Nancy Mitford and Leonard Tancock (London: Penguin, 1978), p. 31; Nathaniel Lee, *The Princess of Cleve*, in *The Works of Nathaniel Lee*, ed. Thomas B. Stroup and Arthur L. Cooke, 2 vols. (New Brunswick: Scarecrow Press, 1955), 2:153, dedication, lines 14–15 (all references are to this edition). For the tangled stage history and the composition of Lee's play, see Robert D. Hume, *The Rakish Stage: Studies in English Drama, 1660–1800* (Carbondale: Southern Illinois University Press, 1983), pp. 113–18.

33. Hume, *The Rakish Stage*, pp. 118–27. In *Nathaniel Lee*, Twayne's English Authors Series (Boston: Twayne, 1979), pp. 155–61, J. M. Armistead argues that Nemours is really a composite portrait of Rochester and Buckingham meant to satirize a "type" as much as any specific individual.

34. See Hume, *The Rakish Stage*, p. 120n, for a brief discussion of Restoration attitudes towards homosexuality.

35. Rochester, "Love a woman? You're an ass," in *The Complete Poems*, p. 51.

36. Armistead, *Nathaniel Lee*, p. 154.

37. Hume, *The Rakish Stage*, pp. 122–23.

38. Ibid., pp. 123–27; Armistead, *Nathaniel Lee*, pp. 156–57.

39. Hume, *The Rakish Stage*, pp. 130, 131, 120–21.

40. Sir George Etherege, *The Man of Mode; or, Sir Fopling Flutter*, in *The Dramatic Works of Sir George Etherege*, ed. H.F.B. Brett-Smith, 2 vols. (Oxford: Basil Blackwell, 1927), vol. 2, I.i.200–205. All references are to this edition.

41. For a general survey of such plays, see Robert D. Hume, "Marital Discord in English Comedy from Dryden to Fielding," *Modern Philology* 74 (1977): 248–72.

42. John Dryden, *Marriage A-la-Mode*, in *The Works of John Dryden*, vol. 11, I.i.9–10.

43. Colley Cibber, *The Careless Husband*, in *Colley Cibber: Three Sentimental Comedies*, ed. Maureen Sullivan (New Haven: Yale University Press, 1973), I.i.64–75. All references are to this edition.

44. In his edition of Etherege's poems, Thorpe includes this "Song" in his section "Poems of Doubtful Authorship." Though he feels that "it seems impossible to determine the author," he concludes that Charles Blount "seems the best guess" (pp. 134–35).

45. Giacomo Casanova, Chevalier de Seingalt, *History of My Life*, tr. Willard R. Trask, 6 vols. (New York: Harcourt, Brace and World, 1966), 1:31–32.

46. Donatien Alphonse François de Sade, *Justine, or, Good Conduct Well Chastised*, in *The Marquis de Sade*, tr. Richard Seaver and Austryn Wainhouse, 2 vols. (New York: Grove Press, 1965), 1:646–47.

CHAPTER THREE: THE PHILOSOPHICAL LIBERTINE

1. Rochester to his wife at Adderbury, 1679?, in *Letters*, p. 228.

2. Rochester to Elizabeth Barry, 1675?, in *Letters*, p. 99.

3. J. S. Spink, *French Free-Thought from Gassendi to Voltaire* (London: Athlone Press, 1960), p. 4.

4. For a consideration of Gassendi's relation to the rehabilitation of Epicurus, see Spink, *French Free-Thought*, pp. 85–171, and Samuel Holt Monk, ed., *Five Miscellaneous Essays by Sir William Temple* (Ann Arbor: University of Michigan Press, 1963), pp. xviii–xxiv.

5. Charles Blount to Rochester, 7 February 1680, in *Letters*, p. 241.

6. Charles Blount and Charles Gildon, *The Oracles of Reason* (London, 1693), pp. 109–10.

7. Sir William Temple, "Upon the Gardens of Epicurus; or, Of

Gardening, in the Year 1685," in Monk, *Five Miscellaneous Essays*, pp. 10 and 6. For a discussion of Temple's relation to libertine thought, see Clara Marburg's *Sir William Temple: A Seventeenth-Century "Libertin"* (New Haven: Yale University Press, 1932).

8. Saint-Évremond, Charles de Marguetel de Saint-Denis, seigneur de, "Of Pleasures," in *Miscellany Essays: By Monsieur St. Euremont . . . With A Character By A Person of Honour . . . , Continued by Mr. Dryden*, 2 vols. (London: Printed for John Eberingham, 1695), 2:46.

9. Saint-Évremond, "Epicurus his Morals," in *Miscellanea; or, Various Discourses . . . ,* trans. Ferrand Spence (London: Printed for Sam. Holford, 1686), p. 75.

10. Ibid., p. 102.

11. Saint-Évremond, "The Life of Petronius Arbiter," in *The Satyrical Works of Titus Petronius Arbiter . . .* (London: Printed for Sam. Briscoe, 1708). All references are to this edition.

12. For a study of the late seventeenth-century ideal of the gentleman, see Jean Gagen, "Congreve's Mirabell and the Ideal of the Gentleman," *PMLA* 79 (1964): 422–27.

13. Novak, *William Congreve*, p. 18.

14. Congreve to Joseph Keally, 29 November 1708, in *William Congreve: Letters and Documents*, ed. John C. Hodges (New York: Harcourt, Brace and World, 1964), p. 53.

15. Etherege to the earl of Dover, 14 June 1688, in *Letters*, pp. 206–7.

16. Etherege to William Jephson, 24 May 1688, in *Letters*, pp. 200–201.

17. For a discussion of this tradition, see Richard E. Quaintance, "French Sources of the Restoration 'Imperfect Enjoyment' Poem," *Philological Quarterly* 42 (1963): 190–99.

18. Etherege, "The Imperfect Enjoyment," in *Poems*, p. 8, line 50. For a brief comparison of Etherege's poem to Beys' original, see Thorpe's notes to the poem, ibid., pp. 77–79, and Quaintance, "Restoration 'Imperfect Enjoyment' Poem," pp. 192–95.

19. Rochester, "The Imperfect Enjoyment," in *Complete Poems*, p. 36, line 62.

20. The *Oxford English Dictionary* provides examples of this usage—"To take the part of, stand up for, contend on behalf of"—from 1652–1748.

21. Charles Sackville, "The Antiquated Coquette," in *Poems*, p. 34, lines 38–43.

22. "In Praise of a Mask," in *Westminster-Drollery; or, A Choice Collection of the Newest Songs and Poems At Court and Theaters. By*

a Person of Quality, 3d. ed. (London: Printed for H. Brome, 1674), pp. 90–91.

23. James Thompson, "Congreve's Dramatic Songs: 'O I am glad we shall have a Song to Divert the Discourse,'" *Philological Quarterly* 62 (1983): 372.

24. Brian Corman, "'The Mixed Way of Comedy': Congreve's *The Double-Dealer*," *Modern Philology* 71 (1974): 358; B. Eugene McCarthy, "Providence in Congreve's *The Double-Dealer*," *Studies in English Literature* 19 (1979): 407–19.

25. Traugott, "Rake's Progress from Court to Comedy," p. 404.

26. John Dennis, "To Matthew Prior, Esq; Upon the Roman Satirists," in *The Critical Works of John Dennis*, ed. Edward Niles Hooker, 2 vols. (Baltimore: Johns Hopkins Press, 1939–43), 2:218–19.

27. Hugh Blair, *Lectures on Rhetoric and Belles Lettres* (1783; rpt. Carbondale: Southern Illinois University Press, 1965), p. 528.

28. Aubrey L. Williams, *An Approach to Congreve* (New Haven: Yale University Press, 1979), p. 131.

29. For an examination of how Congreve's four comedies use wit combat to reveal their characters' attempts to achieve a mastery over conventional social norms, see Harold Love, *Congreve*, Plays and Playwrights Series 1 (Oxford: Basil Blackwell, 1974).

30. The last decade has seen a growing controversy over the role of Christian providential order in the plays of Congreve. In "Poetical Justice, the Contrivances of Providence, and the Works of William Congreve," *ELH* 35 (1968): 540–65, and *An Approach to Congreve*, Aubrey L. Williams has argued that "the playwright's imaginative vision is consistent with a Christian normative order" (*An Approach to Congreve*, p. x). John Barnard, "Passion, 'Poetical Justice,' and Dramatic Law in *The Double-Dealer* and *The Way of the World*," in *William Congreve*, ed. Brian Morris (London: Ernest Benn, 1972), pp. 93–112, and B. Eugene McCarthy, "Providence in Congreve's *Double-Dealer*," have argued against this position. Recently Harriet Hawkins has entered the fray on the side opposing Williams; see her "The 'Example Theory' and the Providentialist Approach to Restoration Drama: Some Questions of Validity and Applicability," *The Eighteenth Century: Theory and Interpretation* 24 (1983): 103–14.

31. Anthony Gosse, "Plot and Character in Congreve's *Double-Dealer*," *Modern Language Quarterly* 29 (1968): 274–88.

32. Peter Holland bases his discussion of this play on a similar perception of the total disorder that infects the comic world: "That world itself has by then been shown to be more than foolish; it is also inverted, a clear case of the world upside-down. . . . Old men try to be

young rakes; women rule the men; the world is topsy-turvey" (*The Ornament of Action*, p. 230).

33. Ibid., p. 229.
34. Williams, *An Approach to Congreve*, p. 193.
35. Ibid., p. 207.
36. Richard Steele, *The Conscious Lovers*, ed. Shirley Strum Kenny, Regents Restoration Drama Series (Lincoln: University of Nebraska Press, 1968), I.ii.16.
37. See Jocelyn Powell's perceptive analysis of this scene in *Restoration Theatre Production*, pp. 187–89. He explores how Betterton and Barry, in "comic roles for tragic actors of great power," develop Fainall and Marwood as "two people caught in their own traps."
38. Thompson, "Congreve's Dramatic Songs," p. 378.
39. Ibid., p. 377.

CHAPTER FOUR: THE FEMALE LIBERTINE ON THE RESTORATION STAGE

1. Macfarlane, "Witchcraft in Tudor and Stuart Essex," in Cockburn, *Crime in England*, pp. 79–80; Larner, *Enemies of God*, pp. 89–94.
2. Larner, p. 92.
3. Ibid., p. 10.
4. "A General Satyr on Woman," in *Female Excellence; or, Woman Displayed, in Several Satyrick Poems*, by "A Person of Quality" (London: Printed for Norman Nelson, 1679), p. 3.
5. Lawrence Stone, *The Past and the Present* (London: Routledge and Kegan Paul, 1981), p. 165.
6. Thomas Dekker and Thomas Middleton, *The Roaring Girl*, in vol. 3 of *The Dramatic Works of Thomas Dekker*, ed. Fredson Bowers, 4 vols. (Cambridge: Cambridge University Press, 1953–61), III.i.133–34. All references to Dekker are to this edition.
7. Stephen Greenblatt, *Renaissance Self-Fashioning: From More to Shakespeare* (Chicago: University of Chicago Press, 1980), p. 9.
8. Linda Bamber, *Comic Women, Tragic Men: A Study of Gender and Genre in Shakespeare* (Stanford: Stanford University Press, 1982), p. 15.
9. Rosemary Masek, "Women in an Age of Transition: 1485–1714," in *The Women of England, from Anglo-Saxon Times to the Present: Interpretive Bibliographical Essays*, ed. Barbara Kanner (Hamden, Conn.: Archon Books, 1979), pp. 138–82.
10. Hilda L. Smith, *Reason's Disciples: Seventeenth-Century English Feminists* (Urbana: University of Illinois Press, 1982), p. 20.

11. Mary Astell, *An Essay in Defence of the Female Sex* . . . (London: Printed for A. Roper and E. Wilkinson . . . and R. Clavel, 1696), p. 23.

12. Christopher Hill, *Milton and the English Revolution* (New York: Viking Press, 1978), p. 118.

13. Smith, *Reason's Disciples*, p. 9. There are, of course, those who would not agree with Smith's understanding of seventeenth-century feminism. Joan Kelly, in "Early Feminist Theory and the *Querelle des Femmes*, 1400–1789," *Signs* 8 (1982): 4–28, argues that "feminists of the *querelle* remained bound by the terms of that dialectic" with misogyny: "What they had to say to women and society was largely reactive to what misogynists said about women" (p. 27). Ellen Pollak, in *The Poetics of Sexual Myth: Gender and Ideology in the Verse of Swift and Pope* (Chicago: University of Chicago Press, 1985), also takes issue with Smith: "But the ideological dominance of the view that female self-preservation was coextensive with the preservation of the female as a spiritual icon was such that even early defenses of female education . . . finally had to recognize its terms" (p. 47).

14. This argument was first made by Alice Clark, *Working Life of Women in the Seventeenth Century* (1919; rpt. London: Routledge and Kegan Paul, 1982). The topic is touched on by Masek, "Women in an Age of Transition," pp. 143–46; Hill, *Milton and the English Revolution*, ch. 9; Sheila Rowbotham, *Women, Resistance, and Revolution* (London: Allen Lane, Penguin Press, 1972), ch. 1; Smith, *Reason's Disciples*, pp. 11, 27–29; and Pollak, *Poetics of Sexual Myth*, pp. 27–31.

15. Masek, "Women in an Age of Transition," p. 144.

16. Astell, *Essay in Defence of the Female Sex*, p. 3.

17. Rowbotham, *Women, Resistance, and Revolution*, p. 35.

18. François, Duc de La Rochefoucauld, *Seneca Unmasqued; or, Moral Reflections*, tr. Aphra Behn in *Miscellany: Being a Collection of Poems by several Hands. Together with Reflections on Morality, or Seneca Unmasqued* (London: Printed for J. Hindmarsh, 1685), pp. 366 and 355.

19. Jean de La Bruyère, *The Characters; or, The Manners of the Age*, tr. "by several hands" (London: Printed for John Bullord, 1699), pp. 55 and 69.

20. Anthony Hamilton, *Memoirs of the Comte de Gramont*, tr. Peter Quennell (London: George Routledge and Sons, 1930), p. 171.

21. Lorenzo Magalotti, *Relazione d'Inghilterra*, published in English as *Lorenzo Magalotti at the Court of Charles II*, tr. and ed. W. E. Knowles Middleton (Waterloo, Ontario: Wilfrid Laurier University Press, 1980), p. 70.

22. Hamilton, *Memoirs of Gramont*, p. 215.

23. Smith, *Reason's Disciples*, p. 10.

24. Rowbotham, *Women, Resistance, and Revolution*, p. 25.

25. Hill, *Milton and the English Revolution*, p. 135. See also Keith Thomas, "Women and the Civil War Sects," *Past and Present* 13 (1958): 42–62.

26. Patricia Higgins, "The Reactions of Women, with Special Reference to Women Petitioners," in *Politics, Religion, and The English Civil War*, ed. Brian Manning (New York: St. Martin's Press, 1973), pp. 220–21. For a consideration of the many active roles women played during the Revolution, see Antonia Fraser, *The Weaker Vessel* (New York: Knopf, 1984), pp. 163–264.

27. Higgins, "The Reactions of Women," pp. 210–11.

28. *To the Supreme Authority . . . Petition of divers well-affected Women* (1649) B.M. 669 f. 14(27), quoted by Higgins, p. 217.

29. Higgins, p. 222.

30. Mary Poovey, *The Proper Lady and the Woman Writer: Ideology as Style in the Works of Mary Wollstonecraft, Mary Shelley, and Jane Austen* (Chicago: University of Chicago Press, 1984), p. 7.

31. Arthur H. Scouten, review of Fidelis Morgan's *The Female Wits: Women Playwrights on the London Stage, 1660–1720*, in *The Scriblerian* 15 (1982): 62–63.

32. Angeline Goreau, *Reconstructing Aphra: A Social Biography of Aphra Behn* (New York: Dial Press, 1980), p. 150. J. M. Armistead, in *Four Restoration Playwrights: A Reference Guide to Thomas Shadwell, Aphra Behn, Nathaniel Lee, and Thomas Otway* (Boston: G. K. Hall, 1984), maintains that the attacks on Behn began in earnest only after her death: "Mrs. Behn was in good repute, both as artist and as person, with most of the contemporaries who cared to comment on her in print. . . . Very soon after her death, however, she began to be seen as a purveyor of the worst sort of lewd, unprincipled entertainment" (p. xviii).

33. Goreau, *Reconstructing Aphra*, pp. 173–74.

34. William Van Lennep, "Thomas Killigrew Prepares His Plays for Production," in *Joseph Quincy Adams: Memorial Studies*, ed. James G. McManaway, Giles E. Dawson, and Edwin E. Willoughby (Washington: Folger Shakespeare Library, 1948), pp. 803–8.

35. Thomas Killigrew, *Thomaso; or, The Wanderer*, in *Comedies, and Tragedies* (London: Printed for Henry Herringman, 1664), p. 371. All references are to this edition.

36. James Howard, *All Mistaken; or, The Mad Couple* (London: Printed by H. Brugis, for James Magnes, 1672), p. 19.

37. Rochester, "Woman's Honor," in *The Complete Poems*, p. 14.

38. Astell, *Essay in Defence of the Female Sex*, p. 22.

39. *Marriage Asserted: In Answer to a Book Entituled Conjugium Conjurgium: Or, Some Serious Considerations on Marriage . . . By William Seymar, Esq.*[pseudonym] (London: Printed for Henry Herringman, 1674), p. 17.

40. Marin Cureau de La Chambre, *The Art of How to Know Men*, tr. John Davies (London: Printed by T.R. for Thomas Dring, 1665), pp. 26, 29, and 30.

41. Lady Mary Wortley Montagu to Lady Mar, 31 October 1723, in *The Complete Letters of Lady Mary Wortley Montagu*, ed. Robert Halsband, 3 vols. (Oxford: Clarendon Press, 1965–67), 2:32.

42. According to the editors of *The London Stage, 1660–1800*, Part I, 1660–1700, ed. William Van Lennep, Emmett L. Avery, and Arthur H. Scouten (Carbondale: Southern Illinois University Press, 1965), "The date of the first performance is not known, and the play is one of a large group commonly assigned to September–December 1690. As the Prologue implies an autumn production, it has been placed at late September, although the premiere may have been October" (p. 389). Judith Milhous and Robert D. Hume argue for a November date in their "Dating Play Premieres from Publication Data, 1660–1700," *Harvard Library Bulletin* 22 (1974): 398.

43. Thomas Southerne, *Sir Anthony Love; or, The Rambling Lady* (London: Printed for Joseph Fox and Abel Roper, 1691), sig. A2. All references are to this edition.

44. Holland, *The Ornament of Action*, esp. chs. 3 and 5.

45. Ibid., p. 145.

46. Victor Oscar Freeburg, *Disguise Plots in Elizabethan Drama: A Study in Stage Tradition* (1915; rpt. New York: Benjamin Blom, 1965), esp. chs. 3–4.

47. An indication of the inevitability of this pattern is given by Freeburg when he notes that up to 1611 he has found only two examples in English drama of female pages who serve their lovers unrewarded (*Cupid's Revenge* and *Philaster*). Robert L. Root, Jr., *Thomas Southerne*, Twayne's English Authors Series (Boston: Twayne, 1981), ch. 3, pp. 45–46, notes other women who remain in male disguise both before and after the Restoration.

48. For a rather extravagant account of the sexual implications of the breeches role, see Jan Kott, *Shakespeare Our Contemporary*, tr. Boleslaw Taborski (New York: Anchor Books, 1966), pp. 293–342.

49. Freeburg, *Disguise Plots in Elizabethan Drama*, pp. 72–80, discusses the many ways in which the female page affirms her femininity even while disguised as a man.

50. Margaret Lamb McDonald, *The Independent Woman in the Restoration Comedy of Manners*, Salzburg Studies in English

Literature 32 (Salzburg: Institut für Englische Sprache und Literatur, 1976), p. 170. The unusualness of Sir Anthony's character can be apprehended by contrasting McDonald's extreme judgment to that of G. Wilson Knight in *The Golden Labyrinth: A Study of British Drama* (London: Phoenix House, 1962): Knight argues that the play's "prevailing tone is kindly, even warm; the outspoken impudency of Sir Anthony's talk marks a health; on her lips pretended licentiousness is its own purification. She does nothing but good, satirizing and serving the others" (p. 140).

51. Thomas Southerne, *The Wives Excuse; or, Cuckolds Make Themselves* (London: Printed for Samuel Brisco, 1692), p. 47. All references are to this edition.

52. Though Wilding delivers this judgment of Wittwoud while ignorant of her identity, the truth of the remark nonetheless stands.

53. Sarah Fige, *The Female Advocate; or, An Answer To a Late Satyr Against the Pride, Lust and Inconstancy of Woman. Written by a Lady in Vindication of her Sex* (London: Printed by H.C., 1687), p. 23.

54. Choderlos de Laclos, *Les Liaisons dangereuses*, tr. P. W. K. Stone (London: Penguin, 1961), pp. 28 and 188.

55. Ibid., p. 179.

56. Ibid., p. 392.

CHAPTER FIVE: SEXUAL DISCOURSE IN THE EIGHTEENTH CENTURY

1. Philip Dormer Stanhope, fourth earl of Chesterfield, *The Letters of the Earl of Chesterfield to His Son*, ed. Charles Strachey, 2 vols. (London: Methuen, 1901), 2:82–83.

2. See Hagstrum, *Sex and Sensibility*, pp. 5–11, for a survey of the various meanings that *sensibility* and related terms could take in the eighteenth century.

3. Chesterfield, *Letters*, 1:350.

4. Peter Wagner, "The Pornographer in the Courtroom: Trial Reports about Cases of Sexual Crimes and Delinquencies as a Genre of Eighteenth-Century Erotica," in *Sexuality in Eighteenth-Century Britain*, ed. Paul-Gabriel Bouce (Manchester: Manchester University Press, 1982), p. 135.

5. Roy Porter, "Mixed Feelings: The Enlightenment and Sexuality in Eighteenth-Century Britain," in Bouce, *Sexuality in Eighteenth-Century Britain*, p. 20.

6. Tony Tanner, *Adultery in the Novel: Contract and Transgression* (Baltimore: Johns Hopkins University Press, 1979), p. 17.

7. Robert Wallace, "Of Venery; or, Of the commerce of the two sexes," printed in Norah Smith, "Robert Wallace's 'Of Venery,'"

Texas Studies in Literature and Language 15 (1973): 433–34. For a discussion of Wallace's place in eighteenth-century thought, see Norah Smith, "Sexual Mores in the Eighteenth Century: Robert Wallace's 'Of Venery,'" *Journal of the History of Ideas* 39 (1978): 419–33.

8. G. S. Rousseau, "Nymphomania, Bienville, and the Rise of Erotic Sensibility," in Bouce, *Sexuality in Eighteenth-Century Britain*, pp. 105–6.

9. For a discussion of critical misapprehensions that have governed our understanding of the eighteenth-century theatre, see Hume's *The Rakish Stage*, particularly chs. 7, 9, and 10.

10. Arthur H. Scouten and Robert D. Hume, "'Restoration Comedy' and Its Audiences, 1660–1776," *Yearbook of English Studies* 10 (1980): 45–69.

11. For an intriguing consideration of the relationship between a "declining" theatre and "rising" novel, see Laura Brown, *English Dramatic Form, 1660–1760: An Essay in Generic History* (New Haven: Yale University Press, 1981), esp. chs. 5 and 6.

12. George Lillo, *The London Merchant*, ed. William H. McBurney, Regents Restoration Drama Series (Lincoln: University of Nebraska Press, 1965), IV.xviii.57–59. All references are to this edition.

13. Lawrence Marsden Price, "George Barnwell Abroad," *Comparative Literature* 2 (1950): 127.

14. Richard E. Brown, "Rival Socio-Economic Theories in Two Plays by George Lillo," *Tennessee Studies in Literature* 24 (1979): 99.

15. Alexander Pope, "Epistle to Bathurst," in *The Poems of Alexander Pope*, vol. 3, pt. 2:93, lines 69–78.

16. For an essay dealing with the history of and attitudes towards wrecking, see John G. Rule, "Wrecking and Coastal Plunder," in *Albion's Fatal Tree: Crime and Society in Eighteenth-Century England*, ed. Douglas Hay et al. (New York: Random House, 1975), pp. 167–88.

17. Roberta F. S. Borkat, "The Evil of Goodness: Sentimental Morality in *The London Merchant*," *Studies in Philology* 76 (1979): 303.

18. Daniel Defoe, *The Fortunes and Misfortunes of the Famous Moll Flanders*, ed. G. A. Starr (Oxford: Oxford University Press, 1971), pp. 68–69. All references are to this edition.

19. Marlene LeGates, "The Cult of Womanhood in Eighteenth-Century Thought," *Eighteenth-Century Studies* 10 (1976): 28–29.

20. From a letter by Dickens in John Forster, *The Life of Charles Dickens*, ed. J. W. T. Ley (London: Cecil Palmer, 1928), p. 611n. Dickens' remark is discussed by Anne Robinson Taylor, *Male Novel-*

ists and Their Female Voices: Literary Masquerades (New York: Whitston Publishing, 1981), p. 2.

21. Ian Watt, *The Rise of the Novel: Studies in Defoe, Richardson, and Fielding* (Berkeley and Los Angeles: University of California Press, 1957), p. 113.

22. Ian Watt, "The Recent Critical Fortunes of *Moll Flanders*," *Eighteenth-Century Studies* 1 (1967): 112.

23. Dorothy Van Ghent, *The English Novel: Form and Function* (1953; rpt. New York: Harper and Row, 1967): p. 59.

24. John J. Richetti, *Defoe's Narratives: Situations and Structures* (Oxford: Clarendon Press, 1975), p. 101.

25. G. A. Starr, *Defoe and Casuistry* (Princeton: Princeton University Press, 1971), p. 150. The question of Moll's ambiguous sexuality has recently been reexamined in a feminist context by Miriam Lerenbaum, "Moll Flanders: 'A Woman on her own Account,'" in *The Authority of Experience: Essays in Feminist Criticism*, ed. Arlyn Diamond and Lee R. Edwards (Amherst: University of Massachusetts Press, 1977), pp. 101–17, and Nancy K. Miller, *The Heroine's Text: Readings in the French and English Novel, 1722–1782* (New York: Columbia University Press, 1980), pp. 3–20.

26. Patricia Meyer Spacks, "'Ev'ry Woman is at Heart a Rake,'" *Eighteenth-Century Studies* 8 (1974): 43.

27. Richetti, *Defoe's Narratives*, pp. 106–8.

28. Michael Shinagel, *Daniel Defoe and Middle-Class Gentility* (Cambridge: Harvard University Press, 1968), p. 154.

29. Juliet McMaster, "The Equation of Love and Money in *Moll Flanders*," *Studies in the Novel* 2 (1970): 133.

30. Ibid., p. 137.

31. Robert A. Erickson, "Moll's Fate: 'Mother Midnight' and *Moll Flanders*," *Studies in Philology* 76 (1979): 85.

32. John Gay, *The Beggar's Opera*, ed. Edgar V. Roberts, Regents Restoration Drama Series (Lincoln: University of Nebraska Press, 1969), I.ii.9–14. All references are to this edition.

33. Hume, *The Rakish Stage*, p. 251.

34. Rochester, "A Satyr Against Reason and Mankind," in *The Complete Poems*, pp. 94–101, lines 6–7 and 115–16.

35. Brigid Brophy, "Mersey Sound, 1750," *New Statesman* 66 (15 November 1963): 710; Leo Braudy, "*Fanny Hill* and Materialism," *Eighteenth-Century Studies* 4 (1970): 37.

36. Nancy K. Miller, "'I's' in Drag: The Sex of Recollection," *The Eighteenth Century: Theory and Interpretation* 22 (1981): 49.

37. Robert Markley, "Language, Power, and Sexuality in Cleland's *Fanny Hill*," *Philological Quarterly* 63 (1984): 345.

38. Robert Scholes, *Semiotics and Interpetation* (New Haven: Yale University Press, 1982), pp. 134–35.

39. John Cleland, *Memoirs of a Woman of Pleasure*, ed. Peter Sabor (Oxford: Oxford University Press, 1985), p. 144. All references are to this edition.

40. Michael Shinagel, "*Memoirs of a Woman of Pleasure:* Pornography and the Mid-Eighteenth-Century English Novel," in *Studies in Change and Revolution*, ed. Paul J. Korshin (Yorkshire: Scolar Press, 1972) p. 225.

41. Ibid.

42. Miller, *The Heroine's Text*, p. 60.

43. Pablo Neruda, "Body of a Woman," in *Twenty Love Poems and a Song of Despair*, tr. W. S. Merwin (London: Jonathan Cape, 1969), p. 9.

44. Markley, "Cleland's *Fanny Hill*," p. 347.

45. Thomas Stretzer, *A New Description of Merryland, Containing a Topographical, Geographical, and Natural History of that Country*, 6th ed. (Bath: Printed by J. Leak and E. Curll, 1741), p. 6.

46. Markley, "Cleland's *Fanny Hill*," p. 349.

47. Porter, "Mixed Feelings," p. 11. Frank E. Manuel and Fritzie P. Manuel, *Utopian Thought in the Western World* (Cambridge: Harvard University Press, 1979), concur with Porter's suggestion that the Enlightenment signaled a profound change in attitudes towards sexuality: "The audacious and scandalous ideas voiced during the Enlightenment, even if not meant to be taken literally, reflected a fundamental change in attitude toward sexual fulfillment for the individual. These ideas, moreover, were not restricted to an aristocratic class, but had resonances in the rich gutter literature of the age" (p. 536).

48. Porter, p. 15.

INDEX

DESIGNED BY BRUCE GORE
COMPOSED BY THE COMPOSING ROOM, INC., APPLETON, WISCONSIN
MANUFACTURED BY BRAUN-BRUMFIELD, INC., ANN ARBOR, MICHIGAN
TEXT AND DISPLAY LINES ARE SET IN TRUMP MEDIAEVAL

ⅢⅢ

Library of Congress Cataloging-in-Publication Data
Weber, Harold.
The restoration rake-hero.
Includes bibliographical references and index.
1. English drama—Restoration, 1660–1700—History
and criticism. 2. Libertines in literature. 3. Sex
in literature. 4. English drama—17th century—History
and criticism. 5. English literature—18th century—
History and criticism. 6. England—Social life and
customs—17th century. I. Title.
PR698.L52W4 1986   822'.4'093520692   86-40063
ISBN 0-299-10690-X